trees
shrubs *&* hedges

FOR YOUR HOME

TREES, SHRUBS & HEDGES FOR YOUR HOME, THIRD EDITION

SENIOR EDITOR	Kathie Robitz
PRINCIPAL AUTHOR	Jacqueline Hériteau
CONTENT EDITOR	Nancy T. Engel
JUNIOR EDITOR	Angela Hanson
CONSULTING HORTICULTURAL EDITOR	Elizabeth P. Stell
GRAPHIC DESIGNER	Kathryn Wityk
GRAPHIC DESIGN INTERN	Larissa Stuts
PHOTO COORDINATOR	Mary Dolan
TECHNICAL REVIEWERS	Ken Badgley, Carole Ottessen, Mike Stoll, Brian Trimble
DIGITAL IMAGING SPECIALIST	Frank Dyer
INDEXER	Schroeder Indexing Services
COVER DESIGN CONCEPT	Kathryn Wityk
FRONT COVER PHOTOGRAPHY	*left* Virginia Hamrick/Dreamstime.com; *top right* Richard Shiell/Deminsky Photo Associates; *bottom right* Neil Soderstrom
BACK COVER PHOTOGRAPHY	*left* Angie Westre/Dreamstime.com; *top right* Larry Lefever/Jane Grushow/ Grant Heilman Photography, Inc.; *bottom right* Larry Lefever/Grant Heilman Photography, Inc.

CREATIVE HOMEOWNER

VICE PRESIDENT AND PUBLISHER	Timothy O. Bakke
MANAGING EDITOR	Fran J. Donegan
ART DIRECTOR	David Geer
PRODUCTION COORDINATOR	Sara M. Markowitz

Manufactured in the United States of America

Current Printing (last digit)
10 9 8 7 6 5 4 3 2

Trees, Shrubs & Hedges for Your Home
Previously Published as *Complete Trees, Shrubs & Hedges*
Library of Congress Control Number: 2010921869
ISBN-10: 1-58011-507-1
ISBN-13: 978-1-58011-507-0

CREATIVE HOMEOWNER®
A Division of Federal Marketing Corp.
24 Park Way
Upper Saddle River, NJ 07458
www.creativehomeowner.com

Planet Friendly Publishing
✔ Made in the United States
✔ Printed on Recycled Paper
Text: 10%   Cover: 10%
Learn more: www.greenedition.org

GREEN EDITION

At Creative Homeowner we're committed to producing books in an earth-friendly manner and to helping our customers make greener choices.

Manufacturing books in the United States ensures compliance with strict environmental laws and eliminates the need for international freight shipping, a major contributor to global air pollution.

And printing on recycled paper helps minimize our consumption of trees, water, and fossil fuels. *Trees, Shrubs & Hedges for Your Home* was printed on paper made with 10% post-consumer waste. According to the Environmental Defense Fund Paper Calculator, by using this innovative paper instead of conventional papers we achieved the following environmental benefits:

Trees Saved: 21

Water Saved: 9,448 gallons

Solid Waste Eliminated: 574 pounds

Greenhouse Gas Emissions Eliminated: 1,962 pounds

For more information on our environmental practices, please visit us online at www.creativehomeowner.com/green

Safety First

Though all concepts and methods in this book have been reviewed for safety, it is not possible to overstate the importance of using the safest working methods possible. What follows are reminders—do's and don'ts for yard work and landscaping. They are not substitutes for your own common sense.

▌ Always use caution, care, and good judgment when following the procedures described in this book.

▌ Always determine locations of underground utility lines before you dig, and then avoid them by a safe distance. Buried lines may be for gas, electricity, communications, or water. Start research by contacting your local building officials. Also contact local utility companies; they will often send a representative free of charge to help you map their lines. In addition, there are private utility locator firms that may be listed in your Yellow Pages. **Note:** previous owners may have installed underground drainage, sprinkler, and lighting lines without mapping them.

▌ Always read and heed the manufacturer's instructions for using a tool, especially the warnings.

▌ Always ensure that the electrical setup is safe; be sure that no circuit is overloaded and that all power tools and electrical outlets are properly grounded and protected by a ground-fault circuit interrupter (GFCI). Do not use power tools in wet locations.

▌ Always wear eye protection when using chemicals, sawing wood, pruning trees and shrubs, using power tools, and striking metal onto metal or concrete.

▌ Always read labels on chemicals, solvents, and other products; provide ventilation; heed warnings.

▌ Always wear heavy rubber gloves rated for chemicals, not mere household rubber gloves, when handling toxins.

▌ Always wear appropriate gloves in situations in which your hands could be injured by rough surfaces, sharp edges, thorns, or poisonous plants.

▌ Always wear a disposable face mask or a special filtering respirator when creating sawdust or working with toxic gardening substances.

▌ Always keep your hands and other body parts away from the business ends of blades, cutters, and bits.

▌ Always obtain approval from local building officials before undertaking construction of permanent structures.

▌ Never work with power tools when you are tired or under the influence of alcohol or drugs.

▌ Never carry sharp or pointed tools, such as knives or saws, in your pockets. If you carry such tools, use special-purpose tool scabbards.

Metric Equivalents

All measurements in this book are given in U.S. Customary units. If you wish to find metric equivalents, use the following tables and conversion factors.

Inches to Millimeters and Centimeters

1 in = 25.4 mm = 2.54 cm

in	mm	cm
1/16	1.5875	0.1588
1/8	3.1750	0.3175
1/4	6.3500	0.6350
3/8	9.5250	0.9525
1/2	12.7000	1.2700
5/8	15.8750	1.5875
3/4	19.0500	1.9050
7/8	22.2250	2.2225
1	25.4000	2.5400

Inches to Centimeters and Meters

1 in = 2.54 cm = 0.0254 m

in	cm	m
1	2.54	0.0254
2	5.08	0.0508
3	7.62	0.0762
4	10.16	0.1016
5	12.70	0.1270
6	15.24	0.1524
7	17.78	0.1778
8	20.32	0.2032
9	22.86	0.2286
10	25.40	0.2540
11	27.94	0.2794
12	30.48	0.3048

Feet to Meters

1 ft = 0.3048 m

ft	m
1	0.3048
5	1.5240
10	3.0480
25	7.6200
50	15.2400
100	30.4800

Square Feet to Square Meters

1 ft² = 0.092 903 04 m²

Acres to Square Meters

1 acre = 4046.85642 m²

Cubic Yards to Cubic Meters

1 yd³ = 0.764 555 m³

Ounces and Pounds (Avoirdupois) to Grams

1 oz = 28.349 523 g

1 lb = 453.5924 g

Pounds to Kilograms

1 lb = 0.453 592 37 kg.

Ounces and Quarts to Liters

1 oz = 0.029 573 53 L

1 qt = 0.9463 L

Gallons to Liters

1 gal = 3.785 411 784 L

Fahrenheit to Celsius (Centigrade)

$°C = °F - 32 × 5/9$

°F	°C
-30	-34.45
-20	-28.89
-10	-23.34
-5	-20.56
0	-17.78
10	-12.22
20	-6.67
30	-1.11
32 (freezing)	0.00
40	4.44
50	10.00
60	15.56
70	21.11
80	26.67
90	32.22
100	37.78
212 (boiling)	100

Contents

Introduction 6

PART 1
LANDSCAPING 8
WITH TREES, SHRUBS, AND HEDGES

Plan and Grow 10
with Care

PART 2
ALL ABOUT TREES 68

Main Facts and Key Details 70

Tree Profiles 86
Alphabetized by genus (scientific name)

Introduction

Choosing the right low-maintenance, disease-resistant plants for your location is the first step toward success, followed by proper planting and care. *Trees, Shrubs, and Hedges for Your Home* **can be your guide to a beautiful garden of your own creation.**

Trees, shrubs, and hedges make up the living framework of your garden. Trees provide shade, screen out unsightly views, make a visual link between land and sky, and filigree winter's open horizon. Shrubs, on the other hand, fill the middle heights between the trees and the lawn or flower beds. Not just a backdrop for herbaceous flowers, shrubs contribute shape, color, and texture throughout the year, even when blanketed by snow. When used as hedges, trees and shrubs make living fences. Woody plants are bargains when you consider their ease of maintenance and enduring contribution to the landscape. Even though they may be the most expensive plants in your garden and some may require years to mature, the investment is worth making.

The plants in this book are among the best of their kind. This means they have lasting beauty and low maintenance needs, and most are pest- and disease-resistant. Yet some woody plants, such as the finicky roses, are so desirable that we plant them even though we know they will need extra care. Still, you can prevent many problems if you choose your plants to fit the soil, sunlight, and climate your property provides.

Trees, shrubs, and hedges are the most important plants in your landscape. While the loss of a zinnia or a peony bush—even a patch of lawn—is a nuisance, the loss of the shade and shelter provided by trees and shrubs usually requires significant restructuring of your garden design. This book provides information on choosing the right woody plants for your property. It also explains how to get your plants off to a good start and give them the care that's best for a long and healthy life. Such plants will reward you with "good bones," the structure a landscape needs, and beauty that will be enduring. —*Jacqueline Hériteau*

Rhododendron is a broad-leaved deciduous evergreen that produces clusters of pink, purple, or red flowers in the spring.

In March and April, a flowering plum tree is abloom with small white or pink flowers before leaves appear.

Solid hedge walls add structure to a path leading up to the house and soften the look of the brick. The hydrangeas, with their pudgy purple-pink flowers, are in bloom at the height of the summer.

PART 1

Landscaping with Trees, Shrubs, and Hedges

Trees, shrubs, and hedges are the backbone of a home landscape, so the time you spend planning to incorporate them into a new or an existing design will be well spent. Don't skimp on the planning stage. The more intimate you become with the landscape, the more satisfying your changes will be. Walk the property. Study the existing groupings of large plants—the trees and shrubs—from various perspectives and at different times of day—at sunrise and sunset and in the rain—absorbing the way the garden feels, smells, and looks.

Plan and Grow with Care

Become familiar with the textures of bark and leaves, the development of flowers and berries, and the seasonal changes in plant silhouettes. These details will help you choose the plants that will give you pleasure for many years.

There are Japanese maples for nearly all regions of North America. Most landscapes benefit from at least one of these maples somewhere.

Design Considerations

There's an amazing number of wonderful plants from which to choose, but most homeowners limit themselves to the same 50 or so popular ornamentals. Few discover the fragrant viburnum's intoxicating sweet clove scent; or experience one of spring's great moments—the blooming of a cherry against a background of evergreens; or witness fall's fiery foliage display of maples, barberries, euonymus, black gums, and serviceberries.

Before making an addition to your garden, learn all you can about available plants. The information is easy to ac-

quire, and your garden will be more varied and interesting for your effort. Visit the arboreta and public gardens in your region to study the plants growing there. Talk to successful gardeners in your neighborhood. Also inquire at local garden centers; many offer free design services. For an additional charge, they might deliver, plant, and provide a replacement warranty. But when your design plans require reshaping the contours of the land or changing the grade, it's wise to consult a landscape architect. A garden center that maintains a landscaping division employs experienced landscape architects and can be of great help. Or ask friends or neighbors for recommendations.

Edge, where lawn meets woods, offers an opportunity to blend a fence line with herbaceous plants, such as these lupines, and native trees, such as this spruce and clump of birches, opposite top.

Trees and shrubs help create a structure from which you can build the rest of your landscape, left. They not only provide visual interest, they also section the landscape into separate activity areas.

Flowering trees, such as this plum below, look striking against evergreens. Fallen flower petals make the pathway especially inviting.

PLANTS CHANGE SIZES

To decide whether a woody plant is right for your property, first consider its size at maturity. Growing conditions will make a difference. A mature tree grown in an open, sunny landscape may be 30 to 50 percent shorter and spread considerably wider than the same species growing in a forest, where it competes for light with its tall neighbors. On the other hand, a tree growing under favorable conditions in a garden may be a giant compared with its dwarfed and deformed counterpart growing on a wind-blown rocky mountaintop. Climate also has an effect. Plants in the warm parts of their range may grow taller and reach maturity sooner than those of the same species growing in areas with shorter, cooler growing seasons. Once you have a sense of a plant's eventual size, try to picture its effect on your site when fully mature. That is, consider whether it will be in scale.

Dwarf and pendulous conifers in various hues can give you year-round color without outgrowing their site, above and right.

CREATING BALANCE

Balanced plantings create a sense of security and well-being. To achieve balance, you first need to know what the mature plant's eventual size and shape will be.

For an informal balance, you might repeat clumps of shrubs and trees that have similar size and structure but are different species. On the other hand, you could achieve a formal balance by using only one species, the plants symmetrical or exactly the same size, such as a line of columnar trees or a closely clipped hedge. Then, too, series of graceful weeping trees or of shrubs, with branches loosely layered like clouds, can soften the line and create a balance somewhere between formal and informal.

This planting features 'Blue Carpet' juniper, 'Garnet' Japanese maple, and various lighter-hued conifers.

Balance is an important design factor. Weeping trees are graceful and dramatic, but more than one is only suitable for a large landscape.

Scale and Structure in Your Landscape

Scale refers to a plant's size and mass relative to the objects around it. The right scale determines a plant's appeal. For example, a massive tree is breathtaking set off by a large expanse of lawn that might dwarf and diminish the charm of smaller trees. A young blue spruce may look perfectly suited to a small yard, but as it soars toward maturity, it will be increasingly out of scale, making the yard look smaller. This isn't to say that a big plant never looks good in a small space. *Structure*—the growth habit of a plant—is as important as size. Where a large, dense, imposing evergreen would overwhelm a small space, a single open, airy one, such as a tall, leggy rhododendron, might be the only woody plant a small patio garden needs. However, to enjoy the interest created by several diverse plants in a small space, you could choose a group of small or dwarf species. The dwarf cultivars (*culti*vated *vari*eties) of boxwood, holly, juniper, and pine add texture without the bulk of standard sizes.

There are tricks of scale you can use to create the illusion of space. As shown in the accompanying illustrations, you can make a shallow garden seem deeper if you place plants with larger leaves up close and plants with smaller leaves farther away, and drastically reduce the size of the plants toward the back. Or you might suggest greater depth by pruning a hedge so that it narrows as it recedes. So, too, you could narrow the path between a pair of hedges as they recede.

Leaf sizes and textures can be used to help small spaces look much larger—and long, narrow expanses seem wider. If you place larger-leaved plants in the foreground and gradually diminish leaf size in the distance, you will create the illusion of greater depth. Conversely, the same plantings viewed from the opposite direction make distant plants appear closer.

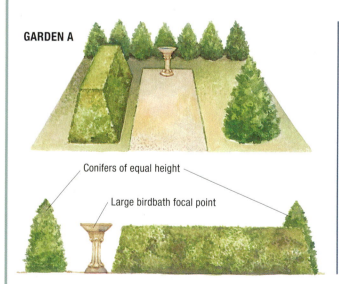

GARDEN A

Conifers of equal height

Large birdbath focal point

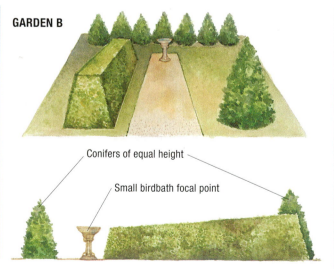

GARDEN B

Conifers of equal height

Small birdbath focal point

Which garden is larger? At first glance you might think that Garden B is larger than Garden A. But as the side views on the bottom pair of illustrations show, the two gardens are of equal size. In Garden B, the designer employed visual tricks. For example, the width of the path is reduced as it approaches the conifers, and the

hedge is made narrower. In addition, the hedge in Garden B is pruned to gradually reduce its height as it recedes. The conifer in the foreground is larger than those at the back, and the birdbath is smaller than the one in Garden A. All of these features combine in Garden B to suggest a larger space.

Keep scale and structure in mind when designing your landscape. This massive tree is set off by the expansive lawn.

Types of Plants

If a plant's mature size will be suitable, consider other assets it will bring to the design. A property needs both evergreen and deciduous plants to be attractive year-round. Study the plant's silhouette, and decide whether it will add a contrasting element or conform to and reinforce an existing pattern. Also decide whether the plant's texture—the size, shape, and mobility of its foliage, the twigginess of its branches, the growth patterns of its bark—will contribute to the overall design. Lastly, look for color in its foliage, flowers, fruit, and bark. The best plants have assets in more than one season, which is especially important in a small garden.

EVERGREENS

Evergreens are major players in landscape design. They serve as permanent color accents, as backdrops, and as year-round screening, and they are the most effective plants for hedges. Evergreens come in an astonishing variety of forms and textures. And their year-round color anchors the garden.

There are two main groups of evergreen trees and shrubs: coniferous (narrow-leaved) and broad-leaved. Coniferous evergreens are cone-bearing plants, most of which have either needlelike leaves, such as pines, or scalelike leaves, such as junipers. Coniferous evergreens can have strikingly different hues and textures. Those with gray-and-silver foliage draw the eye and moderate the intensity of showy garden flowers. Those with blue-gray foliage soften nearby greens, enhance the rose in pink flowers, and intensify nearby purples and blues. In winter, many juniper varieties take on tints of plum or purple. Some golden cultivars of the Hinoki false cypress (*Chamaecyparis obtusa*) are so yellow they can assume the role of a flowering shrub, and their color lasts throughout the year. In a

Evergreen trees and shrubs such as this weeping eastern white pine (*Pinus strobus*) provide year-round color and interest.

small landscape one of these especially colorful evergreens is beautiful—and sufficient.

Broad-leaved evergreens have foliage strikingly different from that of the conifers, ranging from the smooth-edged tiny leaves of little-leaf boxwood to the spiny white-margined leaves of variegated English holly and the big, dark leathery leaves of rhododendron. Many broad-leaved evergreens, such as rhododendrons and camellias, are prized for their flowers, and others, such as hollies and cotoneasters, produce colorful berries. Semievergreen species, such as abelias and some magnolias, keep their foliage all winter in the warm parts of their range but lose it in cooler parts. Some broad-leaved genera—barberry, rhododendron, and holly, among others—include both evergreen and deciduous species, an important difference.

The term evergreen has caused misconceptions. Although the plants are always green, their individual leaves are not. Older leaves are shed, but not all at once and often unnoticeably. The yellowing of the inner, older leaves of a pine or hemlock is a normal part of its cycle of renewal. On the other hand, larches and a few other conifers are deciduous; larch needles turn a glorious yellow-gold in autumn and drop as winter arrives.

Evergreens can be broad-leaved, such as the rhododendron at right, or narrow-leaved, such as the spruce at left.

HABIT

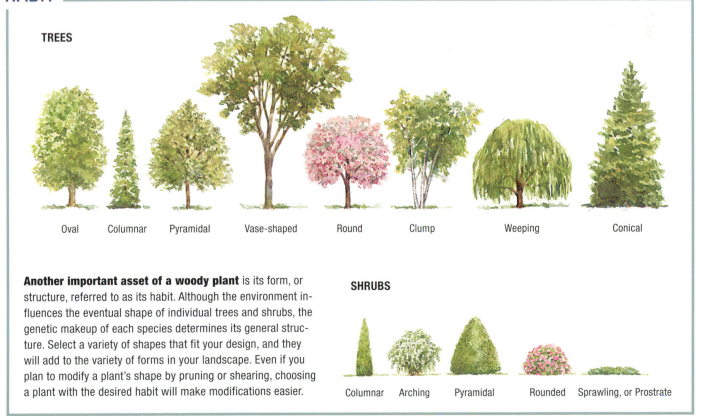

TREES

Oval   Columnar   Pyramidal   Vase-shaped   Round   Clump   Weeping   Conical

Another important asset of a woody plant is its form, or structure, referred to as its habit. Although the environment influences the eventual shape of individual trees and shrubs, the genetic makeup of each species determines its general structure. Select a variety of shapes that fit your design, and they will add to the variety of forms in your landscape. Even if you plan to modify a plant's shape by pruning or shearing, choosing a plant with the desired habit will make modifications easier.

SHRUBS

Columnar   Arching   Pyramidal   Rounded   Sprawling, or Prostrate

DECIDUOUS PLANTS

Deciduous trees and shrubs lose their leaves at the end of each growing season. In winter, the branching structures and twiggy silhouettes of naked trees and shrubs have intrinsic beauty and can contribute as much to a landscape's composition as their fresh green foliage in spring and their bright colors in fall. Bark can be an asset in all seasons. The rugged fissured trunk of an ancient oak, the beautiful exfoliating bark of the Heritage river birch, and the colorful stems of shrubby red- and golden-twigged dogwoods are especially important in winter. Tartarian and red-osier dogwoods (*Cornus alba* and *C. stolonifera*) stand out in snowy landscapes.

During the growing season, deciduous trees and shrubs contribute foliage, flowers, and fruit. Many deciduous trees and shrubs are prized primarily for their foliage. Some, such as the maples, provide welcome shade in summer; others, such as the graceful weeping willow, are valued for their beautiful form. These "foliage" trees and shrubs add texture and color to the garden, and some provide color accents all season long. Some striking examples include purple European beech (*Fagus sylvatica* 'Cuprea'), lemon yellow spirea (*Spiraea japonica* 'Limemound'), purple smoke tree (*Cotinus coggygria* 'Royal Purple'), and the red, bronze, and violet Japanese maples. Autumn can be a breathtaking high point for deciduous trees and shrubs—the brilliant foliage of maples, black gums, viburnums, witch hazels, and many others sets fire to the fall landscape.

Giant dogwood
(*Cornus controversa* 'Variegata')

Hundreds of showy flowering deciduous trees and shrubs contribute color from earliest spring through early fall and, in milder climates, throughout the year. The wealth of species and cultivars and the variety of colors, forms, and blooming periods are staggering.

The challenge is to decide the trees, shrubs, and hedges you like best of those likely to fit in and to succeed in your landscape plan. For example, the flowers of some make giant bouquets; you'll get outstanding seasonal color in spring from the flowering fruit trees and in summer from the hydrangeas. There are witch hazels that send out their ribbonlike flowers in fall or winter. The flowers of some trees and shrubs, such as the variegated dogwoods and purple-leaved cherries, are accompanied by distinctive foliage. The flowers of others, such as fragrant viburnums, mock oranges, and osmanthus, yield a heady perfume.

SPRING

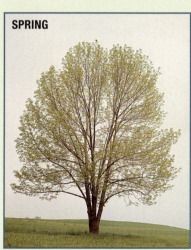

SUMMER

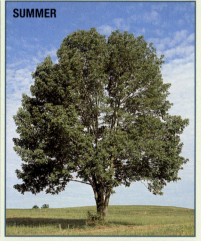

FALL

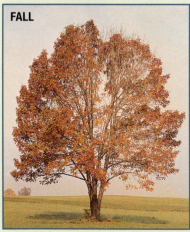

WINTER

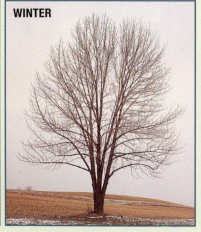

Deciduous trees change with the seasons. The same tree is pictured here as it appears, in spring, summer, fall, and winter.

As the blooming seasons end, many flowering trees and shrubs develop colorful fruits. In fact, showy fruits may be the primary reason to select some species. For example, winterberry's brilliant orange-red berries compensate for its unremarkable leaves and inconspicuous flowers. Others, such as the dogwoods and viburnums, add colorful fruits to their already impressive list of assets.

Most ornamental plants bear male and female sex organs in the same flower or are monoecious and bear them in different flowers on the same plant. Yet some horticulturally important ornamentals, including many of the hollies, are dioecious, meaning the sexes are borne on different plants. To ensure berries on female hollies, you must plant a compatible male nearby. One male can pollinate several females; check with your supplier about optimal plant spacing. In the case of the dioecious ginkgo, you can have its arresting form and golden fall color while avoiding the female's foul-smelling fruit by selecting only male trees.

In planning for fall color, consider the effect of a single deciduous tree, such as a ginkgo, shown at left, or a Japanese maple, shown below against a wall of dark conifers.

Holly plants are either male or female. If you want your female hollies, left, to set fruit, you will need at least one male of a compatible cultivar nearby to provide pollen. Female flowers have a large green knoblike pistil. Males, right, have a tiny pistil and yellowish stamens with pollen.

Choosing the Right Plant

The right plant in the right place is the plant most likely to be healthy and beautiful. The right trees, shrubs, and hedges for you are those that grow vigorously in your environment and require almost no help in fighting pests or diseases. Many such plants are new hybrids of popular ornamentals developed by far-sighted researchers and commercial breeders. Look for improved dogwoods, pest-resistant crabapples, mildew-free crape myrtles, even disease-resistant elms. Other good plants are the rugged—but lovely—native trees and shrubs that are becoming available as nurseries recognize the growing interest in naturalized landscapes and the hardiness and utility of native species. Nature's diversity ensures survival. Monoculture, where many individuals of one species are planted together, invites pests and diseases. You can help avoid infestations by selecting species different from those most common in

The dove tree's eventual 20- to 40-ft. size may serve your plans. Its white flowerlike bracts, above, bloom lavishly every other year.

Few trees feature flower-and-leaf combinations as large as those of the tulip tree, right, but the species grows so fast and tall you'll soon need binoculars to view bees at work. Dwarf forms keep their flowers in closer proximity.

your neighborhood. Often the most popular and overbred plants, such as roses, are the most vulnerable. Look for cultivars advertised as pest- or disease-resistant in your area, and deal with a reliable local nursery. Or consult your local U.S. Department of Agriculture (USDA) Cooperative Extension Service.

With the exception of certain conifers, trees and shrubs grown from cuttings or grafted onto a sturdy rootstock more consistently reproduce desirable characteristics than seed-grown plants. A stem or bud from a desirable species grafted onto the root system of a plant selected for strength and disease resistance almost always results in a superior plant. There are some exceptions, however. For spruces, pines, firs, and larches, you're better off buying seed-grown stock because the cuttings don't train upright reliably. If you want special cultivars of these conifers—say, dwarf, pendulous, or colored—shop for plants grown from cuttings.

Young ash trees are handsome in small spaces, but mature trees, such as this green ash, can reach at least 50 ft. tall. Anticipating eventual size will save headaches later.

Is the Light Right?

When you plan your landscape, consider the availability and intensity of light throughout the year. Most plants tolerate a range of light but have specific conditions in which they perform at their best. Large trees generally grow best in full sun. Many flowering trees and shrubs require full sun for abundant blooms, and some require full sun to bloom at all. Those that evolved in the partial shade of tall trees—for example, small trees such as redbud and dogwood—perform equally well in partial or dappled shade and some even in full shade. Shade-loving plants may thrive in the weak sunlight of spring and fall, but they're likely to suffer in the bright, harsh summer sun, especially in warmer regions. To determine optimal light conditions for particular trees and shrubs, consult the profiles later in this book as well as your local supplier or garden center. The following definitions will help you determine the conditions that you have on your property.

❑ **Full sun**—a daily minimum of six hours of direct unobstructed sun.

❑ **Semisunny or partial shade**—a daily minimum of four to six hours of direct sun.

❑ **Light shade or dappled shade**—sunlight under tall trees and under trees with sparse foliage.

❑ **Shade or full shade**—no direct sun; this occurs on the north side of structures and under dense leaf canopies.

❑ **Dense shade**—shade so deep no shadows are cast; this occurs between tall buildings and under low, close branches.

THE SUN'S PATH

How the sun's path affects sun and shade. The top three drawings show the effects of sunlight on a property with its front yard facing south. The bottom three drawings show the sun's effects on the same property if its front yard were facing east. Before you select woody plants for various sites, try to create a perspective sketch of your own property, with its south side in the foreground and its north side in the background. Include your house and other shade-casting structures.
Note: the sun tracks from east to west. Its angle from the horizon is about twice as high in midsummer (as shown) as in midwinter. Plantings on the north side of a house can be in shade most of the day. Those on the east side of the house receive morning sun and afternoon shade. Those on the west side receive afternoon sun and morning shade. And those on the south side may receive sun nearly all day, unless structures or plantings cast shade there. These are important points to remember when planning your landscape—in the warm South, all-day sun can be too intense for plants near the limit of their heat tolerance, for example.

Hardiness Zone Maps

Average Annual Minimum Temperature

Temp. (°C)	Zone	Temp. (°F)
–45.6 & below	1	below –50
–42.8 to –45.5	2a	–45 to –50
–40.0 to –42.7	2b	–40 to –45
–37.3 to –40.0	3a	–35 to –40
–34.5 to –37.2	3b	–30 to –35
–31.7 to –34.4	4a	–25 to –30
–28.9 to –31.6	4b	–20 to –25
–26.2 to –28.8	5a	–15 to –20
–23.4 to –26.1	5b	–10 to –15
–20.6 to –23.3	6a	–5 to –10
–17.8 to –20.5	6b	0 to –5
–15.0 to –17.7	7a	5 to 0
–12.3 to –15.0	7b	10 to 5
–9.5 to –12.2	8a	15 to 10
–6.7 to –9.4	8b	20 to 15
–3.9 to –6.6	9a	25 to 20
–1.2 to –3.6	9b	30 to 25
1.6 to –1.1	10a	35 to 30
4.4 to 1.7	10b	40 to 35
4.5 & above	11	40 & above

The USDA Hardiness Map divides North America into 11 zones according to average minimum winter temperatures. Hardiness zones are used to identify regions to which plants are suited based on their cold tolerance, which is what "hardiness" means. Many factors, such as elevation and moisture level, come into play when determining whether a plant is suitable for your region. Local climates may vary from what is shown on this map. Contact your local Cooperative Extension Service for recommendations for your area.

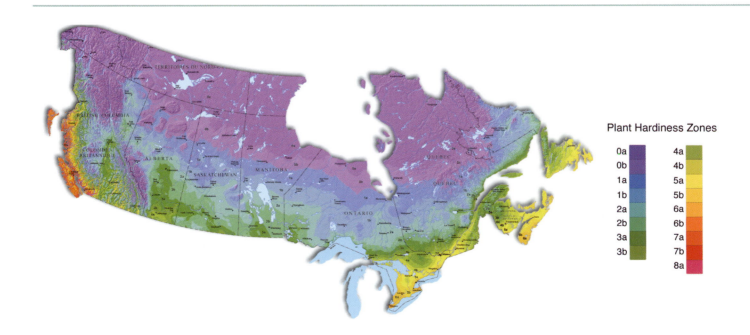

Plant Hardiness Zones

0a		4a	
0b		4b	
1a		5a	
1b		5b	
2a		6a	
2b		6b	
3a		7a	
3b		7b	
		8a	

Heat-Zone Map

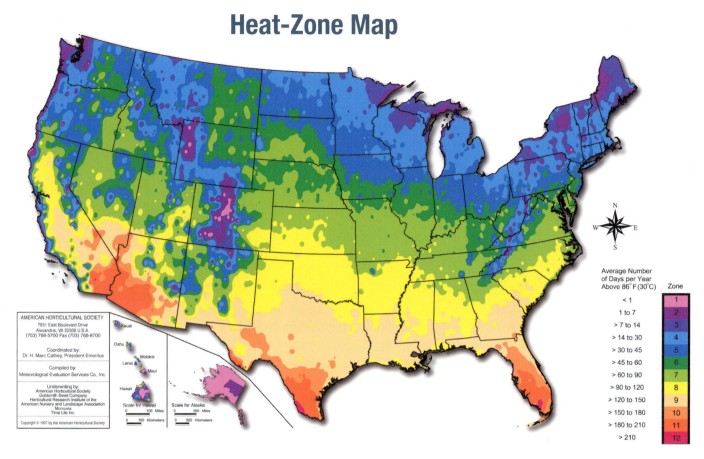

Average Number of Days per Year Above 86°F (30°C)	Zone
< 1	1
1 to 7	2
> 7 to 14	3
> 14 to 30	4
> 30 to 45	5
> 45 to 60	6
> 60 to 90	7
> 90 to 120	8
> 120 to 150	9
> 150 to 180	10
> 180 to 210	11
> 210	12

AMERICAN HORTICULTURAL SOCIETY
7931 East Boulevard Drive
Alexandria, VA 22308 U.S.A.
(703) 768-5700 Fax (703) 768-8700

Coordinated by:
Dr. H. Marc Cathey, President Emeritus

Compiled by:
Meteorological Evaluation Services Co., Inc.

Underwriting by:
American Horticultural Society
Goldsmith Seed Company
Horticultural Research Institute of the
American Nursery and Landscape Association
Monrovia
Time Life Inc.

Copyright © 1997 by the American Horticultural Society

The American Horticultural Society Heat-Zone Map divides the United States into 12 zones based on the average annual number of days a region's temperatures climb above 86°F (30°C), the temperature at which the cellular proteins of plants begin to experience injury. Introduced in 1998, the AHS Heat-Zone Map holds significance, especially for gardeners in southern and transitional zones. Nurseries, growers, and other plant sources will gradually begin listing both cold hardiness and heat tolerance zones for plants, including grass plants. Using the USDA Plant Hardiness map, which can help determine a plant's cold tolerance, and the AHS Heat-Zone Map, gardeners will be able to safely choose plants that tolerate their region's lowest and highest temperatures.

Canada's Plant Hardiness Zone Map outlines the different zones in Canada where various types of trees, shrubs, and flowers will most likely survive. It is based on the average climatic conditions of each area. The hardiness map is divided into nine major zones: the harshest is 0 and the mildest is 8. Relatively few plants are suited to zone 0. Subzones (e.g., 4a or 4b, 5a or 5b) are also noted in the map legend. These subzones are most familiar to Canadian gardeners. Some significant local factors, such as micro-topography, amount of shelter, and subtle local variations in snow cover, are too small to be captured on the map. Year-to-year variations in weather and gardening techniques can also have a significant impact on plant survival in any particular location.

Planting and Transplanting

The methods for planting and maintaining woody plants are similar for most trees and shrubs. For more specific information, see the information about Trees (page 70) and Shrubs (page 150), also paying close attention to profiles on plants of most interest to you throughout this book.

Trees and shrubs are sold in three different ways. Young woody plants are often sold as container-grown plants, usually in plastic pots. More mature specimens that have been growing in the ground are sold balled-and-burlapped, with the root ball wrapped in burlap. Mail-order plants are usually shipped small and bare-root, without any soil.

Before you buy locally, try to examine both the shoots and the roots of the plant. Select only plants that appear healthy and well maintained. Reject plants with damaged, discolored, or diseased foliage, stems, branches, or roots.

Avoid root-bound container-grown plants. They have tightly tangled roots that completely fill the pot, as shown on page 27. For a given container size, smaller plants are less likely to be root-bound and are more likely to succeed. Balled-and-burlapped (B&B) plants may be heavy, unwieldy, and tricky to place in the planting hole, but they benefit from having a large intact root ball.

Return dried-out bare-root plants with broken or heavily snarled roots; those with dry, brittle twigs; and those that you receive too late for optimal planting. Bare-root plants are shipped dormant in the spring. They usually do well if you follow planting instructions carefully. Upon receipt, soak the roots of bare-root plants in a pail of water for 12 to 24 hours prior to actually planting the plant. If planting will be delayed for longer than 24 hours, heel bare-root plants into a trench, as shown below.

Keep your container-grown and balled-and-burlapped plants well watered until you are ready to plant them, but plant them as soon as possible.

Plant bare-root plants and trees described as hard to transplant, such as magnolias, hornbeams, and white and red oaks, in late winter and early spring before vigorous growth begins. Well-maintained container-grown or balled-and-burlapped (B&B) plants can also be planted throughout the summer. Early fall is a good time to plant evergreens, as well as many deciduous species, provided the roots will have at least a month to tie into the soil before falling temperatures (below 40°F) arrest root growth. (Soil cools more slowly than air, so roots continue to grow after the leaves fall.) Water at planting time and again throughout the fall whenever the soil begins to dry out.

Planting

You can keep upright balled-and-burlapped plants for longer periods before planting if you employ the trick used at garden centers. Set each plant on a bed of wood mulch, and cover the root-ball with more mulch. Kept well watered, the mulched "B&B" plants may fare well for weeks or even months. Still, they'll do better if planted promptly. If you can't plant a bare-root tree or shrub immediately, be sure you keep the roots moist. Immediately plunge bare-root plants into a bucket of water. If you need to hold them longer than 24 hours, heel them into the ground in a shallow trench with one angled side. Lay the plants in the trench, resting on their sides. Cover the roots loosely with soil, and keep the soil moist until planting. Plant as soon as possible. Caution: if you wait too long to plant a heeled-in plant, its branches will begin growing vertically, resulting in a lopsided specimen at planting time.

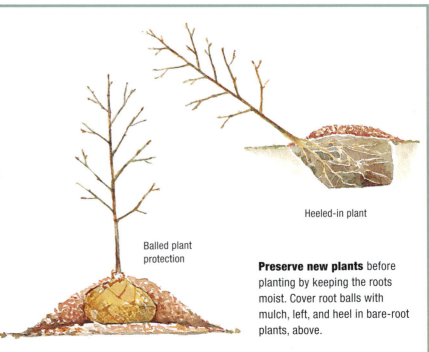

Heeled-in plant

Balled plant protection

Preserve new plants before planting by keeping the roots moist. Cover root balls with mulch, left, and heel in bare-root plants, above.

Trees and shrubs purchased from home centers and garden centers are usually sold in containers or with a root ball wrapped in burlap. Mail-order sources ship bare-root plants, which do not contain soil.

EVALUATING PLANT ROOTS

Before you purchase a woody plant, inspect the condition of its root system. Bare-root plants should be damp upon purchase and should be immediately plunged into water. Container and balled-and-burlapped (B&B) plants should show evidence of regular watering; the goal when planting should be to keep their root balls intact, preventing soil from falling away, creating drying air pockets. Here are examples of features to favor and to avoid.

BARE-ROOT

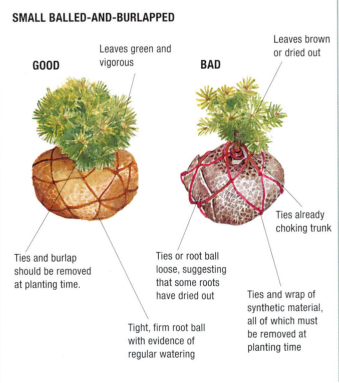

GOOD

BAD

Roots with constricted, bound-up appearance

Most basal roots with numerous fibrous feeder roots

BAD

Balanced, evenly spreading root system

Roots lopsided

CONTAINER

GOOD

BAD

Symmetrical, well-established root system

Excessive, encircling "potbound" roots, some perhaps even emerging from base of container

SMALL BALLED-AND-BURLAPPED

Leaves green and vigorous

Leaves brown or dried out

GOOD

BAD

Ties already choking trunk

Ties and burlap should be removed at planting time.

Ties or root ball loose, suggesting that some roots have dried out

Ties and wrap of synthetic material, all of which must be removed at planting time

Tight, firm root ball with evidence of regular watering

LARGE BALLED-AND-BURLAPPED

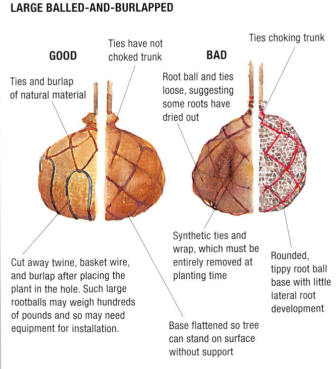

Ties have not choked trunk

Ties choking trunk

GOOD

BAD

Ties and burlap of natural material

Root ball and ties loose, suggesting some roots have dried out

Cut away twine, basket wire, and burlap after placing the plant in the hole. Such large rootballs may weigh hundreds of pounds and so may need equipment for installation.

Synthetic ties and wrap, which must be entirely removed at planting time

Rounded, tippy root ball base with little lateral root development

Base flattened so tree can stand on surface without support

BUYING CONTAINER AND BALLED-AND-BURLAPPED PLANTS

Younger trees and shrubs, such as the mugo pine, above left, may be sold in containers and a lot less than plants of the same species that may be just a year or two older, above right. The burlapped plant probably spent its life in the ground instead of in a pot. Younger trees can catch up to older trees of their species before many years pass.

Small shrubs and trees, above, are usually sold either in containers, such as the rhododendron, above, or balled-and-burlapped. When transporting plants home, protect them from drying effects of wind by placing them inside your vehicle or wrapping them in plastic.

Roots emerging from the base of a container, above right, may indicate excessive, densely tangled roots that can strangle the plant later.

Preparing Planting Sites

The first step in site preparation is to ensure good drainage. Few trees and shrubs can stand saturated soils. To check the drainage at a planting site, dig a hole 24 inches deep and fill it with water. If the water is gone in 24 hours, the drainage is good enough. If more than a little water remains, consider planting species that tolerate poor drainage, or choose another site. If portions of your site are poorly drained, you may wish to try one of the methods shown below. Or you can plant each tree and shrub on individual, slightly raised mounds.

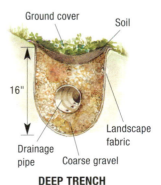

Ground cover
Soil
16"
Drainage pipe
Coarse gravel
Landscape fabric

DEEP TRENCH

8"
Rock or coarse gravel

SHALLOW TRENCH

18"
8"

MOWABLE SWALE

8"

BERM

Solving Drainage Problems. The four methods are described here roughly in relation to their capacity to carry water. The deep trench is first lined with landscape fabric, and then given an initial layer of coarse gravel before the plastic drainage pipe is laid, which is followed by more fill. A shallow rock-filled trench also has a good capacity to move water. A mowable swale is created by digging, and then seeding with grass. Where runoff isn't too heavy, a berm overplanted with ground cover may be enough to redirect unwelcome water.

SOIL TESTING

In the past, planting instructions for trees and shrubs routinely recommended adding humus, to increase water retention, or sand, to improve drainage, to the planting hole. More recent research has shown that the roots of big woody plants set out in holes filled with organic-amended soil tend not to grow outward into the natural soil beyond the hole. Instead, they remain confined as if planted in containers. Mixing sand into the hole may actually decrease drainage and aeration in clay soils. Instead of changing the soil to suit the plant, it's wiser to select plants suitable for the soil.

However, special pH and nutrient requirements of some plants may require that you amend a planting hole or a bed. (See "Basics of Fertilization" on page 47.) For instance, rhododendrons, azaleas, mountain laurels, and other members of the heath family require well-drained, humus-rich, moist acid soil. In this case you can create a raised bed for several shrubs, with plenty of acidic humus and plenty of room for their roots. It may also be practical to amend the soil for hedges, if the plants are set in beds wide enough to contain their mature root systems. (See "Planting a Hedge," page 206.) Shrubs and small trees maintained in containers require improved soils, as described on page 42.

The term acid, and its opposite, sweet, or alkaline, when applied to soil refer to soil pH. The pH of soil affects the availability of nutrients to plants, as explained in the chart on page 30. Most trees and shrubs do well in soils that are slightly acid to neutral, pH 5.5 to 6.8. Some, such as rhododendrons and other heaths, and some hollies and oaks, are among those that require an acid soil pH of 4.5 to 5.5. Lilacs thrive in near-neutral soils. Forsythia, beauty bush, osmanthus, and European beech (*Fagus sylvatica*) are among those that tolerate moderately acid to moderately alkaline soils, up to pH 8.0.

Different species within the same genus may have different soil pH preferences. For example, American beech (*Fagus grandifolia*), unlike its European relative, grows best in acid soils, pH 5.0 to 6.5. Bigleaf hydrangea (*Hydrangea macrophylla*) requires acid soil, but smooth and panicle hydrangeas (*H. arborescens* and *H. paniculata*) are pH adaptable and grow well in alkaline, as well as acid, soils.

In general, acid to neutral soils predominate in areas

TESTING SOIL YOURSELF

To collect samples for testing, take soil from several depths in the location where your trees or shrubs will be planted. First, lift aside several inches of sod, as shown. Then use a clean trowel or shovel to scoop up a representative sampling. Collect the sampling, mix it in a container, and let the soil air dry.

Typically, soil test kits provide a color panel, a test tube for the soil, and a bottle of lime solution. After shaking up the soil and lime, let the mix settle. Then compare its color to colors on the panel. In this test, the orange-red solution, above, corresponds to a panel color indicating mildly acid soil that is slightly less than pH 6. This is the pH level at which many woody plants are able to absorb essential soil nutrients.

These yellow forsythia tolerate moderately acid to moderately alkaline soils. It's wise to test the soil from the location where you plan to plant. Remember: different species within the same genus may have different soil pH preferences.

where the climate is moist—in eastern North America and the Pacific Northwest. Alkaline soils predominate in regions with drier climates. Soils overlying granitic rocks tend to be acid, while those overlying limestone are often alkaline. Locally, soil pH may be quite variable, however, so test your soil before you plant and perhaps again later to assess the effects of soil treatments. You can purchase easy-to-use kits to test soil pH and soil nutrients from garden centers and mail-order suppliers. Laboratory tests may be more accurate; your Cooperative Extension Service, located through telephone information, can provide a list of soil-test labs.

Small changes in soil pH are easier to achieve and maintain than large ones. To raise the pH of acid soil, apply finely ground limestone or dolomitic (magnesium-rich) limestone at the rate recommended on the package. You can mix limestone with soil from the planting hole. Limestone applied to the soil surface annually or semiannually will leach to root level, gradually raising the soil pH there. Proceed slowly and test the soil periodically to measure its progress. An acidic mulch of cottonseed meal, composted sawdust, bark, leaves, or pine needles can effect a slow, but long-lasting, reduction in alkalinity. Mulching may be practical for modest changes in pH for large plantings of shrubs, but to be effective, it must cover the extent of the root systems. Alkaline soils present a difficult problem for many trees and shrubs, and efforts to maintain a pH significantly lower than that of the native soil usually fail. Instead, select from the pH-adaptable species and cultivars available or those species native to alkaline soils. Again, whether your soil is acid or alkaline, you're more likely to succeed if you choose the plant to suit the soil.

How pH Affects Plants

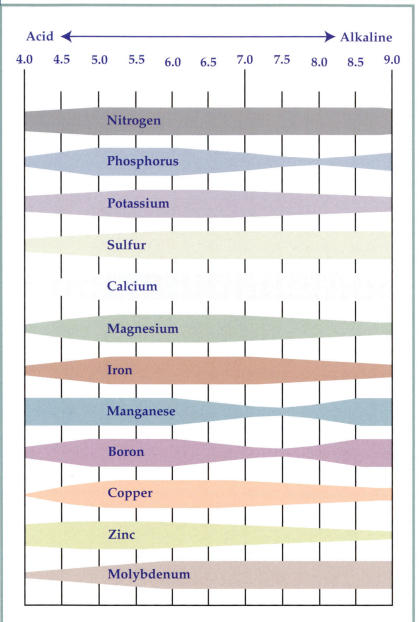

This chart suggests the importance of conducting a soil test before setting out new trees or shrubs or attempting to chemically amend existing problems. For most garden and ornamental plants, the ideal soil pH ranges from moderately acidic (5.5) to neutral (7.0). A low pH number (4.5 or lower) indicates high soil acidity; a high pH number (10.0 or higher) indicates high soil alkalinity. Relative acidity greatly affects the availability of nutrients to the plants.

The bar widths in this chart approximate the availability of essential nutrients at various pH levels; the narrower the bar width, the less available the nutrients. The first six elements are needed in larger amounts. Based on USDA charts showing nutrient availability in various kinds of soils, the chart represents only an approximation of nutrient availability in a hypothetical "general" soil.

Rhododendrons require well-drained, humus-rich, moist soil with an acid pH of 4.5 to 5.5. You can amend a planting hole or bed to meet these nutrient and special pH requirements.

For the most success, choose plants that suit the soil. Lilacs flourish in near-neutral soils with a pH near 7.0.

Planting Trees and Shrubs

Dig a planting hole two to three times wider than the spread of the roots and deep enough so that the crown (where the trunk meets the roots) will be a couple of inches above ground level. (See "Setting the Plant," below.) The soil in the bottom of the hole must be firm to prevent settling; many plants, especially evergreens, are susceptible to crown rot if the plant settles and water saturates the soil around the crown. Use a spading fork to roughen the sides of the hole to assist root penetration as the plant grow. To promote vigorous root growth, some experts suggest you mix a balanced fertilizer and superphosphate into the soil dug from the planting hole. (See "Basics of Fertilization" on page 47.)

For a container-grown plant, follow the instructions on page 34. Tip the container on its side, and tap it to loosen the roots. Ease the plant gently from the container, or use shears to cut the container off. If the plant is root-bound, carefully loosen, unwrap, and spread the roots if possible, and cut away any roots wrapped around the crown. Make 1-inch-deep slashes from top to bottom on all four sides of the root ball to stimulate the growth of new roots. Gently loosen the outer surface of the root ball.

DIGGING TOOLS

A transplanting spade allows deep thrusts, useful for severing roots and working underneath root balls. A garden spade is highly versatile, able to perform service similar to that of the transplanting spade, while also useful for edging and leveling work. A spading fork serves well for loosening soil and turning compost. The round-head shovels are primarily designed for moving gravel, sand, and crushed rock. But they are also formidable digging tools. A crowbar, or wrecking bar, is invaluable for jobs like loosening hard-packed soil, prying up large stones, and prying up old stumps.

Transplanting spade

Garden spade

Spading fork

Round-head shovels

D-handle

Long handle

Crowbar

Setting the Plant

When planting any tree or shrub, the crown should remain an inch or two above ground level after planting. So for bare-root trees and shrubs, dig the hole a little less deep than the length of the roots. Place the bottoms of container-grown or balled-and-burlapped plants on firm undisturbed ground; this helps prevent settling later. Planting holes should be two to three times as wide as the root mass. Make a berm to capture and hold water for the roots, and mulch to within 3 to 6 inches of the trunk to retard weed growth and conserve soil moisture.

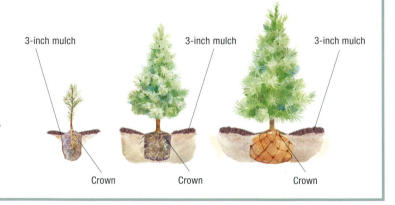

3-inch mulch

3-inch mulch

3-inch mulch

Crown

Crown

Crown

Meticulously shaped and maintained hedges create a graceful frame for a soft and curvaceous garden path.

how to

Transplant Container Plants

DIFFICULTY LEVEL: EASY

Here are transplanting steps for container plants, including procedures to save root-bound plants. Whether you know upon purchase or discover later that a plant is root-bound, planting procedures are the same. If you have a root-bound plant, with roots densely wrapped and tangled, as shown between steps 1 and 2 below, the roots won't spread into surrounding soil efficiently and could eventually strangle the plant unless you cut and redirect them.

1 **With moist soil in the container,** lay the container on its side, left, and slide the plant out. If necessary, tap or massage the container to release the plant. This badly rootbound plant, right, needs emergency surgery.

2 **Make four or more vertical** cuts deep into the soil mass before firmly teasing the roots outward by hand. In the case of this rootbound mass with thick, heavily tangled exterior roots, more and deeper cuts were necessary.

3 **Recheck the planting hole** depth by laying a shovel across the hole. With roots resting firmly on undisturbed soil, the crown should be about 2 in. above ground level. If necessary, build up the soil under the root mass.

4 **Return about half of the soil** to the hole bottom, and gently tamp it to promote plant stability without compacting the soil and thereby removing air pores.

5 **Pour enough water** into the half-filled hole so that it pools. Wait for the water to disappear before returning remaining soil to the hole. Note the soil-conserving use of a tarp.

6 **Create a shallow, moatlike depression** around the trunk. Add more water and let that settle. Note that the trunk's crown remains above ground level.

This red oak seedling will grow into a massive and grand tree of 60 to 70 ft. in about 20 years. It's one of the most popular of all landscaping trees; it transplants easily, and it's hardy.

Balled-and-burlapped plants suffer the least amount of damage if placed in the hole with the burlap still intact. If the plant is heavy, you can pull it into the hole on a piece of plastic and then slide the plastic out. When the plant is in the hole, remove all ties or wires, and cut away as much burlap as possible. If the burlap is treated or synthetic, remove all of it. Gently loosen the surface of the root ball.

Place bare-root plants on a cone or mound of undisturbed or compacted soil in the planting hole, with the roots spread out on the cone. Adjust the height of the cone so that the roots are at the depth at which they grew in the nursery and the crown is about 2 inches above ground level, to allow for settling. Remove broken or damaged roots on all plants. (Also see instructions on planting trees, shrubs, and hedges in the introductions to those sections of this book.)

Having placed the plant in the hole, backfill with soil from the planting hole. For bare-root plants, work the soil in among the roots with one hand while supporting the plant at its proper planting depth with the other. When the hole is half full, water generously. When that water has drained, fill the hole with soil, and tamp the soil down firmly, sloping it away from the plant. Build up a low ridge of soil at the border of the planting hole to make a water-catching basin, and then water slowly and thoroughly. Top the area beginning about 6 inches from the stems or trunk with an organic mulch 3 inches deep. (See "Mulches," on page 44 for more information.)

Experts no longer recommend routinely staking newly planted trees unless they are top heavy or their root balls aren't sufficient to provide stability. Trees left un-staked can sway with the breeze, and this helps them develop stronger trunks and root structures. (See page 77 for more information on staking.)

Watering

Lack of water is probably the biggest single cause of failure of newly planted trees and shrubs because it's then that they are most vulnerable to drought. Water well during the first growing season to promote the growth of big, healthy root systems. Monitor the soil moisture. A useful rule of thumb is to water when the top inch of soil has become dry. Sandy soils dry out faster than clayey or humus-rich soils. Water slowly and deeply; the water must reach the roots. Sprinkling the leaves can reduce stress on newly planted trees and shrubs in hot weather. Trees and shrubs lose moisture through transpiration from their leaves, and watering them can help. Watering also cools the plants. It is best to sprinkle leaves in the morning or late in the day. Watering at midday allows more moisture to be lost to evaporation. Night watering was once thought to make foliage more susceptible to fungal disease, but today it is considered to be as natural as the morning dew.

To check soil moisture, insert a dry stick into the soil, and pull it up after an hour or so. If the bottom of the stick looks and feels damp, the soil is moist enough.

For established trees and shrubs, local climate, soil conditions, and the drought resistance of your plants determine when and how often to water. If you have wisely chosen plants suitable for your soil and climate, rainfall should meet their water needs except during severe droughts. During dry periods, watch for effects of drought—shoots drooping, leaves beginning to wilt or curl, shiny leaves turning dull. Many plants droop on hot summer days, but if they do not recover overnight, it's time to water. Drip-irrigation hoses, soaker hoses, and other systems that deliver water slowly, right to the soil, are preferable to overhead sprinklers for watering trees and shrubs. Frequent shallow watering of lawns can be harmful to trees and shrubs—to repeat, water deeply so that the water reaches their root systems.

Except during severe droughts, rainfall should meet the watering needs of established trees and shrubs, especially if you have chosen plants that are suitable for your climate and soil.

how to

Remove an Existing Shrub or Tree for Transplanting

The best time to remove a smaller woody plant for transplanting is usually in early spring before growth begins. If you have time during the spring before transplanting, sever the roots in a circle, as shown, using a long-bladed spade. New roots will grow that season within the circle, helping reduce stress on the plant after you transplant it in the spring.

1 **If you are removing a shrub,** tie the stems together so you have plenty of head-room. Then scrape turf and debris away from the work area.

2 **Shape the top and sides of a root ball** about as large as you'll be able to wrap and transport later. This shape will make wrapping easier.

6 **Remembering to first flop the burlap over** so the rolled side faces down, tip the root ball enough to slide the roll just beyond the middle of the ball.

7 **Now, tipping the root ball in** the opposite direction, unroll the burlap. This gentle method ensures the desired minimal breakup of the root ball.

8 **Tie opposite corners of the burlap,** checking first to ensure that the entire wrap fits snugly around the bottom of the root ball, leaving no room for soil to break loose.

3 **Use pruning shears** to cleanly cut protruding roots. Otherwise, the protrusions will make wrapping with burlap more difficult.

4 **Undercut the root ball** on all sides until you've cut all roots free. You can test for readiness by tipping and wiggling the plant with your spade.

5 **Using a square sheet of burlap,** wide enough to wrap all the way around the root ball, roll up one end of the sheet to midway, as shown.

9 **Complete the burlap wrap** by tying the two remaining corners. If the plant is smaller than this one, this degree of wrapping may be sufficient.

10 **For plants of this size and larger,** further secure the burlap with twine so that the twine supports at least four quadrants. The goal is a tight, compact ball.

11 **When securing the twine** over the top of the root ball, tension it to keep the soil from loosening during handling. The twine should not constrict the trunk or stems.

how to

Plant a Bare-Root Tree or Shrub

DIFFICULTY LEVEL: EASY

At planting time, it's usually better to limit pruning to suckers, damaged roots, diseased wood, and inward or crossing branches. Avoid removing healthy end buds, which create hormones that stimulate root growth and result in leafing that creates food for the plant. Also, because branches growing low on the trunk promote trunk girth and strength, it's usually better to delay pruning them until after the tree is well established.

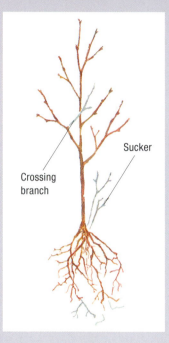

Crossing branch

Sucker

Crown 2 in. above ground level

1 **Keep bare roots in water** until planting time. Place the roots on a cone of undisturbed soil in the bottom of the hole, and spread them over this soil. The firmness of the cone will keep the crown from settling below ground level later. Laying a stick across the hole makes it easy to see whether the crown is elevated enough.

2 **After removing any broken or damaged roots,** use your hands and fingers to pack soil into and around the root network, trying not to leave air pockets.

3 **When the hole is about half full of soil** and the root ends are pretty well covered, fill the hole with water and let that settle before adding the remaining soil.

4 **Add remaining soil,** and create a saucerlike depression and a mounded rim around the edge to catch water. Tamp it down firmly but not so heavily that you press out all air.

5 **Apply and maintain a 3-in.-deep carpet of mulch around the plant,** keeping the mulch about 6 in. from the trunk. The mulch will help suppress weeds, reduce evaporation of moisture from the soil, and nourish the soil as the mulch decomposes on the underside. Water the plant well during its first growing season.

This young maple is turning red in autumn.

GROWING TREES AND SHRUBS IN CONTAINERS

Small trees and shrubs can thrive in outdoor containers, if the containers and soil meet each plant's special needs. For a young tree or a small shrub, such as a gardenia, a suitable container is 14 to 16 inches in height and diameter. Because soil insulates, that amount of soil is usually enough to keep roots from freezing as far north as Zones 6 and 7. A larger plant, such as a dwarf flowering crabapple, can do well for years in an 18- to 20-inch tub. A tub that size holds enough soil to protect the roots in most winters as far north as Zones 4 and 5. A larger plant could start in a 14- to 16-inch tub but will eventually require a big tub, perhaps 30 inches high and 24 inches in diameter. Larger tubs allow more root development, which helps the plant grow bigger. A large tub makes maintenance easier, too, because it will need watering only once or twice a week, even during the summer. During hot, dry, windy periods, smaller containers must be watered daily, even when the soil is a really good organic mix.

HORTICULTURAL PERLITE

HORTICULTURAL POLYMER

PEAT MOSS

Commercial soilless mixes are often used in containers because they are lightweight and easy to move. Yet a fertile semisoilless mix provides a better diet for the plants. You can mix your own by thoroughly combining 1 part good topsoil, 1 part horticultural perlite, and 1 part coarse peat moss. For every 7 inches of planter height, add 1 cup of dehydrated cow manure and ⅓ cup of slow-release 5-10-5 fertilizer. Mixing in horticultural polymers helps keep the soil humid. A horticultural polymer is a jelly-like granule that holds many times its weight in water and releases moisture as soil dries. Mix thoroughly with the soil.

Before planting, soak the container mixture two or three times until water runs out the bottom. After planting, top the soil with a 2- to 3-inch layer of mulch to minimize moisture loss and keep the mix from blowing about. Frequent watering leaches nutrients from the soil, so compensate by giving the plants light applications of a water-soluble fertilizer.

Large containers can reduce watering frequency and help insulate roots.

Fertilizing Container Plants. If you did not amend the soil with a slow-release fertilizer at planting time, scatter it over the soil surface. Apply a dilute solution (about 1 teaspoon of 20-20-20 per gallon of water) of a balanced soluble fertilizer once a week or a far more dilute solution every time you water. Every year, topdress the container soil with 2 or 3 inches of improved soil or compost.

Root-Pruning Container Plants. Container plants can become root-bound. This means that there is too much root material relative to the container and soil mix. Root-pruning every two or three years keeps a plant growing well and helps retard its growth without impairing its form. Root prune in late winter before growth begins.

With a small tub, remove the mulch and tip the tub onto its side before slipping the root ball out. Disentangle the roots wound around the root ball, prune them back, and then cut away the roots growing straight down the sides of the root ball. Next, add fertile soil mix to the tub, slide the root ball back inside, and set the tub upright. Push fresh soil down around the sides, and add 2 or 3 inches to the top of the root ball before replacing the mulch. Water thoroughly. If the tub and plant are too big to turn the tub on its side, use a hand pruning saw to sever all roots growing around the outside of the root ball.

This container-grown threadleaf Japanese maple (*Acer palmatum*) can be transplanted in early spring. It has exquisitely cut leaves and an often-weeping form that gives it a refined appearance.

Using Mulch

Maintain throughout the year the 3-inch layer of mulch that you spread at planting. If the layer is thinner, you'll need an underlayment of water-permeable landscape fabric to prevent weeds from growing upward through the mulch.

Mulches conserve soil moisture, moderate hot and cold soil temperatures, keep weeds at bay, and give the planting a finished appearance. Organic mulches include bark, wood chips, compost, leaf mold (partially composted leaves), sawdust, straw, lawn clippings, buckwheat hulls, and pine needles. The finer the mulch, the faster it decomposes, allows weeds to take hold, and needs to be replenished. Decomposing organic mulches add humus to the soil but deplete soil nitrogen, a necessary nutrient; fine, uncomposted mulches deplete nitrogen most rapidly. Watch for signs of nitrogen deficiency, which include pale new shoots and leaves. An application of a high-nitrogen fertilizer (such as 20-10-10) should correct the condition. Applying a generous mulch of composted leaves or manure, or a mix of both, adds a rich balance of nutrients to the soil without depleting its nitrogen.

For landscape mulches, a sampling of the many available and attractive types, colors, and textures is shown below. There are pine, fir, cedar, hemlock, and various hardwood barks that may be ground, chopped, chipped, or shredded—fine to coarse particle size. Pine needles and conifer bark are often used as acidic mulches; do not use them to mulch plants that prefer somewhat alkaline soils. Low-maintenance inorganic mulches, such as stones, crushed rock, pebbles, gravel, and lava rock or brick, are often used on level terrain and in formal, Japanese, and arid landscapes.

Counterclockwise from upper left: Inorganic mulches include gray granite, yellow beach pebbles, crushed red brick, crushed marble, light brown lava, red lava, and "jade" beach stones.

Counterclockwise from bottom: The organic mulches include aged hardwood chips, fresh hardwood chips, red-dyed shredded cedar, shredded cedar, western pine-bark nuggets, shredded pine bark, shredded hemlock, pine needles, and shredded cypress.

The finer the mulch, the faster it decomposes. If the mulch is organic, it will deposit nutrients into the soil, but it can also deplete nitrogen. To avoid this problem, use composted leaves or manure.

Composting

A mixture of decomposed organic materials, compost is an excellent soil conditioner and mulch. Just dig the stuff a few inches into the soil or spread it on top of the ground as mulch. Compost is the best way to dispose of garden wastes, autumn leaves, and plant-based kitchen refuse.

Some people get pretty scientific and painstaking when making compost. They use heat-trapping containers, measure heat inside the pile, and create precise mixes of additives to accelerate the process and control the end product. Yet compost can be made simply by letting a pile of plant wastes decompose on its own, with the aerating help of an occasional turning with a spading fork. The resulting compost is excellent, though the process takes longer.

You can cut the time by half or more if you chop the waste into small pieces (grinding up leaves in a lawn mower, a leaf blower-vacuum, or a shredder), keep the pile somewhat damp, and aerate it once or twice a week by turning or fluffing the mass with a spading fork. You can fur-

ther speed the process, and improve the compost, by adding 2 cups of a water-soluble high-nitrogen fertilizer to each 10-quart bag of leaves. If you have clayey soil, add 2 cups of gypsum as well. Substitute acid-type fertilizer if you plan to use the compost with acid-loving plants.

ADDING LEAVES

Fallen leaves are good compost ingredients if shredded. Rake or blow the leaves into a pile, and shred them with a lawn mower, leaf blower-vacuum, or shredder to help them break down more quickly. If they aren't shredded, leaves tend to decompose slower than most other materials. So it's better to pile unshredded leaves separately and turn them occasionally as they break down at their own pace into leaf mold over the next year or so.

Electric leaf blower-vacuum

Leaf rake

how to

Make a Wire-Mesh Compost Bin

DIFFICULTY LEVEL: EASY

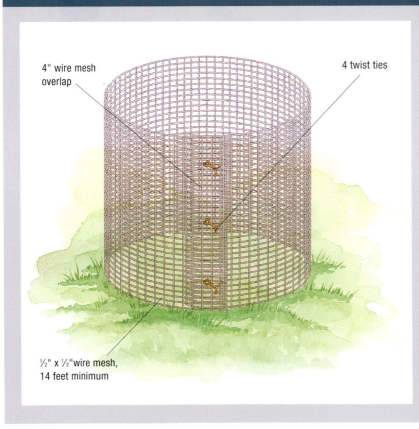

4" wire mesh overlap

4 twist ties

½" x ½" wire mesh, 14 feet minimum

This bin keeps compost materials from blowing around, promotes aeration, and confines a mass that retains heat inside the pile. If you turn the layered contents occasionally to promote aeration, you will have compost in a year or so. **Note:** leaf compost, consisting only of leaves that haven't been shredded, may take one to three years, depending on leaf sizes and types, and the climate.

1 **Form the ½-in. wire mesh** into a cylindrical bin about 4 ft. in diameter by overlapping about 4 in. of the ends and securing them with heavy-duty twist ties.

2 **Place the bin directly on the soil.** Or to deter foraging rodents, place the bin on a paved surface or on a square of ½-in. wire mesh. Use a plywood lid to shade the pile from drying sun and to shed rain whenever the pile becomes too soggy.

BASICS OF FERTILIZATION

Plants absorb most of the elements they require for healthy growth from the soil. Nitrogen (N) is essential for stem and leaf production, phosphorus (P) promotes root growth as well as the growth of flowers and fruits, and potassium (K) promotes flowering and fruit production. These three are the primary nutrients—those needed in the largest amounts and used the fastest. Commercial fertilizers, whether organic or chemical, supply these nutrients and often secondary nutrients and trace elements as well, in combinations called "balanced fertilizers." Their packages list the proportions of the primary nutrients in terms of the N-P-K ratio. An all-purpose balanced fertilizer might have a rating of 20-20-20, with all three elements in equal proportion. Flowering plants usually benefit from fertilizers with higher proportions of phosphate and potassium, such as 5-10-10.

The rate at which a fertilizer releases its nutrients determines the way you use it. Slow-release fertilizers deliver their nutrients over several months and are applied annually. Manufactured slow-release balanced fertilizers deliver nutrients in 6, 8, or 12 months. Organic slow-release fertilizers include limestone, dolomite, superphosphate, and rock phosphate.

Where soil is infertile and when planting shrubs and small flowering trees and hedge plants, add to the hole (or bed) a combination of 8-month (spring plant-ing) to 12-month (fall planting) slow-release fertilizer, as well as rock or superphosphate, which sustains root growth. After the second year, restore used up nutrients in midfall or late winter to early spring by applying a slow-release balanced fertilizer. This, in addition to an annual application of a rich organic mulch of composted leaves or manure, or a mixture of both, provides all the nutrients needed for healthy growth.

Quick-release fertilizers are used to give short-term boosts, if needed, during the growing season. Quick-release fertilizers include balanced "chemical" fertilizers and organic emulsions made from "natural" materials such as seaweed, fish, and manure. Manure steeped in water is known as "manure tea." Most quick-release fertilizers are water soluble and can be sprayed onto leaves, a process known as foliar feeding.

Too much fertilizer of any type, but especially the chemical fertilizers, can burn tender roots and shoots, so never apply more than the amount suggested by the container label. With fertilizer, less is better than more. That's because excess fertilizer can cause rapid weak growth that makes the plant vulnerable to wind damage, drought, temperature extremes, pests, and diseases. Besides, fertilizer runoff from lawns and gardens pollutes water systems.

Poor growth, discolored leaves, and failure to flower or fruit are signs of possible nutrient deficiencies, but they can be caused by other factors as well and are often hard to diagnose. Foliage plants with yellow leaves most likely need nitrogen, but the yellowed foliage of evergreens (yellow with dark veins in broad-leaved evergreens) suggests an iron deficiency. Poor flowering may be due to a lack of potassium and phosphorus or insufficient light. A soil test can help identify the source of the problem. Check the pH, because pH affects the availability of nutrients and adjusting it may solve the problem without the need for fertilizer. If soil tests indicate a need for fertilizers, try applications of a quick-release form of a soluble fertilizer. Also, consider the chart on page 30.

The three numbers on a fertilizer bag indicate the proportions of the three major nutrients, from left to right, nitrogen (N), phosphorus (P), and potassium (K). Flowering plants thrive with fertilizers that have a higher proportion of phosphate and potassium, like this fertilizer. Foliage plants do better with a higher proportion of nitrogen.

How to Prune Plants

Pruning, or selective removal of plant parts, can improve the health and shape of trees and shrubs and make them stronger and more beautiful. Pruning controls size and rampant growth, improves flowering and fruiting, removes diseased parts, and corrects damage . Severe pruning revitalizes many woody plants and regular pruning shapes and maintains hedges.

Although deciduous plants respond better than evergreens to corrective pruning, it may take years to reshape a badly formed tree or shrub. So before you buy a woody plant, study the lines of its trunk or stems and main branches. Choose a plant that, with perhaps some reasonable amount of initial pruning, will grow into the shape you want. If you choose plants to fit your site's space and plants that will adapt to your property's environment, pruning will become only a minor annual chore.

Hand-Pruning Tools

Price is often a reliable gauge of tool quality. Still, some modestly priced tools can give a lifetime of service if you treat them well. Keep blades sharp, and oil joints periodically. After use, wipe dirt from blades, and remove sap using a solvent such as kerosene. Store tools in a dry place, safely away from children. To prevent rust, oil all metal before long-term storage.

FOLDING PULL SAW

PULL SAW

Pull saws, also known as *Grecian saws,* cut on the pull stroke. They are great in tight quarters and easy to use overhead. Folding versions can be safely carried in a pocket. Fixed-blade saws are more safely transported in specially designed scabbards.

Pastured cattle can keep conifers looking compact because they nibble only the young new shoots each spring, sparing the less tender older growth. So too can hand pruning keep growth of conifers and broad-leaved evergreens in check.

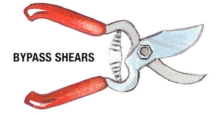

BYPASS SHEARS

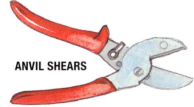

ANVIL SHEARS

Folding pruning knives are handy for a range of tasks, from cutting wood to severing twine.

Bypass pruning shears employ two curved blades consisting of a cutting blade that passes close by a flat-edged branch-gripping blade. Springs reopen the blade effortlessly for the user. For cleanest cuts at branch crotches, position the blade nearer the collar of the limb you wish to save. Bypass shears are designed for wood up to about ½ inch in diameter, as are anvil shears. **Anvil pruning shears** employ a straight cutting blade that presses against the flat surface of a mating anvil-like blade. These shears provide good cutting force relative to exertion. The cutting blade stops at the anvil. However, anvil shears tend to crush stems and don't allow the precise close fit in branch crotches that bypass pruners do, and their anvils almost always damage branch collars.

At planting time, prune back to a main stem only broken branches of new trees and shrubs. Instructions supplied with bare-root plants often recommend cutting back one-third of the branches to compensate for a reduced root system, but this long-accepted practice is now in question. Research has shown that severely pruning the tops of newly planted trees actually retards root growth—the leaves are needed to supply the food to grow abundant roots.

There are two basic kinds of pruning cuts: heading cuts and thinning cuts. A heading cut shortens a stem or branch by cutting off its tip. It removes the dominant end bud, which encourages buds farther back on the stem to grow into new shoots, resulting in a bushier plant. A thinning cut removes an entire stem or branch back to where it joins the main stem or trunk or a larger branch. Use this kind of cut to remove damaged and dead wood, to get rid of crossed branches, or to open up the interior of the plant to let in more light and air.

Bow saws equipped with high-quality blades make quick work of limbs up to several inches in diameter. The position of the handle, above the line of the blade, allows forceful thrusts on the push stroke. The pointed bow saw allows cutting in tight quarters but can limit depth of cut. D-shaped bow saws come in lengths from 21 to more than 40 inches, allowing deeper cuts and even two-person sawing.

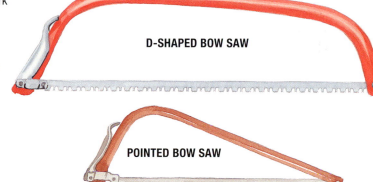

D-SHAPED BOW SAW

POINTED BOW SAW

Pole trimmers have either a long wooden shaft or an extendable shaft of slip-fitting fiberglass tubing that can be locked at various extensions. For small high branches, a pole trimmer reduces the need for a ladder or tree climbing. Trimmers with extendable shafts extend 10 to 14 feet. On branches up to ½ inch or so, you can cut with the rope-pull lopper. On branches up to an inch or so, the saw blade works pretty well. A preliminary undercut, on the bottom side of the limb, will reduce chances that the falling limb will rip bark from the trunk.

Loppers are essentially heftier variations of bypass and anvil pruning shears. They require two-hand operation and can cut larger branches. They are especially handy for pruning in hard-to-reach places. The bigger loppers have ratchet mechanisms that increase cutting force without increasing cutting effort. Some models can handle branches up to 1½ inches in diameter. Whatever the design, use it only on limbs that fit deeply into the cutting jaws, allowing maximum cutting efficiency without overtaxing stress points. The leverage provided by long handles encourages strong people to overtax their lopper, which can break or bend handles and blade assemblies.

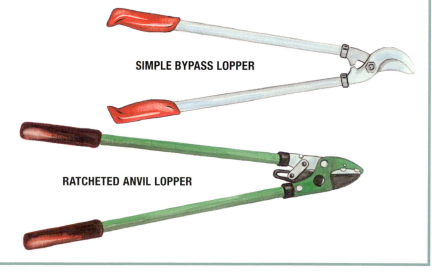

SIMPLE BYPASS LOPPER

RATCHETED ANVIL LOPPER

Shears

In skilled hands, **manual hedge shears** can handle the range of tasks from light flat trims to elaborate curves of topiary. The challenge is to eyeball smooth cutting planes while your hands and arms perform a choppy operation.

Electric hedge shears allow low-effort, smooth trimming as you gracefully sweep the tool over intended planes. For best control of the power-cord extension, drape it over the shoulder on the side of your direction of travel.

Power Pruners

Safety Note: For all electric power tools, be sure your extension cable meets manufacturer's specifications and that it is protected by a ground-fault circuit interrupter (GFCI).

A reciprocating saw can be an excellent pruner, especially when you need to annually cut near ground level about a third of the stems in a row of lilacs.

Chain saws are available in electric or gas-powered models. You may not need a chain saw for general pruning, unless you plan to make much firewood on an annual basis. For occasional trees with trunks less than 4 inches in diameter, a bow saw can be an efficient alternative. However, if you need a chain saw and can do most cutting within 100 feet of an outdoor outlet, an electric chain saw is probably all you'll need.

In contrast to bigger, heavier, gas-powered chain saws, electrics emit no exhaust fumes and are low maintenance, low cost, and quieter. They are always ready to go, except that the chain needs sharpening whenever it begins to show signs of dulling, as with a gas-powered saw. (A dull chain produces sawdust-size particles and cuts so slowly that it tempts you to mistakenly apply more pressure to the bar. A sharp chain yields wood chips the size of dry oatmeal and cuts through wood almost as though it were butter. Low-cost sharpening jigs mount on the saw bar and allow you to sharpen each cutter at the same precise angle and depth.)

Caution: A chain saw is one of the most dangerous power tools in common use, particularly in the hands of inexperienced, fatigued, or careless people. The prime single hazard is deep bone-cutting injury resulting from saw kickback, which can occur when the chain arcing around the nose of the bar unexpectedly hits resistance, such as an unnoticed limb or other obstruction. To avoid kickback, always hold the saw by both handles with a firm opposable-thumb grip and with your left elbow extended, not bent. At the very least, study the manufacturer's owner's manual and heed all its safety instructions.

Basic Pruning Cuts

The shaping of trees, shrubs, and hedges requires applications of specific pruning cuts, and deciduous plants are pruned differently from evergreens. Proceed with caution because mistakes can be difficult to correct. For example, many conifers do not grow new shoots from old wood, and a misplaced cut can leave a permanent hole. (For more on the pruning of conifers, see page 85.)

Use pruning to guide growth in directions that will enhance the form of the plant. The photos in this book give examples of the mature shape typical of many featured plants, but no tree will grow to match these photos exactly. For deciduous trees, the best examples may be the winter silhouettes of trees found in arboreta and public gardens. Study the shapes of species that interest you, and train your eye to recognize features that need correction.

For diseased wood, reduce the chances that pruning tools will transmit disease organisms by dipping their cutting edges in a chlorine bleach solution (1 part bleach to 9 parts water) before using the tools and after each cut.

For more on pruning techniques for trees, see pages 80 to 85. For pruning of shrubs, see pages 156 to 159. And for pruning of hedges, see pages 214 to 215.

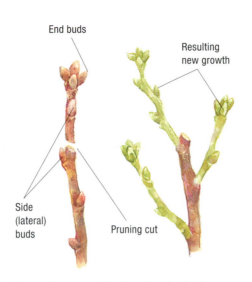

End buds

Resulting new growth

Side (lateral) buds

Pruning cut

Removing an end bud or shoot will stimulate dormant buds below it to grow, producing side shoots and creating a bushier plant. If you allow end buds to remain, they will actually inhibit the growth of side buds, and the stem will continue to grow mainly from the tip.

Resulting new growth

To prune branches with opposite buds, such as those of maple and ash, cut straight across in a line that just clears the bud tips. This will result in fairly uniform growth of both buds.

To prune branches with alternate buds, find a bud pointing in the direction you want your branch to grow. Make your cut about ¼ inch above the bud and on an angle parallel with that bud. There is no need to apply tree wound dressing to cuts, whether small or large.

When pruning with a lopper or with pruning shears, place the blade side nearer the part you wish to save. Cut just outside the branch collar at the angle shown. This will help you avoid leaving a stub and will promote quick healing of the wound.

WHEN TO PRUNE

Pruning stimulates growth in woody plants—just as deadheading and pinching back stimulate flower and foliage production in herbaceous plants. This basic principle, combined with the blooming period of flowering plants, governs the pruning timetables below.

In general, drastic hard pruning shortly before the growing season promotes the most growth; light pruning or late-season pruning encourages less vigorous growth. Avoid pruning after midsummer before the onset of dormancy; pruning at that time can damage a plant by causing a spurt of tender new growth that may not have time to harden enough to withstand winter's cold.

EVERGREENS

In spring, prune
❑ Winter and snow damage before active growth begins.
❑ Pines, firs, spruces, and other conifers to encourage dense branching and improve shape by shearing the light green new growth in early spring. Cut off the tips or half the new growth of pine shoots, or candles.
❑ To slow or dwarf the development of coniferous evergreens, prune new growth once or twice more at intervals of a week. This will also help avoid unsightly cuts.
❑ Plants that bloom on new wood (many of which flower in summer). To encourage flowering, prune old wood in late winter or early spring before growth begins.
❑ To renovate overgrown broad-leaved shrubs, prune no more than one-third of the total green foliage in one season.

In summer, prune
❑ Plants that bloom on old wood (many of which bloom in spring); prune just after the flowers have faded, and then let the plants grow new branches and flower buds that will bloom the following season.
❑ To shape or slow the growth of broad-leaved evergreens. Prune in early summer, after flowering. Prune hollies in mid- to late summer.

In fall and winter, prune
❑ Coniferous evergreens, when removing branches to correct shape or thin congested growth.
❑ Lightly for holiday greens. (This won't harm the plants.)

Any time, prune
❑ Dead, damaged, or diseased branches.
❑ Lightly, for decorative greens and flowers.

DECIDUOUS TREES AND SHRUBS

In spring, prune
❑ Plants that bloom on new wood (many of which flower in summer). Prune before new growth begins, in late winter or early spring, to promote flowering.

In summer, prune
❑ Plants that bloom on old wood (many of which flower in spring). Prune immediately after the blooms fade to avoid cutting off newly formed flower buds and to stimulate growth of more buds for next year's bloom.
❑ Young foliage plants (in early summer) to encourage dense branching. Cut back by half the succulent stems that are beginning to grow lateral shoots.
❑ To slow or dwarf growth in summer after the seasonal growth is complete.
❑ To control height when plants have reached the desired size, after the new growth has fully developed. (Extend the cuts back a bit into old wood.)
❑ Trees that bleed, such as maples and birches

In fall and winter, prune
❑ Trees when dormant, to shape and train.
❑ To renovate overgrown shrubs, when dormant.

Any time, prune
❑ Dead, diseased, or damaged wood. (Prune dead wood before leaves fall; otherwise you may have a hard time distinguishing it from dormant wood.)
❑ Lightly, for indoor use as decorative greens, flowers, and winter branches.

Fall and winter are good times for pruning deciduous trees. When trees or shrubs are dormant, you can shape them or train them to grow a certain way.

Pests and Diseases

Your best defense against pests and diseases is to choose plants suited to your soil and climate, particularly plants that are bred or known to be naturally pest and disease resistant. Research has shown that plants that are inherently healthy and growing in compatible soil and climate are strengthened by normal stresses. Well-grown, strong trees and shrubs live through droughts without supplemental watering, and they sway in heavy winds and bend under ice and snow without breaking. You can further minimize the likelihood of pest infestations by following good gardening practices—including planting a diversity of plants in your landscape; avoiding overhead watering in hot, humid, windless situations; removing decaying vegetation from the grounds and the flower beds in fall and in early spring; and removing by hand and destroying diseased plant materials and habitats, such as the tents of tent caterpillars.

TAKING ACTION

It's reassuring to know that most insect infestations last only days or weeks before disappearing. Monitor, but don't rush to respond to, a few leaf holes or spots. In some seasons, you should even tolerate a defoliation of whole plants. New summer growth covers the leaf depredations of even the gypsy moth caterpillar. Consider discarding a new planting that suffers continual infestations, but wait a year or two before acting; the problem may be caused by weather conditions that won't often repeat.

The next line of defense against pests, as well as diseases, should be a control friendly to the environment rather than a chemical that may have an unfortunate effect on beneficial visitors. Among welcome visitors are beneficial insects, such as praying mantids and ladybugs. Flowers that produce lots of pollen and nectar, such as daisies and butterfly bush, favor beneficial insects. Most birds eat insects, and some vegetarian birds have insect-eating young. You can invite visiting birds to stay by planting trees and shrubs that provide them with dense cover and nesting sites; by planting berry-producing plants, such as dogwood, barberry, and viburnums; and by allowing your flowers to set seeds. Birds will compete with you for edible berry crops, so you may need to cover them with netting. But bird song and the flutter of wings will add aesthetic appeal as well as practical benefits.

Not all of nature's visitors are as welcome to the gardener. Notable nuisances include rabbits, raccoons, squirrels, moles, and voles. Frequent fresh applications of black pepper and garlic powder have some deterrent effect, but outdoor cats can do a better job of keeping small creatures at a distance.

A bigger problem is a growing deer population, especially in winter when these graceful animals will eat almost any leaf they can get at, including your prized rhododendrons. The best year-round deterrent is deer fencing, and it is relatively inexpensive. Another preventive, according to tests run by Cornell University, is fresh Milorganite, a soil amendment made of composted sewage sludge, which has been certified by the USDA as suitable even for food plants. But like pepper and garlic, Milorganite must be reapplied after heavy rains and is ineffective when covered by snow. A dog trained to chase deer out of the garden can be effective, but it must also be trained not to dig up, lie down on, or gallop through the perennials.

When friendly creatures and natural controls fail, as they do so often with roses, for example, seek help from your local Cooperative Extension Service or well-respected local garden center. First, ask staff to identify the problem and make sure it really does need to be treated. If action is needed, ask for a control that is biodegradable, that breaks down quickly to harmless substances.

A CRAWLING PEST

Tent caterpillars emerge from their protective web nest several times a day to feed on emerging buds and leaves. Physically remove all you can reach and drown them in a bucket of dilute chlorine bleach.

Dealing with Deer

Throughout North America, people complain that deer devour their plants, introduce ticks to the neighborhood, and cause car accidents. These problems increase as deer populations increase. Most wildlife managers agree that many regions suffer from deer overpopulation.

DEER OVERPOPULATION?

The total North American deer population fluctuates around 25 million—which approximates estimates of the deer population when the Pilgrims landed. However, by 1900 the deer population had crashed to a mere half million, mainly the result of year-round, unrestricted market hunting. Thus, the population has rebounded phenomenally well—too well for many observers.

Ironically, suburban sprawl and gentrification of the countryside have established ideal deer habitat—open feeding areas with nearby woodsy cover, free of natural predators and off-limits to hunters.

In reddish summer coat, this doe looks incapable of mischief: ravaging gardens, causing traffic accidents, striking with her front hooves at competing deer and even at smaller predators.

Whitetails are named for their large pendantlike tail, which they "flag" upright when agitated and in flight, exposing its bright white underside. Whitetails run with a graceful leaping stride resembling that of gazelles. The buck's antlers have a single forward-sweeping main beam, from which points project.

Overpopulation is usually less troublesome in rural areas, where deer can be hunted and where fence types aren't limited by ordinances.

However, deer overpopulation is disastrous in some forests and parklands. In the eastern states, forest managers suggest that a forested square mile can support a maximum of 15 to 18 deer. Otherwise, deer will overbrowse understory plants essential to that ecosystem. Afflicted forests suffer more than 200 deer per square mile, where malnourished deer devour virtually all plants to a height of 6 feet.

In earlier centuries, natural predators maintained deer populations at the land's ideal biological carrying capacity. Absence of natural predators throws deer populations off balance.

Game managers attempt to adjust deer populations by shortening or lengthening hunting seasons that are often designed to cull at least 30 percent of the herd. However, in states with severe overpopulation, culls of 40 to 50 percent may not be sufficient to return the land's carrying capacities to ideal levels. Populations can be reduced most effectively by increasing the take of female deer. But hunters tend to resist incentives to kill "mothers" and prefer to hold out for a buck with a good set of antlers.

OUR DEER

Technically, the Deer Family (Cervidae) in North America comprises moose, caribou, elk, and smaller cousins we call deer. Although moose and elk sometimes ravage home gardens, their populations are comparatively tiny and their ranges, spotty. Still, many of the same strategies for outwitting deer can succeed with moose and elk.

There are two species of native deer in the genus *Odocoileus* (pronounced oh-dough-COY-lee-us). The more populous are whitetails (*O. virginianus*) of geographically distinct subspecies that occur in all contiguous states and all provinces, though principally east of the Rockies. Mule deer (*O. hemionus*) and its two blacktail subspecies live in western states and provinces. Their ranges sometimes overlap with those of the westward expanding whitetail.

BEHAVIORS AND PREFERENCES

For habitat, deer favor "edge" where they can emerge from woodsy cover in the evening to feed for an hour or two, and then retreat to lie down and chew their cud before they feed again. Conveniently for deer, nocturnal feeding coincides with the hours during which humans and their dogs are asleep.

Deer establish daily and nightly trails to food sources and tend to travel in matriarchal groups, the dominant doe leading her young of the year and others. Once a lead doe has discovered delectables on your property, it becomes harder to discourage her.

During spring and summer, bucks are reclusive and highly conscious of their sensitive and fast-growing velvety antlers that won't harden until late summer or fall. During this "velvet" period, bucks seem to disappear from the landscape.

Deer favor moist plants, rich in nutrients. And what better place to find them than in a well-watered and well-fertilized garden? During droughts and again in summer as wild plants dry up, a garden is an oasis.

Unless discouraged in some way, garden raids continue until woody plants are badly damaged and herbaceous plants are mere stems. Then, in winter, when evergreen leaves and dormant woody buds are the only available food, starving deer may attempt to breach formidable barriers by working under, over, or through them—even pushing them down.

Mule deer are named for their relatively large ears. The "muley's" ropelike tail may rise only slightly in flight. Muley's run with a stiff-legged, bouncing gate called stotting, all four hooves landing at once. The buck's antlers, as well as those of its Pacific Coast cousins, the blacktails, are bifurcated. That is, they split from the base to form two "Ys."

Before fall's mating season, called the rut, bucks spar with trunks of young trees, much like boxers training for a fight. Known as rubbing, this scrapes away most bark, often mortally wounding the tree. Photographer-naturalist Dr. Leonard Lee Rue III suggests a correlation between trunk diameter and size of buck.

COMMUNITY ACTION

Public meetings on deer attract standing-room-only audiences, representing wide-ranging concerns. At opposite extremes, people may want to get rid of deer, whatever the cost, or protect them, whatever the cost.

Some states have attempted to capture and relocate deer. Such studies in California, New Mexico, and Florida soon resulted in deer mortality rates of 53 percent to 85 percent. Researchers suggest that deer relocated from overpopulated areas are often malnourished and have trouble adapting. Besides, such largely futile operations can cost upwards of $1,000 per deer.

At public meetings, people ask whether relocation wouldn't be a good solution, to which savvy officials might respond, "As long as you relocate far from here."

Lethal Measures. In suburban and town settings, concerns for public safety make standard hunting practices unfeasible. Some communities employ professional sharpshooters who sit in elevated blinds to await deer lured to baits and then dispatch them instantaneously with a bullet to the brain. But this method often faces strong opposition.

Nonlethal Measures. Researchers are experimenting with birth-control darts and with deer feed laced with birth-control agents. Yet, it's unclear how this will affect herd dynamics and even fertility in other species.

As addressed on upcoming pages, many homeowners succeed in protecting plants by employing seasonally adjusted nonlethal measures, including:

- So-called "deer-resistant" plants
- Deer fencing and other barriers
- Repellent substances
- Frighteners

Plants Deer Favor Least

Trees and shrubs are most susceptible to browsing when they are small, so it's smart to protect leader branches, especially, until the plants grow beyond a deer's reach. In winter, starving deer may have no other options than evergreen leaves and dormant buds. And during droughts, deer may have scant other sources of moisture than plants they otherwise don't like.

During favorable conditions, deer are selective browsers. And many factors affect their preferences, including a plant's smell, taste, growth stage, and moisture content—as well as availability of alternatives, distance from dwellings, nutritional needs, and conditioning by Mom.

Each plant in the listings on pages 58–59 is recommended by authorities in multiple regions of North America—east to west, north to south. Still, be sure to inquire with local authorities as to which listed plants grow well in your locality while also seeming of low interest to deer. Curiously, some plants that deer relish in the East, such as hostas and daylilies, sometimes appear on "deer-resistant" lists published by credible sources in the West and Southwest, where soil pH and chemical composition may make that plant less appealing to deer.

Here a deer showed predictable food preference by devouring hosta leaves and spurning variegated bishop's weed (also called "goutweed"). The roughly torn stems incriminate deer, rather than rabbits or woodchucks, which bite stems off cleanly. Deer have no upper front teeth and so must rip leaves and twigs off.

PLANTS DEER FAVOR LEAST

Plants here are arranged alphabetically by scientific name. The abbreviation "spp." means and species and may also apply to cultivars, but not always, as deer have proven. The abbreviation "syn." is for synonym or former name.

TREES LARGE AND SMALL

Firs (*Abies* spp.), 86

Maples (*Acer* spp.), 88

Buckeyes (*Aesculus* spp.), 90

Shadbushes (*Amelanchier* spp.), 131

Birches (*Betula* spp.), 91

Catalpas (*Catalpa* spp.), Z4–9, H9–1

Eastern redbud (*Cercis canadensis*), 96

False cypresses (*Chamaecyparis* spp.), 97

Dogwoods (*Cornus* spp.), 100

American smoke tree (*Cotinus obovatus*), 103

Hawthorns (*Crataegus* spp.), 104

Leyland cypress (x *Cupressocyparis leylandii*), 219

American beech (*Fagus grandifolia*), 107

Ashes (*Fraxinus* spp.), 109

Ginkgo, Maidenhair tree (*Ginkgo biloba*), 110

Hollies (*Ilex* spp.), 113; those with spiniest leaves

Larches (*Larix* spp.), 119

Sweet gum (*Liquidambar styraciflua*), 120

Magnolias (*Magnolia* spp.), 122

Hop hornbeam (*Ostrya virginiana*), Z5–9, H9–2

Sourwood (*Oxydendrum arboreum*), 126

Spruces (*Picea* spp.), 128

Pines (*Pinus* spp.), 130

Sycamores (*Platanus* spp.), Z3–8

Douglas fir (*Pseudotsuga menziensii*), Z5–7, H7–5

Oaks (*Quercus* spp.), 136

Black locust (*Robinia pseudoacacia*), Z4–9, H9–3

Bald cypress (*Taxodium distichum*), Z5–11, H12–5

Hemlocks (*Tsuga* spp.), 145

SHRUBS

Barberry (*Berberis* spp.), 216; except invasive
   Japanese barberry

Butterfly bush (*Buddleia davidii*), 165

Boxwood (*Buxus* spp.), 218

Allspice, Sweetshrub (*Calycanthus* spp.), Z5–9

Red-osier dogwood (*Cornus stolonifera* syn. *sericea*), 100

Hazelnut (*Corylus* spp.), 102

Cotoneaster (*Cotoneaster* spp.), 172

Daphne (*Daphne* spp.), 174

Heaths, Heathers (*Erica* spp.), 176

Forsythia (*Forsythia* spp.), 177

Salal & Wintergreen (*Gaultheria* spp.), 180

Goldcup (*Hypericum* spp.), 185

Jasmine (*Jasmimium* spp.), Z6–10

Junipers (*Juniperus* spp.), 114

Mountain laurel (*Kalmia* latifolia), 186

Kerria, Japanese rose (*Kerria japonica*), 187

Beautybush (*Kolkwitzia amabilis*), 188

Crape myrtle (*Laegerstroemia indica*), 118

Leucothe spp (*Leucothe* spp.), 189

Mahonia (*Mahonia* spp.), 190

Heavenly bamboos (*Nandina* spp.), 191

Oleander, Rose bay (*Nerium oleander*), 223

Russian sage (*Perovskia atriplicifolia* & cultivars), Z6–9, H9–6

Pieris, Andromeda (*Pieris* spp.), 194

Yew podocarpus (*Podocarpus macrophyllus*), 226

Cinquefoils (*Potentilla* spp.), 195

Cherries & Plums (*Prunus,* the native spp.), 132

Firethorn (*Pyracantha* spp), 228

Buckthorns (*Rhamnus* spp.), Z6–9, H9–6

Currants & gooseberres (*Ribes* spp.), Z5–10, H10–5

Wild roses (*Rosa* spp.), 198; wild natives and rugosa roses
   suffer least from browsing

Elderberry (*Sambucus* spp.), Z3–9, H9–1

Lavender cotton (*Santolina chamaecyparissus*), Z6–9, H9–4

Spirea (*Spiraea* spp.), 230

Lilacs (*Syringa* spp.), 202

Germander (*Teucrium* spp.), Z4–9, H12–4

Viburnum (*Viburnum* spp.), 203

Yuccas (*Yucca* spp.), Z4–11, H12–5

PERENNIALS (including bulbs)

Yarrow (*Achillea* spp.)

Monkshoods (*Aconitum* spp.)

Onions (*Allium* spp.)

Anemone (*Anemone* spp.)

Columbines (*Aquilegia* spp.)

Sea thrift (*Armeria maritima*)

Wormwood, Mugwort (*Artemesia* spp.)

Wild ginger (*Asarum* spp.)

Milkweed & Butterfly weed (*Asclepias* spp.)

Astilbes (*Astilbe* spp.)

Knapweeds (*Centaurea* spp.)

Snow-in-summer (*Cerastium tomentosum*)

Chrysanthemums (*Chrysanthemum* spp.)

Lily of the Valley (*Convallaria majalis*)

Tickseed (*Coreopsis* spp.)

Montbretia (*Crocosmia* x *crocosmiiflora*)

Crocus (*Crocus* spp.)

Pinks (*Dianthus* spp.)

Bleeding hearts (*Dicentra* spp.)

Coneflowers (*Echinacea* spp.)

Globe thistle (*Echinops* spp.)

Fleabane (*Erigeron* spp.)

Joe Pye weeds (*Eupatorium* spp.)

Spurges (*Euphorbia* spp.)

Queen of the Prairie (*Filpendula* spp.)

Fritillary (*Fritillaria* spp.)

Blanketflower (*Gaillardia aristata, G.* x *grandiflora*)

Scented cranesbill (*Geranium macrorrhizum*)

Baby's breath (*Gypsophilia paniculata, G. repens*)

Hellebores (*Helleborus* spp.)

Rose mallow (*Hibiscus* spp.)

Candytuft (*Ibiris sempervirens*)

Irises, bearded (*Iris* spp.)

Red-hot poker (*Kniphofia* spp.)

Deadnettle (*Lamium* spp.)

Lantana (*Lantana camara*)

Summer snowflake (*Leucojum aestivum*)

Lilyturf (*Liriope* spp.)

Lupines (*Lupinus* spp.) Laz, Roe, LinkWA, AZ

Rose campion, Crown-Pink (*Lychnis coronaria*)

Bee balms (*Monarda* spp.)

Forget-me-not (*Myosotis scorpioides*)

Daffodils (*Narcissus* spp.)

Catmint (*Nepeta* spp.)

Prickly pear (*Opuntia humifusa*)

Peonies (*Paeonea*)

Jerusalem sage (*Phlomis* spp.)

Phlox (*Phlox* spp.)

Mayapple (*Podophyllum peltatum*)

Coneflowers, Black-eyed Susans (*Rudbeckia* spp.)

Salvias (*Salvia* spp.)

Soapwort (*Saponaria* spp.)

Scillas, Squill (*Scilla* spp.)

Groundseal (*Senecio* spp.)

Goldenrods (*Solidago* spp.)

Lamb's ears (*Stachys byzantina*)

Vervain (*Verbena* spp.)

Speedwell (*Veronica* spp.)

Violets (*Viola* spp.)

ANNUALS

Ageratum (*Ageratum houstonianum*)

Snapdragon (*Antirrhinum majus*)

Cleome, Spider Flower (*Cleome hassleriana*)

Larkspur (*Consolida ajacis* syn. *ambigua*)

California poppy (*Eschscholzia californica*)

Sweet alyssum (*Lobularia maritima*)

Poppies (*Papaver* spp.)

Dusty Miller (*Senecio cineraria*); shrub grown as annual

Marigold (*Tagetes* spp.)

Zinnias (*Zinnia* spp.)

GROUNDCOVERS

Bugleweed (*Ajuga* spp)

Wild ginger (*Asarum* spp.)

Junipers (*Juniperus* spp.)

Pachysandra (*P. procumbens, P. terminalis*)

Lungworts (*Pulmonaria* spp.)

Periwinkle (*Vinca* ssp.)

ORNAMENTAL GRASSES

Most ornamental grasses

FERNS

Most ferns

HERBS

Many herbs, especially allium, hyssop, lavender, mint, oregano, marjorum, rosemary, sage, and thyme.

Fences and Other Barriers

Although experts agree that a 9-foot impregnable fence is one of the surest means of keeping deer out, local ordinances may prohibit such tall fences and may also ban electric fences. Before considering barrier options, consider a deer's jumping ability, as well as seasonal behaviors discussed on previous pages.

From a standstill, healthy adult deer are usually capable of jumping 8-foot fences. Given a running start, whitetails have cleared 9-footers. Yet deer don't exert themselves more than they need to. With plenty of nutritious broadleaved plants outside your property, deer might not bother to jump a 4-foot fence. Besides, lingering human scents from perspiration, soaps, deodorants, bug sprays, and dogs can make deer uneasy and therefore content with plants beyond your property.

However, if other plants become overbrowsed or dry, deer will find your beautifully stocked salad bar hard to resist. And once a deer tastes something it likes, it will return for more.

Some questions to ask include: How much browsing is tolerable? Could deer-favored plants somehow be protected without property-line fencing? Could taste and odor repellents be effective? Could you transplant vulnerable plants to protected areas?

"PSYCHOLOGICAL" FENCES

Electric Fences. Designed for snow-free periods, electric fences give harmless shocks that discourage deer from approaching. Powered by a high-voltage, low-impedance charger, an electric fence delivers 4000–5000 volts at low amperage (impedance) in pulses about every second. Low amperage ensures that the electricity merely stings. And pulse durations of less than $1/1000$ second ensure that the electricity doesn't "freeze" its victim on the wire.

Electric fences exploit a deer's preference for going under wires or through them, rather than jumping over. To teach fear of the fence, you can smear peanut butter onto the wires or under small aluminum-foil shelters attached to the wire. A deer's wet nose or tongue touching the bait receives an unforgettable "correction."

Electric fences can feature a single strand of tensioned wire or a single strip of polytape with embedded wires. White or yellow polytape helps ensure that deer see it. But in a home landscape, it resembles crime-scene tape.

Multistrand electric fences are more effective. Even so, deer can work their way through electric fences without feeling shock if their fur provides enough insulation. Then too, dry ground during droughts can prevent electrical flow through the deer into the ground. And, because vegetation touching lower wires can create ground faults, it must be cut regularly. Also, you need to maintain a wide clear swath in front of the fence so deer notice it. Otherwise, they may hit it and break through.

Chargers can be powered by either AC (household current), or a DC battery ranging from 6 to 12 volts, or solar panels. A night timer reduces chances that children will be shocked.

Electric fences serve more as psychological rather than physical barriers, because deer can easily jump all but the tallest ones. However, once deer receive an initial "correction," they fear the entire fence and may not test it unless they are strongly attracted to plants inside. Local code may require prominent labeling.

ORDINANCES

If you live in a rural area, you may be free to erect fencing of any height or type. However, most municipalities have strict ordinances and codes that govern fence types, heights, and setbacks from property lines. For example, a front-yard fence might be limited to a 3- or 4-foot height, while a backyard fence of 5 or 6 feet might be allowed, though still easily jumped by deer.

Fence ordinances are intended to allow a measure of privacy, while also establishing aesthetic standards that help property values. So, before shopping for fencing, inquire with local officials what might be allowed. It's also prudent to consult with neighbors, who may wish to partner in fencing in a style that matches yours and could eliminate need for tall fencing between your properties. Besides, if you wish to erect a fence at variance with ordinances, you may need written approvals of neighbors.

TRUE BARRIER FENCES

Living Fences. Besides their beauty, hedges may be all you need to keep deer out. Hedges usually allow you to circumvent code restrictions on fence height. Even so, you may not need a hedge taller than 4 feet because browsing deer seldom raise their heads higher. Thus, a dense hedge could block a deer's view of your other plantings and discourage a leap into the unknown. Many plants are suitable as hedges or screens. Among suitable evergreens, deer show least interest in firs, hemlocks, pines, spruces, junipers, Leyland cypress, and the hollies with the spikiest leaves. Yet, even if you choose plants that deer relish, such as arborvitae, code may allow you to protect the hedge with a 4- to 5-foot see-through fence.

Wooden Fences. As with living fences, if deer can't see inside, they are less likely to leap into the unknown.

Woven-Wire Fences. Commonly called chain-link fences, those that are 8 feet tall can keep most intruders out. But they look too institutional for most tastes.

Closely spaced uprights in stockade and other types of wooden fences can block a deer's view. Deer are unlikely to jump into the unknown. On level ground, fences such as these could do the job if they are at least 4 or 5 ft. high.

Tensioned-Wire Fences. If wires are closely spaced between closely spaced posts, deer may be discouraged. But deer often work their way through or under wires, unless electrified. The high-tension requires strong and deeply installed corner posts.

Plastic-Mesh Fences. Of the tall fences, plastic mesh is about the easiest and least expensive to install. In ideal settings, the 1- to 2-inch black mesh can look nearly invisible and can be attached to posts of metal, plastic, or wood. It can be stapled to wooden posts and tree trunks.

At a distance, tall plastic-mesh fencing can look nearly invisible, especially when trees serve as support. Because deer have poor vision, attach strips of warning tape or fabric, at least until deer are aware of the fence. Fasten the bottom with ground stakes to keep deer from crawling under the fence.

PLANT PROTECTION

Young trees and shrubs are especially vulnerable to browsing until they reach 5 or 6 feet. On conifers, that height elevates the central leader well beyond reach of browsing deer and just beyond reach of starving deer on hind legs. If deer nip a conifer's leader stem, multiple stems will emerge (like a bad hair day) and begin competing for dominance, requiring that you prune all but a selected new leader.

The forest industry protects young hardwoods and conifers with corrugated polypropylene tubes. But, in the home garden, you can craft nearly invisible protective cylinders of plastic netting or heavier mesh supported by stakes cut from electrical conduit or iron rebar, painted to blend with foliage. (Vegetable gardeners drape planting beds with gauzy-looking polyester row covers each night, which could also work over flower beds and woody plants—presenting a ghostly night garden whose fluttering specters could unnerve both deer and prowlers.)

In late summer, formerly reclusive bucks may rub their antlers on young trees to remove velvet. Then, prior to the rut in fall, bucks begin mock battles that may shred the smallest trees and leave large scars on

Flexible drainpipe that's been slit on one side and fitted around a tree trunk, can discourage antler rubbing in fall. During winter, you can use this device to protect the south-facing side of a tree from sunscald.

Just above the expanse of broadleaved hostas on this hillside, there's a nearly invisible 7½-ft. fence. It consists of ½-inch mesh netting twist-tied to posts of ½-in. galvanized electrical conduit painted green. In soft soil, the 10-ft. lengths of conduit can be driven by gripping it near the top, like a fire pole, and riding it down.

tree trunks of 4- to 6-inch diameter, badly wounding them. You can protect trees from rubbing, either with commercial trunk wraps, or plastic drainpipe slit down one side to fit over the trunk, or with ¼-inch metal mesh. Such wraps also protect young trunks from winter's hungry rabbits that pad over the snow and from voles that tunnel under it.

Prior to winter, you can protect established trees and shrubs with home-crafted surrounds that keep the plant's dormant buds beyond reach of desperately hungry deer until spring, when emerging herbaceous plants become more attractive. Position the surrounds just outside the drip line of low-branching hardwoods and just beyond the bottom spread of conifers. Deer don't like to jump into tight quarters. For this, traditional snow fences are also effective.

This electric fence adjoins an entrance driveway's "cattle-guard" grating, which discourages deer entry and reduces need for a gate. However, in winter, snow can pack sufficiently within grating to create a surface that will support hooves.

You can use chicken wire to make a barrier or protective surround that can keep deer and rabbits away from young trees. In fact, some trees may need this type of protection for a while and until they grow beyond a deer's hind-legged reach of 6 ft.

Sticky snow will overload ½-in. mesh. Thus, in snow country, such "bird netting" serves better as a three-season deer barrier.

Deer Repellents

Repellents originally designed to protect crops and forest seedlings are also available for home gardens. Many repellents work, initially at least, alone or in combination until deer become accustomed to them, or until weather washes them away, or until starving deer are willing to swallow the worst we dish up.

As listed on previous pages, deer tend to avoid strong-scented herbs and toxic plants and so may avoid unfamiliar other plants in close proximity. But there's no guarantee that deer will bypass your yard if they are hungry enough.

DEER-REPELLENT PLANTS

Deer will avoid toxic plants, such as this oleander (*Nerium oleander*), above, and tend to avoid strongly scented herbs, as well as plants with hairy leaves, such as lamb's ears (*Stachys byzantina*), below.

Many authorities cite prickly leaved hollies among evergreens that deer favor least, as on this American holly (*Ilex opaca*), above, and this silver-edged English holly (*Ilex aquifolium* 'Argentea Marginata'), below.

PLANT-APPLIED REPELLENTS

Some repellents give plants a taste deer dislike. Others give plants a repulsive odor. Some products do both. Most are merely topical, doing their job by adhering to the surface of leaves and twigs. Others are systemic, transmitted throughout the plant by its leaves or through the soil.

An innovative researcher in Tennessee protected test plots of soybeans and later his home garden with low-cost repellent "fencing." For his initial tests, he sprayed olfactory repellent on two kinds of "rope," one consisting of ½-inch electric polytape and the other a mere ⅛-inch nylon cord. Around different plots, he stretched his test ropes at a height of two feet and reapplied repellent monthly. Dramatic success! Deer browsing of protected plots was minimal and allowed bountiful harvests.

Some repellent sprays make plants look unsightly, if applied at the wrong temperature or time of day, illustrating the importance of label directions. On a showpiece plant, it's prudent to test repellent on a few leaves and let it dry before spraying the entire plant.

In winter when deer are desperate, combinations of repellents and screening can discourage browsing. On this azalea, researchers test the combined repellency of predator urine (odor) in a plastic vial and leaf spray (bad taste). In the background, burlap stapled to wooden frames hide arborvitae from view—out of sight, out of mind. (Test site: Deer Browse Garden, Institute of Ecosystems Studies, Millbrook, New York)

Available in powder or liquid concentrates, repellents need to be applied in prescribed mixtures when temperatures are above freezing and with no rain forecast. Other label directions may address season, type of plant, and plant parts. Formulations vary widely among manufacturers. Some are based on putrescent eggs with garlic; others on citrus extracts, hot peppers, bittering agents, or dried blood. Although manufacturer claims and customer testimonials can be impressive, independent researchers have found it helpful to change the types of repellents from time to time so deer don't get accustomed to one.

Before purchasing, try to consult with local gardeners who use repellents. Also, owners of nurseries and garden centers sometimes keep track of customer experiences with various repellents and so may have recommendations for specific situations. The Internet is also a good research tool.

As to application methods, manufacturers may suggest dipping an entire tree seedling before planting and then applying solution to emerging shoots and later to dormant twigs. Because of blow-by, spraying may waste some costly repellent. So one manufacturer of an odor repellent suggests applying solution to shoots and twigs with a double-gloved hand—the outer cloth glove serving as the applicator, the inner impermeable glove protecting your hand.

HOME REMEDIES

Gardening magazines continually feature reader letters testifying to the efficacy of strongly scented soaps as well as odors of human hair and stinky clothes. All can be effective repellents at garden access points or near prized plants until their scents have dissipated or deer have become accustomed to them.

NOISEMAKERS AND VISUAL SCARES

In rural areas, beyond earshot of neighbors, nighttime talk radio can give deer the impression that you are up and about. Large farms employ propane gas exploders that fire throughout the night, though deer become accustomed even to loud sounds. The noisier the device, the less your neighbors will appreciate it.

Also, lesser sounds and sudden movements can put deer on the run. These might come from homemade devices connected to trip wires of fish line in the deer's path that fire cap pistols or release jack-in-the-boxes, or set off mousetraps that break balloons. If peanut butter attracts deer to an electric fence, giving them a correction, it should also attract deer to a baited mouse trap on a nonelectric fence. However, peanut butter is also likely to attract raccoons, rats, and bears.

PREDITOR URINE

Predator urine soaked in fabric can emit its unsettling odor for days. A plastic vial with holes punched at the top slows evaporation.

DOGS

Virtually all nurseries employ dogs at night to ward off deer, as well as plant thieves. Even so, the scent of a dog around a property perimeter can be enough to give deer pause, though sometimes not a long pause.

Dogs allowed to range outdoors all night can keep deer away. But barking dogs wake neighbors. Of all dog breeds, border collies may naturally give chase without feeling the neighbor-waking urge to bark.

In any case, the dog needs to be restricted to your property by means of a conventional fence or invisible underground wire that transmits a signal to the dog's shock collar as the dog approaches. Dog tethers are less effective because deer quickly determine how far the exasperated dog can reach.

MOTION DETECTORS

At night, motion detectors are most commonly used to switch on floodlights. However, that motion might be heavy rain, a branch swaying in the breeze, or a deer approaching the branch. Motion detectors can also activate water sprays intended to surprise and insult deer.

Deer may become uneasy when caught in the beam of overhead motion light but may soon adjust to it if not accompanied by an additional surprise. Motion-activated water sprays push deer beyond reach of the spray, if that's the only area you need to protect.

Mature trees frame a lake view from this deck. Rural areas often have less of a deer problem than more densely populated suburban areas because there are more natural food sources for deer in less-populated areas.

PART 2

All about Trees

There are thousands of tree species and cultivars that you can incorporate into your home landscape. We have made the selection process easier by providing detailed information on species that belong to 52 major tree groups called "genera" (plural for "genus"). Within this select group, you will find many options for wherever you live in North America.

You'll find tree genera listed alphabetically by scientific name. So if you know the genus name, you can simply turn to it alphabetically. But if you don't know the scientific name for a species, you can find it by checking the common name in the Table of Contents and the Index. In addition, many common names are listed on page 71.

Main Facts and Key Details

Trees are the longest lived and largest of the garden ornamentals. A tree can define the whole garden, adding eye-catching form, color, and interest year-round. When herbaceous plants have died down each year, a tree remains in view, and most outlive the person who planted it.

Designing Ideas

Trees fill many roles in a well-designed landscape. Along with walls, fences, shrubs, hedges, and other permanent features, trees provide "bones"—the basic landscaping structure. Trees are the big players in the landscape. They modify their surroundings and influence what else you can plant in their vicinity. So it is important to choose trees that will fit into the available space, thrive in growing conditions at the site, and look good in association with other landscape features. If you decide 5 or 10 years hence that you chose the wrong tree, correcting the mistake will be costly and difficult.

You can plant a single majestic tree as a focal point in a lawn, or plant small trees in groups. One or more small trees can anchor a mixed border that will also contain shrubs and flowers. Evergreen trees bring their color to the landscape year-round. Deciduous trees planted near the house can help with climate control, providing cooling shade in summer and allowing more sunlight to reach the house in winter when the branches are bare. Trees can be used to frame a view, to define property lines, and to muffle street noise.

A tree's shape, or habit, helps determine how it can best be used. Weeping trees look graceful and romantic, and can be lovely at a distance and reflected in a pond. Columnar trees tend to look more formal. They are often used along driveways or as vertical accents in formal gardens and large landscapes. Evergreens can also serve as screens or windbreaks.

As you contemplate new trees for your property or consider moving or culling existing trees, try for a variety. Include a tree that has a different size, shape, color, or texture from the others. Or include a tree that's in bloom when the others are not or that has special attributes, such as spectacular fall color, showy fruits or bark, or fragrant flowers.

Very important: make sure the trees you choose are hardy in your zone and suited to the microclimate of your property. And be sure to provide trees the other growing conditions they need to thrive.

Dwarf Colorado blue spruce have silvery blue foliage. These trees grow up to 5 ft. high and 3 ft. wide in Hardiness Zones 3 to 8.

TREES FOR EVERY SEASON AND REASON

When planning your landscape, also consider trees that have exceptional qualities, seasonal interest, and perhaps optional uses, such as trained hedges. **Note:** the plants are alphabetized by scientific name.

FOR FLOWERS
Red Maple (*Acer rubrum*), 88
Red Horse Chestnut (*Aesculus*), 90
Redbud (*Cercis*), 96
Fringetree (*Chionanthus*), 98
American Yellowwood
    (*Cladrastis lutea*), 99
Dogwood (*Cornus*), 100
Hawthorn (*Crataegus*), 104
Dove Tree, Handkerchief Tree
    (*Davidia involucrata*), 105
Franklin Tree
    (*Franklinia alatamaha*), 108
Kentucky Coffee Tree
    (*Gymnocladus dioicus*), 111
Silverbell (*Halesia*), 112
Golden-Rain Tree, Varnish Tree
    (*Koelreuteria paniculata*), 116
Golden-chain Tree, aka Waterer
Laburnum (*Laburnum* x *watereri*
    'Vossii'), 117
Crape Myrtle
    (*Lagerstroemia indica*), 118
Tulip Tree (*Liriodendron*), 121
Magnolia (*Magnolia*), 122
Crabapple (*Malus*), 124
Sourwood, Sorrel Tree
    (*Oxydendrum arboreum*), 126
Flowering Fruit Trees (*Prunus*), 132
Callery Pear, Flowering Pear
    (*Pyrus calleryana*), 134
Japanese Pagoda Tree, Chinese
    Scholar Tree (formerly *Sophora
    japonica* 'Regent', aka
    Styphnolobium japonicum), 139
Stewartia (*Stewartia*), 141
Snowbell (*Styrax*), 142

FOR FRUITS
Incense Cedar
    (*Calocedrus decurrens*), 92
Hornbeam (*Carpinus*), 93
Cedar (*Cedrus*), 65
Several Dogwood (*Cornus*), 100
Filbert (Hazelnuts) (*Corylus*), 102
Smoke Tree (*Cotinus*), 103
Hawthorn (*Crataegus*), 104
Holly (*Ilex*), 113
Golden-Rain Tree, Varnish Tree
    (*Koelreuteria paniculata*), 116
Tulip Tree (*Liriodendron*), 121
Magnolia (*Magnolia*), 122

Crabapple (*Malus*), 124
Black Gum (*Nyssa sylvatica*), 125
Oaks (*Quercus*), 136

FOR EXCEPTIONAL BARK
Chinese Paperbark Maple
    (*Acer griseum*), 59
Birch (*Betula*), 91
Shagbark Hickory (*Carya ovata*), 94
American Yellowwood,
Virgilia (*Cladrastis lutea*), 99
Hawthorn (*Crataegus viridis*
    'Winter King'), 104
Dove Tree, Handkerchief Tree
    (*Davidia involucrata*), 105
Gum Tree (*Eucalyptus*), 106
Beech (*Fagus*), 107
Franklin Tree
    (*Franklinia alatamaha*), 108
Crape Myrtle
    (*Lagerstroemia indica*), 118
American Sweet Gum
    (*Liquidambar styraciflua*), 120
Lacebark Pine (*Pinus bungeana*), 130
Stewartia (*Stewartia*), 141
Chinese Elm, Lacebark Elm
    (*Ulmus parviflora*), 146

FOR FALL COLOR
Maple (*Acer*), 88
American Hornbeam
    (*Carpinus caroliniana*), 93
Fringe Tree (*Chionanthus*), 98
Dogwood (*Cornus*), 100
Smoke Tree (*Cotinus*), 103
Hawthorn (*Crataegus viridis*
    'Winter King'), 104
Burning Bush and Wintercreeper
    (*Euonymus*), 220
Franklin Tree
    (*Franklinia alatamaha*), 108
Ashes (*Fraxinus*), 109
Ginkgo, Maidenhair Tree
    (*Ginkgo biloba*), 110
Crape Myrtle
    (*Lagerstroemia indica*), 118
Japanese Larch (*Larix kaempferi*), 119
American Sweet Gum
    (*Liquidambar styraciflua*), 120
Black Gum, Pepperidge, Sour Gum,
Black Tupelo (*Nyssa sylvatica*), 125
Sourwood, Sorrel Tree

    (*Oxydendrum arboreum*), 126
Callery Pear, Flowering Pear
    (*Pyrus calleryana*), 134
Scarlet Oak
    (*Quercus coccinea*), 136
Stewartia (*Stewartia*), 141

FOR WINTER INTEREST
Incense Cedar
    (*Calocedrus decurrens*), 92
Cedar (*Cedrus*), 95
White Cedar, False Cypress
    (*Chamaecyparis*), 97
Corkscrew Hazel,
    (*Corylus avellana* var. *contorta*), 102
Hawthorn (*Crataegus*), 104
Beech (*Fagus*), 107
Holly (*Ilex*), 113
Juniper (*Juniperus*), 114
Larch (*Larix*), 119
Magnolia (*Magnolia*), 122
Crabapple (*Malus*), 124
Amur Cork Tree
    (*Phellodendron amurense*), 127
Spruce (*Picea*), 128
Pine (*Pinus*), 130
Oak (*Quercus*), 136
Mountain Ash (*Sorbus*), 140
Stewartia (*Stewartia*),141
Arborvitae (*Thuja*),143
Hemlock (*Tsuga*), 145

ALSO USED AS HEDGES
Incense Cedar
    (*Calocedrus decurrens*), 92
European Hornbeam
    (*Carpinus betulus*), 93
Cedar (*Cedrus*), 95
White Cedar (*False Cypress*)
    (*Chamaecyparis*), 97
European Smoke Tree
    (*Cotinus coggygria*), 103
Hawthorn (*Crataegus*), 104
Blue Gum Eucalyptus (*Eucalyptus
    globulus* 'Compacta'), 106
Holly (*Ilex*), 113
Juniper (*Juniperus*), 114
Crape Myrtle
    (*Lagerstroemia indica*), 118
Pine (*Pinus*), 130
Arborvitae (*Thuja*), 143
Hemlock (*Tsuga*), 145

Shape, or Habit

Because a mature tree is large, its eventual shape and size are the most important factors determining its function in the landscape design. Remember that a silhouette is just two dimensional and that trees are three-dimensional forms. When designing a landscape on paper, it may be easier to think in two dimensions, but you need to keep all three dimensions in mind when you are fitting the tree into the landscape. Here are some guidelines for working with different forms and design qualities of trees.

Shade Trees. Generally, a shade tree is wide branching, but not all shade trees have the same shape. And shape can change as a tree matures. The tops of some shade trees, such as the sugar maple, become somewhat pyramidal. Many of the oaks become rounded. The slow-growing Japanese zelkova is vase-shaped when young, and more rounded when mature.

A shade tree's wide branching demands space all around and is especially lovely from a distance. A single shade tree turns a patio into an intimate outdoor living room. Widely separated pairs of shade trees provide a magnificent canopy for a large patio and lend grandeur to an entrance. But it's difficult and not wise to grow flowers under trees because the roots compete for water and nutrients. A shade tree can reduce light so much that even shade-tolerant grasses may have trouble. A solution may be to mulch the area with pebbles or crushed rock.

Columnar Trees. Their branches grow upward and close to the trunk in a symmetrical fashion. These trees often have 'Columnare' (columnlike) or 'Fastigiata' (with erect branches) as their cultivar names. Use them to introduce tall vertical accents near rounded clumps of trees. Columnar trees look right at home in open landscapes similar to those of the Provence region of France or southern Italy. They can also be handsome on the grounds of starkly modern buildings. Unfortunately, Europe's famous columnar Lombardy poplars do not thrive in many parts of North America, but you can substitute columnar cultivars of red maple (such as *Acer rubrum* 'Columnare'), European hornbeam (*Carpinus betulus* 'Columnaris'), and European beech (perhaps *Fagus sylvatica* 'Dawyck'). 'Princeton Sentry' and 'Mayfield' are beautiful columnar ginkgos. Narrow, pointed evergreens, such as American arborvitae or juniper cultivars, are beautiful along walls and are also used for windbreaks. Majestic columns of green add drama aligned along allées or set as a group in a sweep of lawn. Small cultivars make good container specimens for patios, roof gardens, and decks.

OVAL   COLUMNAR   PYRAMIDAL   VASE-SHAPED

ROUND   CLUMP   WEEPING   CONICAL

Weeping Trees. Use weeping trees where a grace note is needed, where the branches will be reflected in water, or where wind can sweep through them. Or simply place them in an expanse of lawn. A single weeping tree can make such a strong impact that one is usually all a small garden can handle. This pendulous form is so popular that many cultivars have been bred or grafted to accentuate it. Today there are weeping crabapples, willows, birches, European beeches, kousa dogwoods, and flowering cherries, to name a few. One of the most beautiful pendulous conifers is the weeping blue Atlas cedar.

Flowering Trees. The blooms of flowering trees take many forms. Yellowwood's delicate drooping white clusters, red horse chestnut's brilliant scarlet spires, and magnolia's big fragrant pink cups or white saucers are just a sampling of the wonderful variety available. Even trees valued primarily for their foliage and form surprise and delight us with their flowers—red maple's small, deep scarlet flowers announce spring's arrival, while weeping willow's graceful branches drip golden catkins. Flowering trees make a tremendous impact in bloom, but because most flower for only a few weeks and some for only a few days, shop for species that have additional assets. Dogwoods, crabapples, and hawthorns bear showy flowers, bright fruit, and colorful fall foliage, and they look interesting even when leafless.

If you have room on your property, you can have at least one tree in flower from early spring through late summer. If you garden in Hardiness Zones 4 to 8, for example, consider early-spring-flowering plums, cherries, and star magnolia; followed by the late spring blossoms of dogwoods, redbuds, new pear cultivars, crabapples, and hawthorns. And brighten summer's landscape with golden-rain and golden-chain trees. In a smaller landscape, place two or three flowering trees against a backdrop of evergreens to carry the garden through the seasons. If you have room for only one tree, consider the beautiful Yoshino cherry or the Sargent cherry, both of which flower in spring.

Fall and Winter Interest. In winter, a tree can show off its stark silhouette, its distinctive bark, and its ornamental fruit. Especially striking are the majestic winter silhouettes of the oaks. Evergreens that blend with deciduous foliage in summer take center stage after the leaves fall.

Weeping cherries can provide both spectacular spring blooms and a grace note. This one is *Prunus subhirtella* 'Pendula Plena Rosea'.

Formal incense cedar, graceful Serbian spruce, and stately cedar of Lebanon all stand out in the winter landscape.

The bark of most trees becomes more rugged and interesting with the years, and some species shed their bark in beautiful patterns. The peeling purple-brown bark of paper-bark maple exposes a rich cinnamon orange beneath. The marbled bark of the lace-bark pine rivals the beauty of the paper birch. Some trees keep their colorful fruits through the winter, including the hollies, hawthorns, and many flowering crabapples. Birds that feed on the fruits also liven up the winter landscape; overwintering birds will often stay around in spring and help control the minority of insects that are harmful.

What and Where to Plant

When choosing a site for a tree, remember that its location must accommodate its needs. Otherwise, adjust the design or pick another species.

Before you buy any tree, draw a plan for your landscape that considers design, along with appropriate species and their placement. Investigate all the characteristics of a tree you are considering using. Consider placement in relation to buildings and other permanent structures. (Site large trees at least 20 feet away from foundations and small ones at least 8 feet away.) Many trees, even small ones, are planted too close to buildings; they eventually outgrow the space, make the building hard to maintain, and can reduce air circulation enough to promote structural rot in your house. Near the house, such trees block light from the structure and often need to be severely pruned. Such severe pruning make the trees appear misshapen and out of place.

In addition to size, consider desirable assets. For example, site a small tree with fragrant flowers near a walk or patio, or site a tree with colorful fruits near a window so you can enjoy both the fruits and visiting birds in winter. If you need a lawn tree, you might avoid a species such as sweet gum, because its prickly round seed pods must be picked up before late-season lawn mowing. And you probably wouldn't plant a hawthorn next to an often-used walkway where dropped fruits would stick to shoes and attract yellow jackets. Also avoid planting near power and water lines, and septic systems.

Many young trees can tolerate light shade when they are small, but most tall trees require full sun as they mature. Small and midsize trees that are native to the woodland understory, such as redbud and American hornbeam, often do well in sun or in light shade. A tree evenly exposed to sun-

Consider Scale

ONE-STORY CONSIDERATIONS

TWO-STORY CONSIDERATIONS

One-story houses usually appear in better scale with small to midsize trees. Tall trees dwarf the house. And the tall conifer visually divides the house in half, while blocking the view from inside year-round. Two-story houses tend to look better with at least a few taller trees. The short trees at bottom left make this house tower. Trees that appear more in scale with the houses lend an informal balance. Low shrubs won't ever block the view from inside.

EXPOSURE

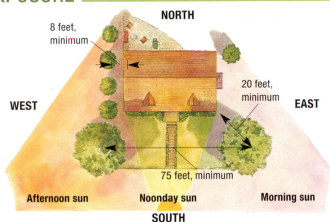

NORTH

8 feet, minimum

20 feet, minimum

WEST

EAST

75 feet, minimum

Afternoon sun Noonday sun Morning sun

SOUTH

Sun Path and Tree Spacing. When siting trees, consider the sun's path from east to west and how it will affect patterns of sun and shade. Position trees that will grow large at least 20 ft. from the house. Position smaller trees at least 8 ft. from the foundation.

Sun Angle and Prevailing Wind. Large deciduous trees in southerly positions can block high-angle, hot sun. In winter, their bare branches allow the low-angle sun to deliver warming sunlight. A row of dense conifers blocks cold winter winds.

light, with room to spread its branches, will most likely develop a symmetrical shape. Use the tree's eventual form and spread to guide you in siting it. For example, columnar trees can be set more closely to one another than pyramidal trees. Be sure to allow space for trees to reach their mature spread. Specimens destined to become large shade trees may need to be spaced 75 feet apart or more. If you wish to create a natural privacy screen, you can achieve a denser look by staggering the trees in a zigzag line.

Strategically located deciduous trees will shade your house in summer, and in winter their bare branches will let sunlight through to warm your home and lower heating bills.

SELECTING TREES

Once you have the location set, and if you are planting new trees, it pays to start small. Young plants are less costly, adapt more easily to transplanting, and grow more quickly. Research has shown that it takes only a few years for trees 7 to 8 feet tall to overtake trees of the same species that were 15 feet tall when planted at the same time. For guidance on selecting trees with various types of root balls—bare-root, container, balled-and-burlapped—see "The Root of the Problem" on page 26.

If you want to plant a big tree, you can hire a landscape service with skilled workers and mechanized equipment to plant it any time the ground is workable. However, if you pay for the planting, be sure to obtain a replacement warranty in writing.

Choosing a Tree

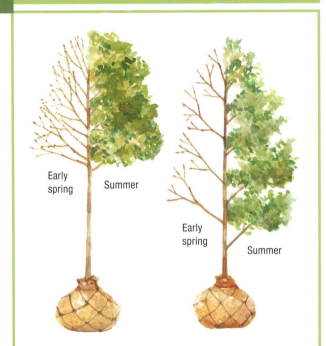

Early spring   Summer

Early spring   Summer

Which tree would you choose? As shown at left, trees from nurseries are sometimes prepruned to present an attractive full head of branches atop a graceful long trunk. But such trees often have closely spaced branches that will soon require major thinning to space out limbs so they won't crowd one another as they thicken. The tree at right shows far better limb spacing for future growth.

Planting and Moving Trees

Prepare the soil, and dig a generous planting hole two to three times the width of the rootball, according to the directions beginning on page 32. Whether you are planting a container-grown sapling or a larger balled-and-burlapped tree, handle the rootball gently when moving the tree into its hole, trying to keep the rootball firm and intact. Be sure to set the crown about 2 inches above the soil line, and slope the soil away from it. Trees that fail within five years of planting often die of crown rot because they are planted too deeply or sink after planting.

It was once standard practice to prune new trees—especially bare-root trees—at planting time. Logic then suggested that cutting back the top growth would help the tree compensate for the roots lost when the plant was dug from the nursery field. But experts no longer recommend pruning at planting time. Research has shown that end buds produce hormones that stimulate root growth and that full leafing helps photosynthesis produce the nutrients the tree needs to grow healthy roots. Thus, severe pruning at planting impedes a tree's ability to extend its root system.

Transplanting a large tree is usually best left to professionals, but you can move a small established tree yourself or with the aid of a helper. You can lift small plants and transplant them promptly, but you are more likely to succeed if you prepare for the move a year ahead as shown on pages 38–39.

Planting Considerations

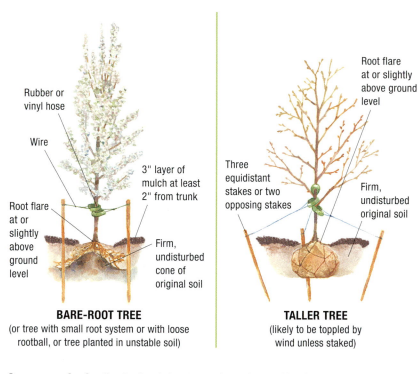

Root flare at ground level or slightly above

3" layer of mulch at least 2" from trunk

Supports looped loosely around trunk so it can sway in wind

Firm, undisturbed cone of original soil

BARE-ROOT TREE
(or tree with small root system or with a loose rootball)

Rubber or vinyl hose

Wire

3" layer of mulch at least 2" from trunk

Root flare at or slightly above ground level

Firm, undisturbed cone of original soil

BARE-ROOT TREE
(or tree with small root system or with loose rootball, or tree planted in unstable soil)

Root flare at or slightly above ground level

Three equidistant stakes or two opposing stakes

Firm, undisturbed original soil

TALLER TREE
(likely to be toppled by wind unless staked)

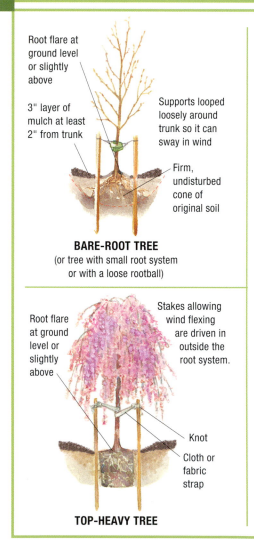

Root flare at ground level or slightly above

Stakes allowing wind flexing are driven in outside the root system.

Knot

Cloth or fabric strap

TOP-HEAVY TREE

As a general rule, dig planting holes two to three times wider than the existing root system but no deeper. Place the root system on firm, undisturbed soil so that the trunk flare remains at or only slightly above ground level and won't later settle. Newly planted trees grow stronger trunks and root systems if allowed to flex in the wind. Yet some trees, especially in windy sites, need staking so that they won't blow over. If staking is needed, it's usually sufficient to support the tree in its lower third. Try to remove the stakes of a spring-planted tree in fall or within one year.

STAKING AND WRAPPING

Staking can help stabilize a tree while its roots are taking hold, and it can help straighten a bent trunk. Trees in windy locations sometimes need the extra support of stakes at first, but research shows that trees forced to depend on their own roots for stability develop better root systems. And the freedom to flex in the wind promotes thicker, stronger trunks than when trees are rigidly staked. Stake only those deciduous trees that are unstable in the wind or need to be straightened. Remove the stakes within a year of planting. When you position support loops consisting of hose or strapping, allow the trunk some room to flex in the wind. Conifers rarely need staking; they usually come with a heavy enough rootball to provide good basal stability.

For broad-leaved and coniferous evergreens in cold windy regions, a burlap windbreak may help prevent excessive drying of the leaves. A protective cylinder of hardware cloth around the trunk will keep rabbits and other mammals from chewing through the bark and thereby killing the young tree. Affix the wire to stakes, and extend it well above the level of expected snow cover so that hungry mammals moving on the snow surface don't inflict any damage. Remove wire or burlap wraps in spring when growth starts. In areas where the winter sun can burn young trunks, a wash of calcium carbonate with resins or a coat of white latex paint can reduce sunscald. Deftly wrapped burlap strips can serve the same purpose during the first year.

If a tree is top heavy and the trunk spindly at planting time, such as this 'Hakuru Nishiki' willow, you may need to stake the upper one-third so that wind doesn't snap the trunk where you place support loops. Make the loops loose to allow desirable flexing of the trunk in the wind.

Use side-cutting pliers to wrap and cut wire, shown at left. Here old garden hose serves as the protective tubing.

Three hose-protected guy wires support a large newly planted tree. For such large trees, you may need to run wires fairly abruptly down to ground level to allow room for mowing.

Adding Mulch and Fertilizer

Trees fare better if their roots need not compete with grass or other plantings for water and nutrients. Besides, digging around the base of a tree to install other plants can damage tree roots. Especially avoid disturbing shallow-rooted plants, such as beeches and fleshy-rooted magnolias. Even with more tolerant, deep-rooted species, use caution and restraint, and limit decorative underplanting to shade-tolerant, shallow-rooted ground covers. You can set them out when you're planting the tree.

Another solution is to encircle the base of your trees with a generous layer of mulch, whether in the form of aged wood mulch, pebbles, or crushed rock. Mulches come in a variety of colors and textures that are attractive themselves, as shown on page 44. For added splashes of color around tree trunks, you can arrange containers of bright flowering annuals.

Fertilize newly planted and young trees as explained on page 47. Established trees usually need little or no fertilizer, and lawn trees may get all the boost they need from nitrogen-rich lawn fertilizers. Too much fertilizer can cause succulent growth that attracts pests. For example, fertilized hemlocks are more susceptible to woolly adelgids, and fertilized tulip trees become more susceptible to aphids.

If your trees show signs of nutrient deficiency, a soil test by a laboratory is the best means of determining whether they need fertilizer, and if so, how much. The lab report will indicate deficiencies and fertilizer application rates.

A good time to apply fertilizer is in late winter before a tree's period of rapid growth. Trees in mild climates can benefit from fertilizer applied in late fall, after their tops have become dormant but while their roots are still growing. (If grass grows under the tree, avoid feeding it by fertilizing with soluble granular nitrogen only when the grass is dormant, in late winter or early spring. Broadcast the fertil-

Supplemental Fertilizing

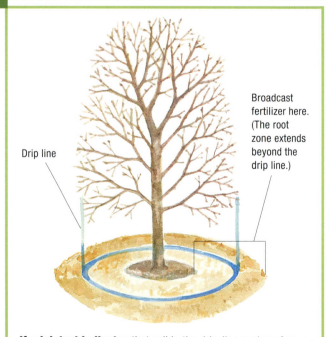

Drip line

Broadcast fertilizer here. (The root zone extends beyond the drip line.)

If a lab test indicates that soil in the drip-line region of your tree lacks sufficient nitrogen, you can amend it by applying the recommended amounts on the surface. However, nitrogen is quickly water soluble, allowing grass plants to absorb much of it. If grass underlies your tree, wait to fertilize until the grass is dormant, giving the nitrogen a chance to soak deeper than the grass roots.

TOOLS FOR AERATING

For ease of use and effectiveness, it's hard to beat a cordless electric drill and a 2-inch-diameter soil auger. But this rig isn't designed for rocky or heavy soils. Instead, pros often use hand augers to produce needed torque. Although long digging bars are great for loosening and prying rocks free, they tend to compact soil around themselves unless adroitly used to loosen soil at hole edges. **Caution:** before boring or digging, check with local utilities to ensure that you will not be working near utility lines.

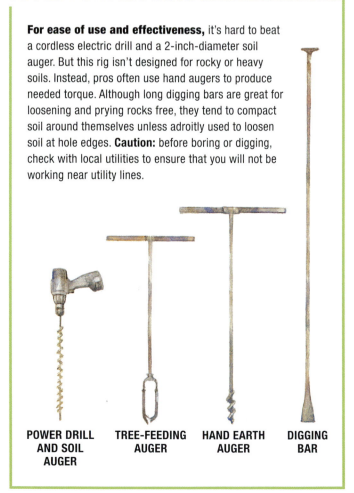

POWER DRILL AND SOIL AUGER

TREE-FEEDING AUGER

HAND EARTH AUGER

DIGGING BAR

izer over the soil beneath the outer two-thirds of the spread of the branches plus half that distance beyond the ends of the branches—the root zone usually extends far beyond the drip line (the perimeter of the area under the branches). Water thoroughly to dissolve the fertilizer and soak it well into the soil.

If a soil test shows that your tree needs a more complete fertilizer that includes phosphate and potassium, apply it in the drip-line zone.

Altering the Site's Grade

Changing the grade near a big tree is a complicated problem, and making a mistake can lead to the death of the tree. If at all possible, make the change outside the tree's drip line. Different tree species have different needs, so before allowing excavators to fill "their way," consult a local arborist or landscape engineer.

To lower the grade, build a retaining wall just beyond the drip line, or even farther out, in locations where winter weather is harsh. Leave the grade at the original level inside the retaining wall, creating a raised bed for the tree, and excavate outside the wall to the desired level.

If you wish to raise the grade within the drip line, the procedure depends on how high you want to elevate it. If you simply cover the root area with soil to raise the grade, the roots could suffocate. Usually you can safely raise the grade up to 4 inches by adding a sandy porous soil, but don't compact it because the tree roots need air.

To raise the grade 4 to 12 inches, you must build a retaining wall at least 3 feet away from the trunk. Leave the soil within that wall at the original grade. Outside the wall, spread porous fill, such as gravel, to within 3 inches of the top of the wall. Then cover this fill with a layer of new soil and grass.

A significant change in grade—a rise of 1 to 2 feet—requires a complicated subsurface ventilating system. For this, you need to build a retaining wall around the trunk and install a series of ventilating drainage pipes into the base that radiate outward as far as the drip line. Cover the pipes with a layer of crushed stone, followed by a layer of gravel, and then a layer of sandy soil.

Changing Grade

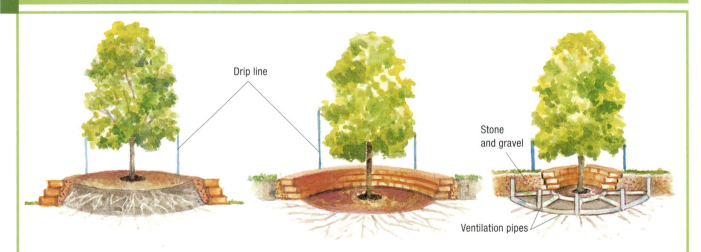

Drip line

Stone and gravel

Ventilation pipes

If you need to lower the grade near a tree, avoid excavating inside the tree's drip line. Because roots usually extend well beyond the drip line, give them as much clearance there as possible.

When raising the grade, avoid filling inside the drip line, mainly because roots need air.

If you must fill more than a few inches inside the drip line, you might be able to save the tree by creating a structural well around it and an elaborate aeration system, complete with ventilation pipes and with aerating crushed stone and gravel. Before allowing excavators to fill "their way," consult an arborist or landscape engineer.

Pruning and Training

The best policy is to select young trees with structures, growth habits, and eventual sizes that will require little or no pruning over the years. If you feel that a new tree needs pruning, wait until the second year after planting before heading back branch ends or removing healthy branches. During the first year after planting, root systems benefit from hormones generated by end buds and from the nourishment produced by leaves.

Prune young trees as they grow to control their shape. With deciduous trees, creating a well-balanced framework of branches results in stronger, healthier, and more handsome trees. But go slowly with the pruning. It takes several years of planned pruning cuts to shape a tree; removing too many branches at one time slows growth and weakens the tree. Remember that for many trees, and certainly conifers, the most beautiful shape is likely to be the one closest to their natural habit.

Conical and pyramidal trees, both evergreen and deciduous, usually have a single leader, or vertical trunk, with all the main side branches extending from it. Open-center trees, also called "branch-headed trees," have a form typically created for fruit trees. But for ornamental trees, most of the pruning will have been done at the nursery. In open-center trees, the trunk divides into several main branches; this branching pattern develops naturally in some deciduous species, but it can also be created at the nursery by cutting back the central leader when trees are young.

Standards, including some shade trees and many smaller deciduous ornamentals, have a length of bare trunk surmounted by a bushy rounded crown. The central leader is removed to create more branching, and the lower limbs are removed gradually over several years to provide clearance beneath the branches. As a tree grows, prune secondary leaders—branches that form tight V-shaped crotches—that are prone to splitting, and those that crowd the interior of the tree or fail to conform to the desired shape. Also prune suckers from the roots and watersprouts growing vertically from the branches, as well as any damaged or dead growth. Use heading cuts to shape the outer edges.

Trees native to a region often have inherent resistance to local pests and diseases. Newer cultivars bred for pest and disease resistance may do well, too. Yet over time, branches on older trees may die or be damaged or broken in storms. Dead, diseased, or damaged wood should be removed.

Same Container Plant—with Different Results

This shows the hypothetical effects of three different pruning philosophies over several years.

Original container tree at planting

Thick, strong trunk

Moderately thick trunk

Slim, weak trunk

Option 1. Unpruned, this tree's energy has gone into side-branch and trunk development, rather than height. At this stage, you can begin removing lower branches gradually over a period of years until you achieve the desired unbranched length of trunk.

Option 2. Here, the lower side branches were pruned back by about one-third at planting time. The result has been moderate growth in height and trunk diameter. At this stage, you can begin removing lower branches gradually over a period of years.

Option 3. All lower side branches were pruned at planting time, so nearly all energy has gone into top growth, leaving a slim, weak trunk. Options 1 or 2 would have been better for the tree.

Pruning Deciduous Trees

For many deciduous trees, the best time to prune is late winter to very early spring, when the trees are dormant, before the sap rises and the buds open. Because birches and maples "bleed" heavily in spring, prune them either when they are fully dormant or in late summer to early fall, when they bleed less. You can also prune in summer to slow rampant growth and to remove suckers and watersprouts. Unless you are repairing storm damage, avoid pruning in fall, when wounds heal more slowly. See pages 48–52 for additional pruning guidelines.

SAME TREE: DIFFERENT RESULTS

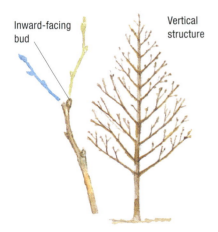

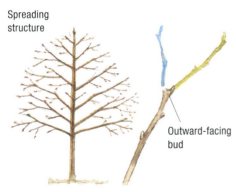

The above two illustrations show resultant growth if the same deciduous tree were pruned differently. In general, pruning cuts mainly above inward-facing buds will produce an inward and essentially vertical branching pattern, as shown at top. Pruning cuts mainly above outward-facing buds will encourage a spreading structure.

ENCOURAGING SIDE BRANCHING

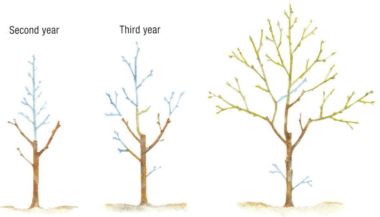

Promote more side branching of a tree with a strong central leader by removing the central leader in the second year. Then remove leaders on all main branches in successive years to achieve the effects you want.

CREATING AN OPEN-CENTERED TREE

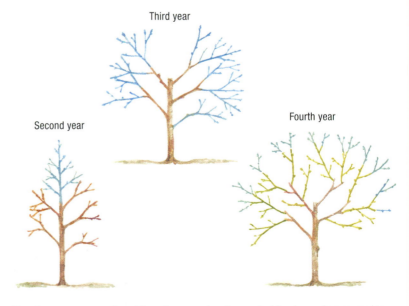

Create an open-centered tree by removing the central leader and encouraging growth that will result in the open-top look.

Pruning and Maintaining Established Trees

Proper pruning cuts just beyond the collar on this kwanzan cherry resulted in the nicely healing wound shown at left and the almost completely healed wound on another branch, shown above.

Improper pruning results are shown here in both pictures. Above left: Careless lopping left a small, protruding chunk of wood that won't heal as quickly as the surrounding edges. Above right: A single top-to-bottom cut resulted in torn bark that exposes the tree to diseases and pests.

These rubbing limbs, left, will eventually abrade the bark on one or both limbs, leaving exposed wood open to pests and diseases. Remove the weaker limb or the one facing inward.

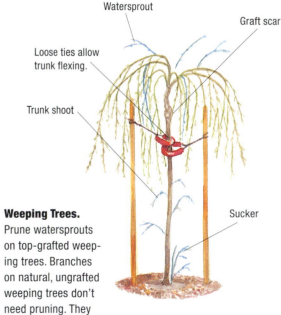

Watersprout

Graft scar

Loose ties allow trunk flexing.

Trunk shoot

Sucker

Weeping Trees.
Prune watersprouts on top-grafted weeping trees. Branches on natural, ungrafted weeping trees don't need pruning. They will eventually weep desirably. Prune dead, lopsided, or congested branches. Rub off soft shoots on the trunk with your thumb, and cut off other shoots and suckers.

Spreading Shoots. Above: You can fashion spreaders from pruned branches, employing broad Y crotches at one end and inserting a galvanized nail, as shown, into the other and then cutting its head off with side-cutting pliers. Right: Growers of fruit trees often spread young shoots to crotch angles greater than 45 deg., both to promote a strong connection at the collar and to keep limbs within reach for picking.

Improper Pruning. The black ridge of bark on this paper birch shows why tight vertical crotches tend to be weaker than crotches with angles greater than 45 deg. Here, the bark of the trunk and branch have grown together, leaving this deep ridge, which has a weaker connection than shallower ridges that result when branches emerge at crotch angles greater than 45 deg. Correct pruning here would involve three cuts, as shown in this drawing. The third cut would begin just outside the bark ridge at the top and proceed at roughly the angle shown by the dotted line.

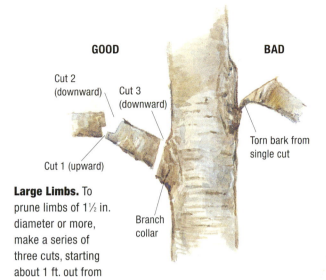

Large Limbs. To prune limbs of 1½ in. diameter or more, make a series of three cuts, starting about 1 ft. out from the collar. If you mistakenly make only one cut, above right, the branch will begin to fall before you're finished, tearing bark away, retarding healing, and exposing wood to disease and pests.

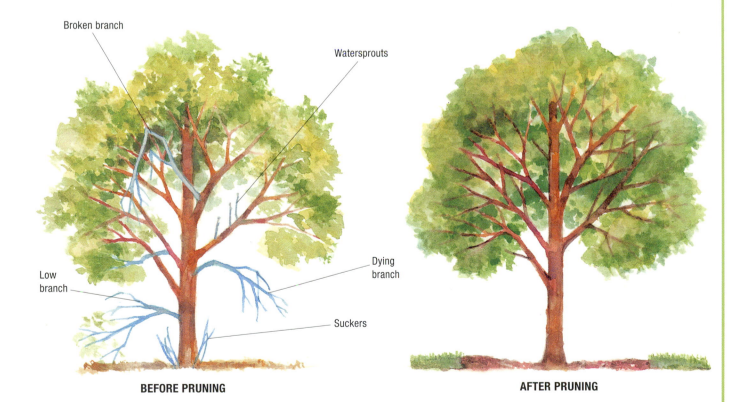

BEFORE PRUNING

AFTER PRUNING

Perfect Pruning. These before-and-after drawings suggest how to prune an established deciduous tree for health and beauty. Always remove dead, broken, diseased, or crossing branches. Also remove watersprouts and suckers.

Creating Special Effects

Pruning can achieve practical and aesthetic purposes beyond general maintenance.

Pleaching. Branches of closely spaced trees can be interwoven to create a tall hedge supported by clean trunks; interweaving upper branches can create arches and tunnels. Though beautiful, pleached forms take a long time and a lot of work to achieve and are time-consuming to maintain.

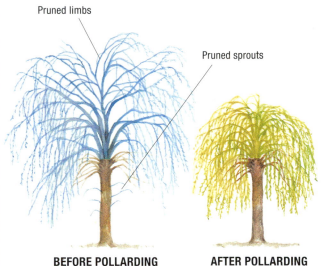

Pruned limbs

Pruned sprouts

BEFORE POLLARDING   **AFTER POLLARDING**

Pollarding. Common in European landscapes, pollarded trees are severely cut back every year or so, often to the main trunk. This allows a tree to mature while retaining an artificially compact form or even hedgelike form. Willows, beeches, and lindens are often given this severe treatment.

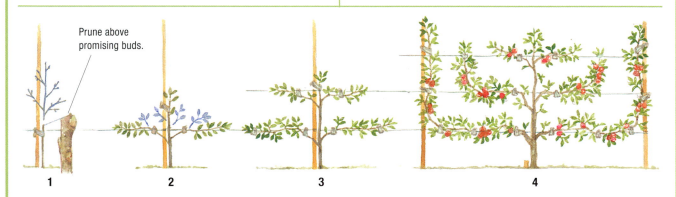

Prune above promising buds.

1   2   3   4

Espalier. The branches of an espaliered tree or shrub are trained flat against a vertical surface in an interesting, usually symmetrical, branching pattern. Espaliers save space, dress up a wall or fence, and provide variety in a small garden. Fruit trees take well to such pruning and bear larger fruit within reach for easy picking. Here are steps in training:

Step 1. After your staked plant's roots are well established, you can drive in end posts at the distance you wish your espalier to spread. Then string a taut galvanized wire between the end posts, crossing the original stake a few inches above the buds of the desired shoots.

Step 2. Prune all but the three best shoots. Tie the two horizontal shoots to the wire, and tie the vertical shoot to the stake. Use nonabrasive ties of biodegradable material.

Step 3. When the vertical shoot reaches the desired height, string the second wire. Select the three best top shoots and secure them as before. Continue securing and training first tier shoots outward, pruning any excess shoots.

Step 4. After some years, the central trunk will support itself and its support stake can be removed. Continue pruning and training over the years.

PRUNING CONIFERS

Try to select conifers with a growth habit and eventual size suitable for your location. Dwarf conifers are especially appropriate for small properties. Although conifers seldom need regular pruning to achieve their natural shape, you can avoid struggling to keep growth in check if you choose carefully. Conifers described in this book are narrow-leaved (needled) and evergreen, except for the larch (*Larix*), which loses its leaves in fall.

All conifers have either of two distinct growth habits: random branching, with branches occurring anywhere, and whorled branching, with multiple branches radiating from the trunk at spaced intervals. (See illustrations bottom.)

Most conifers need little more than removal of dead or damaged branches—or burned foliage (before growth begins). The best time to prune conifers to limit growth or improve shape is just after new growth appears. Some conifers accumulate unattractive, congested growth that should be removed. Also, this minimizes damage from snow and ice. For instructions on pruning competing leaders and training desirable ones, see below left.

LEADERSHIP TRAINING

Prune the less desirable, competing leader.

Replace a broken or damaged leader by splinting the next most desirable branch.

Conifers achieve their characteristic central shaft of trunk because their top leader grows more strongly than other branches. If you want your tree to achieve that characteristic point, prune competing leaders, and replace a damaged leader by splinting it to a support as shown.

Two Types of Conifers

Branching Patterns. Conifer genera have either of two branching patterns: random branching, as shown at left, or whorled branching, as shown far right. Most random-branching conifers can be sheared and pruned to maintain size and to shape them into hedges and topiary art. Of the three whorled-branching conifers, pines don't respond well with new growth when pruned, but you can arrest growth by pinching back new-growth "candles" in spring. The other two whorled-branching conifers, the spruces and firs, can also be pinched back. Yet spruces and firs often have dense enough growth to allow some light shearing, mainly of new growth that won't be noticeable for long.

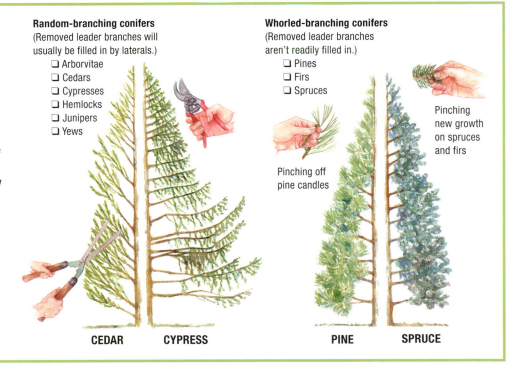

Random-branching conifers
(Removed leader branches will usually be filled in by laterals.)
- ❏ Arborvitae
- ❏ Cedars
- ❏ Cypresses
- ❏ Hemlocks
- ❏ Junipers
- ❏ Yews

Whorled-branching conifers
(Removed leader branches aren't readily filled in.)
- ❏ Pines
- ❏ Firs
- ❏ Spruces

Pinching new growth on spruces and firs

Pinching off pine candles

CEDAR   **CYPRESS**

PINE   **SPRUCE**

The Firs

Abies

The firs are evergreen trees native to high altitudes in cold and temperate climates. Firs resemble spruce, the pyramidal Christmas tree, but the fir silhouette tends to be softer and more graceful. Fir needles are 2 to 3 inches long and rather flat with two white bands on the underside; they last for four or five years before dropping. Crushed, they produce a lemony scent. Fir cones, 3 to 6 inches long and pale green when young, develop a purplish cast as they mature.

Among firs for the home landscape, the long-lived stately white fir (*Abies concolor*) is a popular choice. It's native to the Rockies, Zones 3–7, but adapts to the East, to city life, and to heat and drought. In summer, the dark green needles make a handsome backdrop for the garden, and in fall and winter they lend life to the frozen landscape.

In cultivation, the white fir reaches 30 to 50 feet in height with a spread of 15 to 20 feet; in the wild, it can grow to 100 feet. These are excellent cultivars.

White fir (*Abies concolor* 'Glenmore')

White fir (*Abies concolor*)

FEATURED PROFILE

White, or Colorado, Fir

Botanical Name: *Abies concolor* 'Candicans' **Family:** Pinaceae **Type of Plant:** tall evergreen conifer **Uses:** lawn and park specimen; winter color **Genus Range:** CO, CA, NM **Hardiness:** USDA Zones 3–7 **Height:** 30 to 50' in cultivation; to 100' in the wild **Growth Rate:** slow to medium **Form & Habit:** pyramidal **Flowers:** inconspicuous **Fruits:** green-purple cones 3 to 6" long **Foliage:** 2 to 3" long; silvery bluish green needles usually with two white bands on the underside **Soil & pH:** deep, rich, well-drained, sandy loam; slightly acid **Light & Moisture:** full sun; sustained moisture but tolerates drought

Silver fir (*Abies alba* 'Pendula')
new and old growth

Fraser fir (*Abies fraseri*)

Another fir that thrives in the East is the wonderfully aromatic balsam fir (*A. balsamea*), native from Labrador, Newfoundland, to West Virginia and Minnesota and hardy in Zones 3–5. Southern balsam, or Fraser, fir (*A. fraseri*) is used in the warm Southeast. Hardy in Zones 4–7, it is native to the highlands of West Virginia, North Carolina, and Tennessee.

Culture: firs grow best when transplanted as young container- or field-grown balled-and-burlapped trees. They thrive in deep, rich, moist but well-drained sandy loam that is slightly acid, pH 5.0 to 6.0. Firs do best in full sun but tolerate all-day bright or filtered sunlight.

White fir (*Abies concolor* 'Candicans')

Balsam fir (*Abies balsamea*)

White fir (*Abies concolor* 'Glenmore')

The Maples

Acer

Maples are North America's favorite shade trees, the stars of New England's spectacular fall colors, and the source of delicious maple syrup. The sugar maple (*Acer saccharum*) is Canada's national tree. There is at least one cultivated maple species for every climate but tropical. The larger, slower-growing maples produce hard wood that resists cracking and splitting. These long-lived trees often have strong horizontal branches that can support swings and hammocks.

One of the most widely planted maples is the colorful red, or swamp, maple (*A. rubrum*). Rounded in form, it grows 40 to 60 feet in cultivation. In early spring, garnet-red flower clusters outline the tree's branches; later, red leaf buds appear that open a glossy green. The leaves turn a dazzling gold-orange-crimson in early fall and cling to the branches for weeks. Several types have been bred with tolerances for regional climates, so choose a field-grown specimen from a reliable local nursery. 'October Glory' succeeds in warm regions; 'Red Sunset' withstands winter temperatures to −25°F.

Sugar maple (*Acer saccharum*) in fall

Coloring the hills of New England and southern Canada in fall, the massive sugar maples (*A. saccharum*) provide the sap for maple syrup. Sugar maples reach 60 to 75 feet in cultivation—100 to 120 feet in the wild—and grow more beautiful and imposing with age. These trees are best suited to large properties and open woodlands. They thrive in Zones 3–8 but seem to prefer the eastern reaches of North America. In the Midwest and Pacific Northwest, try cultivars, such as 'Green Mountain' and the smaller 'Rocky Mountain Glow'.

The silver maple (*A. saccharinum*), for Zones 3–9, is sometimes mistaken for the sugar maple. In moist soil the silver maple grows rapidly to a great height and matures into a superb specimen. However, its reputation for rapid growth has too often led to its use as a sidewalk tree. Under such less-than-ideal conditions, silver maple wood is weak, the branches break easily, and the tree never realizes its true potential.

Another popular maple for large landscapes in Zones 3–7 is the Norway maple (*A. platanoides*), reaching 40 to 90 feet. Its dense foliage is generally a lustrous green. The undersides of the leaves of one cultivar, 'Crimson King', are moss green, and the leaves' surface and stems are a shade of maroon that is so dark that it looks almost black. 'Crimson King' makes an eye-catching specimen, even from a distance.

Some excellent maples provide fall color for small

Red maple
(*Acer rubrum*)

Red maple (*Acer rubrum*)
female flowers

Chinese paperbark maple
(*Acer griseum*)

Norway maple (*Acer platanoides*)
samaras

landscapes. One of the loveliest examples is the 25-foot Chinese paperbark maple (*A. griseum*), hardy in Zones 4–8. The fall color is bronze, russet red, or red in warm regions; in cool regions, the color is scarlet. The bark is an enormous asset, mottled in an exquisite combination of cinnamon and forest green. Vine maples (*A. circinatum*) grow wild in the mainly evergreen coastal forests of the Pacific Northwest. They thrive in coastal gardens from British Columbia through northern California, as does the Tatarian maple (*A. tataricum*), an import from Europe and western Asia.

Other attractive maples for the home landscape include the amur maple (*A. ginnala*), which thrives in Zones 3–8, and the Chinese striped-bark maple (*A. davidii*), the miyabi maple (*A. miyabi*), and the nikko maple (*A. nikoense*) in Zones 5–7. For Zones 5–8, choose the three-flowered maple (*A. triflorum*) or the trident maple (*A. buergeranum*). The field, or hedge, maple (*A. campestre*) grows well in Zones 5–9, and the Florida, or Southern sugar, maple succeeds (*A. barbatum or A. floridanum*) in Zones 7–9.

See "Japanese Maple," page 162, for a description of the elegant Japanese maples.

Culture: maples transplant fairly readily, but it is best to choose young container-grown or balled-and burlapped trees and to transplant them in the spring. They flourish in moist but well-drained somewhat acid soils and full sun. During dry spells, mature maples require biweekly watering.

Japanese maples
(*Acer palmatum* 'Fascination' and red 'Fireglow') in spring

FEATURED PROFILE
Red Maple

Botanical Name: *Acer rubrum* **Family:** Aceraceae **Type of Plant:** large deciduous tree **Uses:** shade tree; lawn and park specimen; spring and fall color **Native Range:** east and central North America **Hardiness:** USDA Zones 3–10 **Height:** 40 to 60' in cultivation **Growth Rate:** medium to fast **Form & Habit:** rounded **Bloom Period:** early spring **Flowers:** showy red clusters; female flowers are intensely red **Fruits:** reddish brown winged samaras **Foliage:** reddish new leaves turn green **Soil & pH:** well-drained, somewhat acid **Light & Moisture:** full sun, sustained moisture **Pruning Seasons:** during dormancy

Red maple (*Acer rubrum*)

The Buckeyes

Aesculus

Spring-flowering red horse chestnut
(*Aesculus* x *carnea* 'Briotii')

Summer-flowering bottlebrush
buckeye (*Aesculus parviflora*)

Members of the genus *Aesculus* native to North America are called "buckeyes." The popular European and Asian species are known as "horse chestnuts," but they are not true chestnuts (*Castanea*). Introduced to North America by the colonists, horse chestnuts (*Aesculus hippocastanum*) were planted for their spring flowers and for the dense shade these lovely trees provide. Their glossy brown nuts resemble the edible fruits of the chestnut, but they are so poisonous that even wildlife avoid them. The showiest of the modern cultivars is the red horse chestnut *A.* x *carnea* 'Briotii', a handsome 30- to 50-foot pyramidal tree with upright, 8- to 10-inch rose or salmon red panicles in midspring. Its big bold leaves resemble hands and remain a rich dark green well into October. Though it makes a fine shade tree for the home landscape, 'Briotii' is most often seen along streets and in spacious public grounds.

The North American native buckeyes are hardy in Zones 3–7. Though less spectacular in flower than 'Briotii', buckeyes are popular shade trees and ornamentals in their native regions. Ohio, the "Buckeye State," has chosen the smaller Ohio buckeye (*A. glabra*), which has pale gold flowers, as its state tree. In Zones 4–8, the shrubby bottlebrush buckeye (*A. parviflora*) is among the loveliest summer-flowering shrubs. Native from South Carolina through Alabama and Florida, it grows 8 to 12 feet tall and bears white flowers in July. The large shrub or small tree called the "California buckeye" (*A. californica*) is widely grown on the West Coast.

Culture: transplant container-grown or balled-and-burlapped horse chestnuts in early spring into moist but well-drained soil with a pH of 6.5 or less. The tree will succeed in full sun or light shade.

Common horse chestnut
(*Aesculus hippocastanum*)

FEATURED PROFILE
Ohio Buckeye

Botanical Name: *Aesculus glabra*
Family: Hippocastanaceae **Type of Plant:** deciduous tree **Uses:** shade; lawn and park specimen; naturalizing **Native Range:** southern U.S. **Hardiness:** USDA Zones 3–7 Height: 20 to 40' **Growth Rate:** medium **Form & Habit:** rounded to broad-rounded **Bloom Period:** early to mid May **Flowers:** greenish yellow panicles 4 to 7" long **Fruits:** 1 to 2" long, light brown capsule **Foliage:** bright green changing to dark green **Soil & pH:** well-drained, slightly acid **Light & Moisture:** full sun or light shade; sustained moisture **Pruning Seasons:** early spring

Ohio buckeye (*Aesculus glabra*)

The Birches

Betula

Paper birch (*Betula papyrifera*) in fall

Japanese white birch
(*Betula platyphylla* variety *japonica*
'Whitespire')

Birches are tall, slender trees known for their beautiful bark. They have graceful crowns and small pointed leaves that rustle with every breeze and turn yellow and yellow-green in fall. Widely distributed over the Northern Hemisphere, birches are usually found in moist soil near cold rivers and lakes. In cultivation, they establish quickly and are fast growing. They are also rather short lived, especially in temperate regions where they are susceptible to birch leaf miner and bronze birch borer.

The most beautiful bark belongs to the paper, or canoe, birch (*Betula papyrifera*), which thrives in chilly Zone 2 and, under good conditions, survives as far south as Zone 6 or 7. Its chalky white bark, striped dark gray or black, can be cut and peeled in big sheets. Native Americans once used it to sheathe their canoes and wigwams. The sap can be boiled down to a sweet syrup, and in the fall the leaves give a golden wash to northern forests. Paper birch can be grown as a single-stemmed or trained as a multistemmed plant. It is more successful in the northern Midwest than the popular multistemmed European birch (*B. pendula*), which requires a regular spray program to survive.

In warm reaches of its hardiness zones—Zones 4–9—the vigorous cultivar of native river birch, *B. nigra* 'Heritage', is especially resistant to pests and diseases. It tolerates soil that is wet a portion of the year but dry in summer and fall. 'Heritage' develops a pyramidal shape and grows 30 to 40 feet tall in cultivation; it can be pruned to develop multiple stems. Of the birches that do well in warm areas, 'Heritage' bark is the color closest to white. Paper thin and buff pink, the bark peels away to expose an inner bark that may be salmon pink to grayish, cinnamon, or reddish brown.

The slender Japanese white birch (*B. platyphylla* variety *japonica* 'Whitespire') is a single-trunk cultivar resistant to the borer and adaptable to many temperatures and soils in Zones 2–6 or 7. A superior introduction by John L. Creech, a former Director of the United States National Arboretum, 'Whitespire' has beautiful chalk-white bark with contrasting black triangles at the base of lateral branches. The bark doesn't exfoliate.

Culture: the birches transplant easily in early spring or fall to moist, humus-rich soil that is below pH 6.5. They will grow in full sun or light shade. Watering during droughts and substantial feeding in early spring help to offset attacks of birch leaf miner.

River birch (*Betula nigra*) catkins

River birch (*Betula nigra* 'Heritage')

Incense Cedar
Calocedrus decurrens

Young incense cedar (*Calocedrus decurrens*)

The incense cedar (*Calocedrus decurrens*) is the only North American native in the genus *Calocedrus,* which comprises three species. Often mistaken for the beautiful evergreen American arborvitae (*Thuja occidentalis*), incense cedar is a stately symmetrical conifer that grows at a slow-to-moderate rate and can live for a thousand years. In the Northwest, where it grows wild, the tree reaches heights of 130 feet and becomes broadly conical with wide-spreading branches. In cultivation, it is narrow, 30 to 50 feet in height, with a spread of 8 to 10 feet. Incense cedars can be grouped to create a tall screen, but the tree is most beautiful featured in a large formal landscape with plenty of space around it. Exceptionally elegant, it has spicy aromatic, shiny dark-green scalelike leaves. In early spring, small attractive cylindrical cones appear, turning reddish or yellowish brown as they ripen, and persist until the next spring. The scaly bark becomes cinnamon red as it matures. The cultivar 'Aureovariegata' is splashed with irregular patches of vivid gold.

With winter protection, incense cedar is hardy to southern New England, Zone 5, and extends its range southward into Zone 8. Southerners prefer incense cedar to arborvitae because it stands up to heat even in Georgia and holds its color in winter.

Culture: incense cedar transplants best as a young tree in spring or early fall. It thrives in well-drained moist soil, cultivated sandy loam, pH 6.0 to 7.0, but adapts to a variety of soils. It withstands salt spray—not road salt— and grows well in full sun or light shade. It does not tolerate drought, wet locations, dry air, or sweeping winds.

Incense cedar (*Calocedrus decurrens*)

Incense cedar (*Calocedrus decurrens*)

Incense cedar (*Calocedrus decurrens*)

FEATURED PROFILE
Incense Cedar

Botanical Name: *Calocedrus decurrens* **Family:** Cupressaceae
Type of Plant: midsize evergreen conifer **Uses:** formal landscaping element; winter color **Native Range:** W. U.S. from OR to NV and S. CA **Hardiness:** USDA Zones 5 or 6–8 **Height:** 30 to 50' in cultivation; to 130' and higher in the wild **Growth Rate:** slow to moderate **Form & Habit:** columnar; regular silhouette **Flowers:** inconspicuous **Fruits:** erect cones 4 to 5" long by 2 to 5" wide; yellowish or reddish brown **Foliage:** scalelike; glossy dark green **Soil & pH:** well-drained, fertile; pH adaptable **Light & Moisture:** full sun to light shade; sustained moisture

The Hornbeams

Carnipus

Ironwood (*Carpinus caroliniana*) in fall

Ironwood (*Carpinus caroliniana*) fruit clusters in summer

The two species of hornbeams most used in landscaping have remarkably tough wood and are beautiful trees year-round. These fairly slow-growing trees tolerate urban conditions well. Hornbeams are related to birches and beeches and resemble them somewhat in their form and foliage.

The European hornbeam (*Carpinus betulus*) is one of the most effective moderate-size trees for urban landscapes in Zones 5–7. The tree is pyramidal when young; in time, it develops an oval-to-round crown made up of many slender branches that arch up from a silvery trunk. It reaches 40 to 60 feet. It can be pruned and sheared repeatedly and is used in tall hedges and pleached allées (in which two parallel rows of trees are trained with their branches interwoven).

The leaves of the European hornbeam are as dainty as a birch's but smaller and more refined. In summer and fall, decorative drooping fruit clusters of single-winged ribbed nutlets appear. Similar to maple samaras, they are strung together by the dozens. In fall, the leaves turn yellow and yellow-green. Among the more beautiful cultivated varieties of hornbeams used in North America are the cut-leaf 'Asplenifolia', with lacy-textured leaves, and 'Incisa', with somewhat coarser leaves. 'Fastigiata', a heat- and drought-resistant pyramidal tree that grows to 35 feet tall, is a popular street tree.

The native species (*C. caroliniana*) known as "muscle-wood" or "ironwood" is a small understory tree 20 to 30 feet tall. Its fine-grained wood is so resistant to splitting that the early settlers used it to make bowls and hammer handles. Musclewood grows wild in Zones 2–9, from Nova Scotia to Minnesota and south to Florida and Texas. Though the European species is the most widely cultivated, the native tree is loved for its spectacular red and orange fall color. Because native hornbeams are often propagated from seed, making the fall foliage color unpredictable, buy the native species in autumn.

European hornbeam (*Carpinus betulus* 'Fastigiata')

Culture: the hornbeams are somewhat difficult to start. Transplant young container-grown or balled-and-burlapped trees in early spring to moist but well-drained, somewhat acid soil. The trees prefer full sun but tolerate shade.

FEATURED PROFILE
European Hornbeam

Botanical Name: *Carpinus betulus* **Family:** Betulaceae **Type of Plant:** shearable deciduous shade tree **Uses:** urban landscaping, specimen, container, hedge, pleached allée **Native Range:** Europe, Asia Minor, east and southeast England **Hardiness:** USDA Zones 5–7 **Height:** usually 40 to 60'; occasionally 70 to 80' **Growth Rate:** slow to medium **Form & Habit:** pyramidal in youth; oval-round at maturity **Bloom Period:** April **Flowers:** inconspicuous male and female catkins **Fruits:** ribbed nut ¼" long; single-winged samara **Foliage:** long, narrow, serrated pointed oval; 2½ to 5" long; dark green in summer; yellow to yellow-green in fall **Soil & pH:** prefers well-drained soil but tolerates a wide range of soils **Light & Moisture:** best in full sun, tolerates dappled shade; keep roots moist **Pruning Seasons:** August or after the leaves fall

European hornbeam (*Carpinus betulus*)

Hickories
Carya

Pecan (*Carya illinoensis*) in bloom

Pecan (*Carya illinoensis*) fruits (nuts)

Hickories comprise a group of big beautiful trees native to the eastern United States and nearby Canada and south to Mexico. Grown for their sometimes flaky shaggy bark and for their copious and sometimes messy nuts, they can be difficult to transplant once established because of their long taproot. The shagbark hickory (*Carya ovata*) is

Shagbark hickory (*Carya ovata*)

the species most widely planted as an ornamental. As a nut-bearer it is second only to its cousin the pecan (*C. illinoensis*), the largest of the hickories. A big, picturesque tree, the shagbark reaches 60 to 70 feet in cultivation; in the wilds of the central-eastern United States, it reaches 100 to 120 feet. The common name refers to the bark's loose, outward-curving sections and the resulting shaggy look. The leaves, a deep yellow-green in summer, change to rich yellow and golden brown in fall. Too large and messy for the average yard, the shagbark is used in Zones 3 or 4–9 as a specimen tree on a large property or allowed to naturalize in suburban woods.

Two hickory trees growing near each other produce more abundant nut crops, even though flowers of both sexes appear on the same tree, making the trees self-pollinating. Settlers learned from Native Americans how to grind and steep the pecan-flavored nuts to extract a flavored oil that was used in making sweet cakes. The hard, slow-burning wood was used to make wooden wheels and ax handles and was made into charcoal. Hickory chips are still used today for smoking ham and bacon and for barbecuing.

The vase-shaped bitternut hickory (*C. cordiformis*) has a delicate branching structure and is used in the Midwest as a shade tree. Its nuts are inedible.

Culture: to avoid transplant difficulties, choose a young container-grown or balled-and-burlapped tree and plant it in early spring in rich, well-drained loam in full sun. Hickories adapt to a wide range of soils, including clay.

Shagbark hickory (*Carya ovata*)

FEATURED PROFILE
Shagbark Hickory

Botanical Name: *Carya ovata* **Family:** Juglandaceae **Type of Plant:** large deciduous nut-bearing shade tree **Uses:** shade; nut crop; attractive bark lends winter interest **Native Range:** Quebec to MN; S. to GA and TX **Hardiness:** USDA Zones 3 or 4–9 **Height:** 60 to 70' in cultivation; to 120' in the wild **Growth Rate:** medium to slow **Form & Habit:** straight trunk with oblong crown **Bloom Period:** early May, with the leaves **Flowers:** male borne in 3-branched catkins; female in small terminal spikes **Fruits:** hard-shelled edible nuts in 4-valved husk **Foliage:** pointed, serrated leaflets 4 to 6" long **Soil & pH:** deep, rich, well-drained; pH tolerant **Light & Moisture:** full sun; sustained moisture

Shagbark hickory (*Carya ovata*)

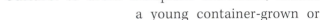

The Cedars

Cedrus

Like most conifers, the cedars are evergreens. Large, handsome, and long-lived, the trees tend to be graceful when young and magnificent when mature. Cedars have few rivals for beauty when given enough space. Their foliage consists of clusters of small needles, and their cones are large and decorative. Two Asian species have been gracing American gardens since Colonial times.

Blue Atlas cedar
(*Cedrus libani* subsp. *atlantica* 'Glauca')

The hardiest of the Asian cedars is the exquisite cedar of Lebanon (*Cedrus libani*), which grows well in Zones 5 or 6–7. Admired since Biblical times, this native of Asia Minor and Turkey starts off pyramidal in shape with dark green foliage, grows quickly to 40 to 60 feet, and eventually reaches 120 feet. It becomes attractively flat-topped and develops a massive trunk; its stiffly held, sweeping horizontal branches make a dramatic statement.

The blue Atlas cedar (*C. libani* subsp. *atlantica*) from northern Africa is closely related to the cedar of Lebanon and reportedly tolerates urban pollution better. The leaves of the species are light green to silvery blue. A pyramidal blue-needled cultivar, 'Glauca', is a striking steel blue. Another dramatic cultivar, 'Pendula', has drooping branchlets that cascade like a waterfall. This weeping cultivar is

Deodar cedar (*Cedrus deodara*)

sometimes damaged by severe winters at the northern edge of its range.

Strikingly arching, drooping branches distinguish the deodar cedar (*C. deodara*), native to the Himalayas. It is hardy in Zones 7–8 or 9. The most graceful of the cedars and the largest, it reaches 200 feet with a spread of 150 feet after many decades. Its fine foliage may be light green, grayish green, or silver. The blue-green cones seem expressly created to decorate Christmas trees.

Culture: the cedars transplant with some difficulty. Transplant a young container-grown or balled-and-burlapped tree in early spring to deeply worked, well-drained, somewhat acid soil. Provide protection from wind; *C. libani* needs an open site. Cedars do not tolerate wet feet, shade, or pollution.

FEATURED PROFILE
Blue Atlas Cedar

Botanical Name: *Cedrus libani* subsp. *atlantica* 'Glauca' **Family:** Pinaceae **Type of Plant:** blue-needled evergreen conifer **Uses:** lawn and park specimen; winter color **Genus Range:** mountains of Algeria and Morocco **Hardiness:** Zones 6–9 **Height:** 40 to 60' **Growth Rate:** fast when young; then slow **Form & Habit:** pyramidal, then pendulous and flat-topped **Flowers:** erect male cones 2 to 3" long **Fruits:** greenish white cones 3" long, maturing to brown in second year **Foliage:** vivid blue to silver-blue **Soil & pH:** well-drained; somewhat acid **Light & Moisture:** full sun; withstands drought

Blue Atlas Cedar
(*Cedrus libani* subsp. *atlantica* 'Glauca')

The Redbuds

Cercis canadensis

A white form of eastern redbud
(*Cercis canadensis* variety *alba*)

Multistemmed Chinese redbud
(*Cercis chinensis*)

Redbuds are midsize native and exotic trees that provide an early flush of color across much of the United States. In the woodlands of the East, the lovely eastern redbud (*Cercis canadensis*) outlines its bare stems and older branchlets with vivid red-purple or magenta buds. The buds open to rose purple-pink flowers. This colorful flowering contrasts vividly with the creamy white bracts of the dogwoods that open at about the same time. Reddish purple heart-shaped leaves usually appear after the flowers bloom and mature to a dark green. In summer, the leaves glow lime green, turning yellow or gold in fall. Flattened pealike seedpods develop and linger until after the leaves fall. At only 20 to 30 feet tall, with a slim profile and dark bark, the redbud is charming at the back of a shrub border.

The most popular cultivated variety is 'Forest Pansy', a purple-leaved redbud. 'Flame' is double-flowered. The leaves of 'Silver Cloud' are splashed with silvery white in early summer and gradually fade to a soft green. 'Royal White' is a beautiful cultivar of *C. canadensis* variety *alba*. The flowers of 'Wither's Pink Charm' are a clear pink.

The eastern redbud is native to Zones 3 or 4–9 of the eastern United States and from the Great Lakes area of Canada south to Oklahoma and Texas. It succeeds in most areas, including the Pacific Coast, but not where summers are cool. Where summers are hot, the tree is worth trying as far north as Zone 3 if given protection from winter winds. A similar plant known as the "Judas tree" (*C. siliquastrum*), native to Europe and Asia, has been cultivated since ancient times.

The showy multistemmed 10- to 15-foot Chinese redbud (*C. chinensis*), hardy only to Zone 6, grows well in the South. In the Southwest, cultivated varieties of two lovely little native redbuds are popular: glossy-leaved 'Oklahoma', a cultivar of *C. reniformis*, is hardy in Zone 8 and grows wild from Texas to New Mexico. 'Texas White' is a white-flowered form. The closely related drought-tolerant western, or California, redbud (*C. occidentalis*) can handle winters in Zone 7.

Culture: transplant a container-grown redbud in the spring while it is still dormant to deeply cultivated, moist but well-drained soil. Redbuds thrive in full or partial sun.

FEATURED PROFILE
Eastern Redbud

Botanical Name: *Cercis canadensis* 'Forest Pansy'
Family: Fabaceae **Type of Plant:** small deciduous flowering tree **Uses:** showy midspring flowers; shrub border; naturalizing **Genus Range:** NJ to FL; W. to MI, TX, northern Mexico **Hardiness:** USDA Zones 5–9
Height: 20 to 30' **Growth Rate:** medium **Form & Habit:** slender trunk, branched close to the ground
Bloom Period: midspring **Flowers:** purple-pink buds open rose pink **Fruits:** 2 to 3" seedpod **Foliage:** new red-purple leaves turn green in summer; yellow or gold in fall **Soil & pH:** well-drained; pH adaptable **Light & Moisture:** full or partial sun; sustained moisture

Eastern redbud
(*Cercis canadensis* 'Forest Pansy')

The White Cedars
also called "False Cypress"

Chamaecyparis

Nootka cypress
(*Chamaecyparis nootkatensis*)

Sawara false cypress (*Chamaecyparis pisifera* 'Filifera Aurea')

Sawara false cypress
(*Chamaecyparis pisifera* 'Golden Mop')

White cedars, also known as "false cypresses," are large evergreen conifers that reach over 100 feet in the wild, but only about 50 feet in the home landscape. The Hinoki false cypress (*Chamaecyparis obtusa*) of Japan and Formosa was introduced to North America in 1861. The foliage is glossy, scalelike, and flat, and the branch tips turn down in an interesting half twist, giving this white cedar a soft appearance and an appealing texture and soft appearance that is unusual for a conifer. The species is valued for its dark, dense, glossy green foliage; its handsome pyramidal form; and its colorful reddish brown bark that sheds in long narrow strips. It thrives in cool regions of the East and West coasts, and some colorful cultivars do well in midwestern and southern landscapes.

Varieties of Hinoki false cypress with yellow foliage are especially handsome against a background of deciduous trees and tall dark evergreens. An excellent yellow form is the golden cypress (*C. obtusa* 'Crippsii'), hardy in Zones 4–8. A dense, pyramidal evergreen, its branchlets are tipped a rich yellow-gold. This slow-growing dwarf needs a decade or two to reach 8 to 10 feet but may eventually reach 30 feet. Another yellow variety of false cypress is the 18- to 20-foot golden threadleaf Sawara false, or Japanese, cypress (*C. pisifera* 'Filifera Aurea'). This yellow species is somewhat hardier than *C. obtusa*—to Zone 3 with protection—and holds its color in summer as well as in winter. A narrow 10-foot threadleaf cultivar, 'Boulevard', is one of the best of the forms. Its grayish blue winter foliage turns a silvery green in summer.

The most arresting form is also one of the few that are native to North America: the young blue- or gray-green Nootka cypress, or Alaska cedar (*C. nootkatensis* 'Pendula'). This weeping form has elegantly arranged pendulous, drooping branches. A species native to cool moist regions of the West Coast in Zones 4–7, it can live more than a thousand years. In cultivation it reaches 30 to 45 feet.

Shrubby forms include the 2- to 3-foot-high dwarf golden Hinoki cypress, *Chamaecyparis obtusa* 'Nana Lutea', which stays a beautiful lemon gold all season. Graceful 4- to 6-foot 'Nana Gracilis' has deep green, lustrous foliage.

Culture: plants that are container grown transplant easily in early spring and early fall in moist but well-drained sandy soil. The false cypresses are most successful in sunny, humid areas.

Golden cypress
(*Chamaecyparis obtusa* 'Crippsii')

FEATURED PROFILE
Golden Cypress

Botanical Name: *Chamaecyparis obtusa* 'Crippsii'
Family: Cupressaceae **Type of Plant:** dwarf evergreen conifer **Uses:** golden accent plant
Genus Range: Japan and Formosa **Hardiness:** USDA Zones 5–8 **Height:** 8 to 10', eventually may reach 30' **Growth Rate:** medium **Form & Habit:** spreading pyramid with drooping branchlets **Bloom Period:** spring **Flowers:** inconspicuous **Fruits:** inconspicuous cones ⅓ to ⅜" around; bluish changing to red-brown **Foliage:** scalelike, dark green, pressed close against the branchlets, tipped a rich yellow-gold **Soil & pH:** loamy, well-drained soil; somewhat acid **Light & Moisture:** full sun; sustained moisture **Pruning Seasons:** rarely needed

The Fringe Trees

Chionanthus

Chinese fringe tree
(*Chionanthus retusus*)

Two types of fringe trees, one native and the other from China, make excellent midsize year-round trees beginning in spring, when a profusion of fleecy white flowers covers them. The botanical name *chionanthus*, derived from the Greek *chion* for "snow" and *anthos* for "flower," truly describes the effect of the tree in bloom. Fringe trees are also decorative in fall, when they are marked by bright leaf color. In winter, they reveal their handsome, gray ridged bark.

Best known is the native white fringe tree (*Chionanthus virginicus*), a slow-growing ornamental 12 to 20 feet tall that follows the dogwood into bloom. As the fringe tree's leaves open in mid- to late spring, a mist of fragrant greenish white fringelike flowers with petals 6 to 8 inches long bloom on the branches. The tree is often as wide as it is tall—about 20 feet—and the leaves remain a strong, fresh green all summer. In fall the leaves turn a luminous yellow-gold, seemingly all at once; if the cold intensifies, they drop almost as suddenly.

Purple fruits that look like tiny plums develop on the female tree, and birds relish them. The flower petals on the male tree are larger and showier than the female flowers. Known in some regions as old-man's-beard, the fringe tree grows wild from southern New Jersey to Florida and west to Texas, usually near water. It succeeds in Zones 3 or 4–9. Tolerant of urban pollution, it's especially pretty near a pond or set off by a large lawn.

The Chinese fringe tree (*C. retusus*) is popular in warm regions. A large handsome multistemmed shrub with leaves smaller than the American species, it covers itself with a fleece of 2- to 3-inch snow-white florets two or three weeks before the native fringe tree blooms. The Chinese fringe tree bears male and female flowers on the same plant and has a more formal appearance.

Culture: young balled-and-burlapped or container-grown fringe trees transplant easily in spring and thrive in moist but well-drained slightly acid soil, pH 6.0 to 6.5. Full sun is best, but partial sun will do. The white fringe tree flowers on the previous season's growth, so prune immediately after it blooms. On the other hand, the Chinese fringe tree flowers on each new season's growth; prune it in late winter before new growth begins.

White fringe tree (*Chionanthus virginicus*)

White fringe tree
(*Chionanthus virginicus*)

FEATURED PROFILE
White Fringe Tree

Botanical Name: *Chionanthus virginicus* **Family:** Oleaceae **Type of Plant:** small flowering tree or shrub **Uses:** scented spring flowers; lawn specimen; in shrub border **Native Range:** S. NJ to FL and TX **Hardiness:** USDA Zones 3–9 **Height:** 12 to 20' **Growth Rate:** slow **Form & Habit:** open, spreading crown **Bloom Period:** May–June **Flowers:** clusters of drooping greenish white 6 to 8" long fringelike petals **Fruits:** bloomy purple fruits obscured by foliage **Foliage:** medium to dark green **Soil & pH:** well-drained; pH 6.0 to 6.5 **Light & Moisture:** full or partial sun; sustained moisture **Pruning Seasons:** immediately after blooming

American Yellowwood
also called "Virgilia"

Cladrastis lutea

American yellowwood
(*Cladrastis lutea*)

American yellowwood (*Cladrastis lutea*)

When the American yellowwood (*Cladrastis lutea*) blooms in spring or early summer, foot-long clusters of fragrant white flowers resembling wisteria droop from its branches, and the bees swarm around them. Slow-growing yellowwood grows little more than a foot each year to reach a height of 30 to 50 feet. The bright yellow-green spring foliage changes in summer to bright green; in autumn, to golden yellow. Low dramatic horizontal branching and a rounded crown make this an excellent shade tree. The smooth pale gray bark looks silvery and, as the tree matures, becomes interestingly furrowed and corky. The outer bark peels away in platelets, exposing the attractive orange-brown bark underneath, which gives it winter interest. Yellowwood is considered an outstanding tree for city landscapes and for larger, more open landscapes. Nurseries offer the pink-flowered cultivar 'Rosea'.

One of the many drought-tolerant native trees, and generally trouble free, yellowwood supports nitrogen-fixing bacteria that improve the fertility of soil. Yellowwood grows wild along the limestone cliffs and ridges of the Southeast, from North Carolina to Kentucky and Tennessee. It thrives where summers are hot and winters are cold in Zones 3 or 4–8. Already rare when it was discovered in 1796, yellowwood is available on the East and West coasts through nurseries that specialize in native plants.

Culture: set out a young dormant yellowwood in early spring. It does best in full sun but tolerates a bit of shade. It accepts soil that is somewhat acid or somewhat alkaline. Cut it back in summer, and then only if it needs shaping, because the tree weeps sap profusely if pruned in winter or spring.

FEATURED PROFILE
American Yellowwood, or Virgilia

Botanical Name: *Cladrastis lutea* **Family:** Fabaceae **Type of Plant:** midsize flowering tree or shrub **Uses:** spring to early-summer flowers; shade; dramatic lawn specimen **Native Range:** NC to KY and TN **Hardiness:** USDA Zones 3 or 4–8 **Height:** 30 to 50' **Growth Rate:** slow **Form & Habit:** somewhat delicate, wide-branching with rounded crown **Bloom Period:** late spring to early summer **Flowers:** fragrant white flowers 1 to 1¼" long, in drooping clusters 8 to 14" long **Fruits:** brown seedpod 2½ to 4" long **Foliage:** 8 to 12" long, composed of 7 to 9 leaflets; yellowish green changing to bright green in summer, to golden yellow in fall **Soil & pH:** well-drained; pH adaptable **Light & Moisture:** full sun; tolerates drought **Pruning Seasons:** only in summer

American yellowwood
(*Cladrastis lutea*)

The Dogwoods

Cornus

Red-osier dogwood (*Cornus sericea*) in winter

The dogwood is an almost perfect flowering tree that provides year-round beauty in the garden. In mid-spring, the dogwood bears dazzling white or pink 3- to 5-inch star-shaped "flowers," which are pointed bracts that surround the tree's true but inconspicuous green flowers. In fall, the foliage turns red to plum-colored, and the tree's bright red berries attract birds.

The popular flowering dogwood (*Cornus florida*) is still the classic choice for northern gardens. This lovely ornamental can reach 40 feet. But if the tree is stressed, as it would be growing in cities, for example, it tends to develop problems.

Increasingly, flowering dogwood is being replaced by resistant Kousa, or Chinese, dogwood (*C. kousa* variety *chinensis*). The dangling fruit of the Kousa dogwood resembles a small strawberry, and the bark exfoliates attractively. Where Kousa dogwoods aren't available, a resistant hybrid of the Kousa and Florida species, *C.* × *rutgersensis*, is used. The flowers of these dogwoods open on top of somewhat drooping branches and bloom for several weeks in early summer. The weeping Kousa varieties, 'Elizabeth Lustgarten' and 'Weaver's Weeping', are breathtaking. There's also a pink Kousa dogwood, 'Satomi'. 'Summer Stars', an introduction by William Flemmer of the Princeton Nurseries, blooms into August and has exceptionally long-lasting flowers.

The Pacific, or mountain, dogwood (*C. nuttallii*) is native from British Columbia to southern California in Zones 6–9 and reaches 75 feet in cultivation. Native Americans once steeped its bark to make a potion for treating fevers. In April, showy white bracts cover the tree; in fall, numerous clusters of orange-red fruits appear, and the foliage turns yellow and scarlet. The tree sometimes blooms again in August. The Pacific dogwood doesn't grow well outside its native range and is sold only through nurseries and plant societies that specialize in native West Coast plants. This big American native is sometimes mistaken for the giant dogwood of China and Japan (*C. controversa*), a 30- to 40-foot tree in cultivation in Zone 5. The giant dogwood is highly valued by European gardeners but almost impossible to find commercially in America.

Less well known but much loved are the yellow-flowered dogwoods. The evergreen dogwood (*C. capitata*) from China has glossy green leaves and large sulfur yellow flowers followed by crimson fruits. It grows to 40 feet and can be somewhat bushy. Also shrubby is the yellow-flowered 20- to 25-foot Cornelian cherry (*C. mas*), widely planted in the Midwest. Its showy scarlet fruit ripens in July and attracts birds. People eat the fruit as well; though acidic in flavor, it was once grown as a food crop and used to make syrups and pre-

Kousa dogwood
(*Cornus kousa* 'Summer Stars')

Flowering dogwood
(*Cornus florida*) in fall

A weeping kousa dogwood
(*Cornus kousa* 'Elizabeth Lustgarten') in fall

Evergreen dogwood (*Cornus capitta*)

Cornelian cherry (*Cornus mas*)

serves. Cornelian cherry, hardy in Zones 4–8, comes in variegated forms.

Two shrub-size twiggy dogwoods are planted in Zones 2–8 for their barks' winter color. The red-barked, or Tartarian, dogwood (*C. alba*), a multistemmed, vase-shaped shrub 8 to 10 feet tall, bears small white flowers in spring followed by blue-white berries in the fall. The leaves often turn reddish plum with late fall cold; in winter, the bark turns a vivid red. The cultivar 'Sidebar' is smaller than the species, and its fall color is a brilliant coral red.

The red-osier, or American, dogwood (*C. sericea* formerly *C. stolonifera*) is similar to *C. alba* and succeeds in Zones 2–7. It is tolerant of wet soils and is found in many northeastern and midwestern gardens. The stems of the cultivar 'Flagstoned', the golden-twig dogwood, turn a striking yellow. To encourage the greatest display of colorful branches, cut these shrubby dogwoods back in late winter to stimulate the growth of young shoots. Bunchberry (*C. canadensis*) is a 6-inch evergreen subshrub.

Culture: plant a young, dormant, container-grown or balled-and-burlapped dogwood in early spring, and handle the rootball with care. Dogwoods prefer moist but well-drained somewhat acid soil, pH 5.0 to 6.5. They thrive in bright or dappled shade and full sun.

FEATURED PROFILE
Pacific Dogwood

Botanical Name: *Cornus nuttallii* **Family:** Cornaceae **Type of Plant:** large deciduous flowering tree **Uses:** spring flowers; fall fruits; fall color; lawn specimen; naturalizing **Native Range:** British Columbia to southern CA **Hardiness:** USDA Zones 6–9 **Height:** 75' **Growth Rate:** slow to medium **Form & Habit:** spreading, layered branches **Bloom Period:** April **Flowers:** tiny purple and green flowers surrounded by showy white or pinkish bracts **Fruits:** clusters of 30 to 40 orange-red fruits **Foliage:** green, turning yellow and scarlet in fall **Soil & pH:** well-drained, pH 5.0 to 6.5 **Light & Moisture:** full sun, sustained moisture

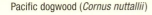

Pacific dogwood (*Cornus nuttallii*)

The Filberts
also called "Hazelnuts"

Corylus

Turkish filbert (*Corylus colurna*)

Harry Lauder's walking stick
(*Corylus avellana* 'Contorta') with male catkins

Though filberts (hazelnuts) are known primarily for the delicious nuts of *Corylus maxima*, several ornamental species of trees and large shrubs are grown for their decorative catkins and cool green summer foliage. The most popular ornamental is the Turkish filbert (*C. colurna*), a handsome, rather formal 35- to 50-foot broadly pyramidal tree that is tolerant of city conditions and, once established, of dry soil. It grows well in Zones 5–7 and thrives even in climates that alternate between dry scorching summers and cold winters.

The Turkish filbert is attractive in every season. In early spring, it bears lovely male catkins. In summer, the foliage remains a rich dark green and fades to yellow-green before dropping in late fall. In winter, the corky tan-to-gray bark shows striking corruga-tions. Three to six small edible nuts in clusters begin to ripen in late summer and are harvested primarily by squirrels. Native to southeastern Europe and western Asia, the species has been grown in gardens in the West since 1582.

The most remarkable is the twisted, often grotesque, corkscrew filbert 'Contorta', an 8- to 10-foot cultivar of the European filbert (*C. avellana*). This horticultural wonder, with its corkscrew branches and twisted twigs, is also known as Harry Lauder's walking stick. The tree's weird branches and drooping yellow catkins attract attention before its leaves appear in the spring.

Culture: transplant a young container-grown or balled-and-burlapped tree in early spring to any well-drained loamy soil in full sun. Maintain moisture around the roots for the first two seasons or until the plant is growing strongly.

FEATURED PROFILE
Corkscrew Hazel, or Harry Lauder's Walking Stick

Botanical Name: *Corylus avellana* 'Contorta' **Family:** Betulaceae **Type of Plant:** small deciduous tree with contorted stems and twigs **Uses:** winter accent plant, collector's item **Genus Range:** Europe, western Asia, North Africa **Hardiness:** USDA Zones 4–8 **Height:** 8 to 10' **Growth Rate:** medium **Form & Habit:** contorted stems **Bloom Period:** March **Flowers:** inconspicuous **Fruits:** yellow catkins **Foliage:** dark green **Soil & pH:** loamy, well-drained, pH adaptable **Light & Moisture:** full sun to light shade, moisture adaptable

Harry Lauder's walking stick (*Corylus avellana* 'Contorta')

The Smoke Trees

Cotinus

The American smoke tree (*Cotinus obovatus*) is a 20- to 30-foot native that is beautiful in three seasons and can be counted on for intense fall color. In June and early July, minuscule yellowish flowers appear. Then by midsummer, clouds of long pinkish gray fruiting panicles envelope the branches in misty halos. The smoky effect is created by thousands of tiny hairs attached to the developing fruit, which dangles in branched clusters at the ends of the branches. Rounded leaves, bluish to dark green in summer, change in later summer to brilliant scarlet, orange, gold, and claret.

The tree grows slowly, and as the bark matures, it becomes corky and quite beautiful. This species is used as a lawn specimen and in shrub groupings. Because the flowers appear on new growth, many gardeners cut the plant back in late winter or early spring to keep it small and to encourage greater flowering. Native to limestone soils in scattered areas from Tennessee to Alaska, it is hardy in Zones 3 or 4–8 or 9.

European smoke tree (*Cotinus coggygria*)

The 15-foot European smoke tree (*C. coggygria*) was a favorite of the Victorians. This smaller species is still popular and is often used in shrub groupings and as a hedge. It is native to Europe and central China. It survives winters as far north as Zone 5; in Zone 4 it dies back to the ground each winter. The European smoke tree is often planted in perennial borders as a background shrub. It is green in summer and red in the fall. The colorful purple cultivars are especially effective as contrasting foliage plants. The leaves of 'Royal Purple' unfold from red to a rich purple that doesn't fade. 'Velvet Cloak' is a luminous purple that turns red-purple in the fall.

Culture: smoke trees transplant easily and thrive in well-drained loamy soil but adapt to dry rocky sites. They need full sun to flower and color well.

European smoke tree (*Cotinus coggygria*)

American smoke tree (*Cotinus obovatus*) in fall

FEATURED PROFILE
American Smoke Tree

Botanical Name: *Cotinus obovatus* **Family:** Anacardiaceae
Type of Plant: small deciduous tree with showy summer aspect and brilliant fall color **Uses:** lawn specimen; shrub border **Native Range:** TN to AL, W. to TX **Hardiness:** USDA Zones 3 or 4–8 or 9 **Height:** 20 to 30' **Growth Rate:** medium to slow **Form & Habit:** multi-stemmed, upright **Bloom Period:** early summer **Flowers:** inconspicuous, yellowish **Fruits:** clouds of pink-gray fruiting panicles **Foliage:** bluish green in summer; scarlet, orange, claret, and gold in fall **Soil & pH:** well-drained soil with high pH **Light & Moisture:** full sun; keep soil on the dry side

The Hawthorns

Crataegus

Hawthorns are picturesque, wide-spreading, spring-flowering twiggy trees or shrubs. The trees are often used to shade small properties, and shrub species are used for screening and as tall hedges. Birds relish the fruit and use the sharp-spined branches as protected nesting sites. These members of the rose family sometimes suffer from the same pests that roses do, so choose only the most resistant types.

An outstanding disease-resistant hawthorn, 'Winter King' is a cultivar of the green hawthorn (*Crataegus viridis*), offered by nurseries in the central and southeastern U.S., where green hawthorns thrive. Twenty to 30 feet tall at maturity, it has a rounded form and silvery bark that exfoliates as the plant matures. In late winter or early spring, flat clusters of tiny white flowers resembling wild roses cover the branches. The flowers are followed in late summer and fall by colorful masses of showy orange-red fruits that persist long into winter. Birds gorge on them. The gray-green foliage turns gold-yellow, scarlet, and pur-

Washington thorn (*Crataegus phaenopyrum*)

ple in autumn. The species is hardy in Zones 4 or 5–7 or 8.

The native Washington thorn (*C. phaenopyrum*) can stand more cold and heat and is one of the best native hawthorns for Zones 3–9. It flowers lavishly in spring; the summer foliage is glossy and green; and the brilliant red fruits persist into winter. It does well planted in city gardens or in hedges and along highways. It is used extensively for naturalizing. Many European species cultivated in America do poorly south of Zone 4 and suffer from a variety of problems, particularly forms of rust.

Caution: most hawthorns have sharp spines, sometimes 3 inches long, and are not recommended for areas frequented by children.

Culture: transplant a young container-grown or balled-and-burlapped tree in early spring. Hawthorns tolerate many soils but do best in full sun in moist but well-drained soil. Prune in winter or early spring.

Green hawthorn
(*Crataegus viridis* 'Winter King') in early spring

Green hawthorn (*Crataegus viridis* 'Winter King')

Dove Tree
also called "Handkerchief Tree"

Davidia involucrata

This small beautiful Chinese import stages an extraordinary show of large creamy white flowers that droop from its branches in mid- to late spring. Likened variously to the wings of a dove, a folded handkerchief, and huge butterflies, the "flowers" are actually two large delicate bracts wrapping small clusters of minute round yellow flowers. One bract, 2 to 3 inches long, droops from the top of the cluster; the second bract, usually 4 to 7 inches long, hangs straight from the bottom of the cluster. With the slightest breeze, the bracts flutter, resembling flapping wings or handkerchiefs. Large heart-shaped leaves resemble those of the linden and remain a deep green until they fall. In cultivation, the broadly pyramidal tree grows at a modest rate to a height of 20 to 40 feet. Its dense branches can cast a pleasant light shade, and its orange-brown bark has an interesting scaly pattern.

Dove tree
(*Davidia involucrata*) flower

The dove tree (*Davidia involucrata*) is hardy through winters as far north as Zone 6 and summers as far south as Zone 8. On the northern edge of its range, it will survive the cold but may not flower well. The tree tends to bloom lavishly only every second year and may take a decade to reach flowering age. It is somewhat hard to find, but the search is worthwhile. A collector's plant, it deserves to be featured where it can be admired.

Culture: plant a young container-grown or balled-and-burlapped tree in early spring or early fall. It will do best in light shade but will tolerate full sun if the soil is moist. The dove tree thrives in slightly acid, well-drained loam amended with peat moss.

Dove tree (*Davidia involucrata*)

Dove tree (*Davidia involucrata*)

Dove tree (*Davidia involucrata*)

FEATURED PROFILE
Dove, or Handkerchief, Tree

Botanical Name: *Davidia involucrata* **Family:** Nyssaceae **Type of Plant:** small to midsize deciduous flowering tree **Uses:** showy mid- to late-spring flowers; light shade; specimen **Native Range:** China **Hardiness:** USDA Zones 6–8 **Height:** 20 to 40' in cultivation; to 65' in the wild **Growth Rate:** medium to slow **Form & Habit:** broad pyramid **Bloom Period:** mid- to late spring **Flowers:** two white bracts of unequal length, 2 to 3" and 4 to 7" long **Fruits:** 1½" green drupe with purplish bloom, changing to rust speckled with red **Foliage:** broad pointed oval to 5" long; scented when opening; bright green in summer **Soil & pH:** well-drained; pH 5.0 to 6.5 **Light & Moisture:** light shade or full sun; roots need sustained moisture **Pruning Seasons:** winter

The Gum Trees

Eucalyptus

Eucalyptus (*Eucalyptus torquata*)

Blue gum eucalyptus (*Eucalyptus globulus*)

Eucalyptus trees are Australian evergreens valued for their beautiful aromatic foliage and colorful exfoliating bark. They have become well established along the West Coast and in warm regions of California and Florida. In their native land, the fast-growing, shallow-rooted, pest- and disease-resistant plants grow quite tall, but here they stay to heights suitable for street trees, screening, and specimens in the home landscape. The fuzzy white or red flowers borne in spring by most species will attract honeybees.

The well-known blue gum eucalyptus (*Eucalyptus globulus*), a tall, handsome, fast-growing but messy tree, has been widely planted along the California coast as a windbreak for citrus groves and in wet areas to help dry them. It is hardy in Zones 9–11. Be aware that blue gum eucalyptus trees exude toxins that kill or inhibit the growth of vegetation around them, particularly grasses and broad-leaved plants. A tidier eucalyptus for the home landscape is the multi-trunked, bushy dwarf *E. globulus*

Eucalyptus
(*Eucalyptus pauciflora*)

'Compacta', which rarely exceeds 40 feet. Plant it as a specimen, a sheared hedge, or a tall windbreak. The aromatic silvery blue leaves are coin shaped in youth and lance shaped at maturity.

Eucalyptus species for colder or drier regions include the snow gum (*E. pauciflora*), which is hardy to Zone 7 and the most cold resistant of the species. Its whitish bark exfoliates; its leaves are small and silvery green. In Zone 8, the slightly smaller silver-dollar tree (*E. cinerea*) makes a lovely tree for the garden; use its branches for cut foliage in arrangements. The bark of this species doesn't shed. Drought-tolerant *E. torquata* is often planted in desert areas. It's a highly ornamental little tree, 20 to 25 feet tall, with coral red and yellow flowers and green, golden long narrow leaves.

Culture: in early spring or fall, transplant the youngest tree available to moist soil in full sun. Eucalyptus trees generally tolerate drought and adapt to different types of soil.

FEATURED PROFILE

Silver-dollar, or Argyle Apple, Tree

Botanical Name: *Eucalyptus cinerea* **Family:** Myrtaceae **Type of Plant:** broad-leaved evergreen tree with aromatic foliage **Uses:** landscaping; tall hedge; windbreak; cut foliage **Native Range:** Australia **Hardiness:** USDA Zones 8–11 **Height:** 35 to 40' **Growth Rate:** fast **Form & Habit:** broad, irregular **Bloom Period:** spring **Flowers:** creamy white **Fruits:** woody capsule **Foliage:** blue-green coin-shaped juvenile leaves on pendulous stems **Soil & pH:** tolerant **Light & Moisture:** full sun, medium-dry soil **Pruning Seasons:** hard pruning in spring encourages growth of attractive young foliage

Silver-dollar tree (*Eucalyptus cinerea*)

The Beeches

Fagus

The beeches are majestic trees with branches that may sweep gracefully to the ground. Two species are cultivated: the silver-barked American beech (*Fagus grandifolia*), which reaches 50 to 70 feet, and the smaller European beech (*F. sylvatica*). In the fall, their shimmering green leaves turn a soft attractive russet-gold-brown and cling to the lower branches well into winter. The symmetrical branching and beautifully smooth bark are especially appealing in winter. Birds and squirrels seek out the nuts. Beeches set a network of shallow roots that make it difficult for anything to grow on the soil surface near them, although small flowering bulbs, such as crocus and grape hyacinth, look attractive nestled among the roots. Both beech species need large open spaces to achieve their potential.

The American beech (*F. grandifolia*), native to eastern North America, is hardy in Zones 3–9. It's a slow-growing, magnificent tree that reaches its greatest size in Ohio and the Mississippi River Valley. Note: it can be difficult to transplant and is not recommended for cities. Few nurseries carry it. This tree needs a large open landscape. It's superb in a natural landscape, and the large oily seeds are relished by birds and animals.

The European beech (*F. sylvatica*) is easier to grow and has been planted since Colonial times in Zones 5–7 and in Zone 4 with some winter protection. Its nuts were once fed to pigs and livestock. Nurseries offer a variety of forms and colors of European beech. The fern-leaved beech 'Asplenifolia', with its delicately cut leaves, is one of the most graceful. Weeping forms are considered gangly in youth, but they come into their own with age. The cultivar 'Pendula' and the purple-leaved 'Purpurea Pendula' are weeping forms that acquire mass and extraordinary presence in maturity. 'Fastigiata', an upright narrowly columnar form, is hardier than the species.

For riveting color accents, columnar *F. s.* 'Dawyck Purple' has purple-bronze foliage; *F. s.* 'Dawyck Gold' is yellow in spring and lime green in summer. The exotic foliage of *F. s.* 'Tricolor' ('Purpurea Tricolor') is a gleaming copper color, edged and tipped with pink and white. River's purple beech (*F. s.* 'Riversii') is a large spreading tree with a deep purple color that usually holds in summer.

European beech (*Fagus sylvatica* 'Fastigiata') columnar form

Culture: transplant a young container-grown or balled-and-burlapped beech with great care in early spring. Beeches thrive in full sun in well-drained, loose soil in the acid range of pH 5.0 to 6.5. In summer or early fall, prune out branches that will grow into the center of the tree or rub against other branches.

River's purple beech (*Fagus sylvatica* 'Riversii')

FEATURED PROFILE
American Beech

Botanical Name: *Fagus grandifolia*
Family: Fagaceae **Type of Plant:** large, long-lived deciduous shade tree with silver-gray bark **Uses:** landscape specimen; tall screen **Native Range:** New Brunswick to Ontario, S. to FL and TX **Hardiness:** USDA Zones 4–7 **Height:** 50 to 70' **Growth Rate:** slow to medium **Form & Habit:** broad pyramid branched to the ground **Bloom Period:** April–May **Fruits:** clusters of tiny edible nuts **Foliage:** silver-green, gold-bronze in fall **Soil & pH:** well-drained; pH 5.0 to 6.5 **Light & Moisture:** full sun; sustained moisture **Pruning Seasons:** summer and fall

American beech (*Fagus grandifolia*) leaves clinging through spring

Franklin Tree

Franklinia alatmaha

Franklin tree (*Franklinia alatamaha*) camellia-like flower

The *Franklinia alatamaha*, a lovely little flowering tree, blooms late in the season with fragrant 3-inch camellia-like white flowers that appear from late July and August into midfall. Only 10 to 30 feet tall, the tree has upright spreading branches and is somewhat oval in form. New growth at the branch tips gives the plant an airy, open look. Long, lustrous leaves unfold in late spring and become bright green in summer; then change to bronze, orange, and red in fall. The bark is interestingly ridged. An exceptionally lovely plant, the Franklin tree deserves a prominent position where its flowers and fall color can be appreciated. Hardy in Zones 5–8 or 9, the tree can be grown as a shrub in colder regions if given winter protection.

Native to the United States, the Franklin tree was first discovered in 1765 by John Bartram, the famous Quaker botanist, when he was plant-hunting along the Alatahama River near Fort Barrington, Georgia. Bartram collected some seeds and soon grew the first cultivated trees at his home in Philadelphia. He named it for his friend and sponsor, Benjamin Franklin. Alas, the tree was last seen in the wild in 1803 by John Lyon, a plant hunter and nurseryman who visited the Georgia area.

Culture: the Franklin tree does best transplanted in early spring as a young container-grown or balled-and-burlapped tree. It requires well-drained, moist humusy loam in the acid range of pH 5.0 to 6.5 but adapts to mildly alkaline soils. It flowers best in full sun but tolerates partial shade.

Franklin tree bark (*Franklinia alatamaha*)

Summer-flowering Franklin tree (*Franklinia alatamaha*)

Franklin tree (*Franklinia alatamaha*) in fall

FEATURED PROFILE
Franklin Tree

Botanical Name: *Franklinia alatamaha* **Family:** Theaceae **Type of Plant:** small deciduous flowering tree **Uses:** scented flowers in summer and fall; fall color **Native Range:** the wilds of Georgia **Hardiness:** USDA Zones 5–8 or 9 **Height:** 10 to 30' **Growth Rate:** slow to medium **Form & Habit:** small airy tree or tall shrub with upright spreading branches **Bloom Period:** July or August into fall **Flowers:** 3" across; fragrant, white, cup-shaped, with showy yellow stamens **Fruits:** segmented woody capsule ⅗ to ⅛" in diameter, composed of wingless seeds **Foliage:** long narrow oval; serrated; in summer shiny dark green; in fall orange to red **Soil & pH:** well drained; pH 5.0 to 6.5 **Light & Moisture:** full sun; sustained moisture

The Ashes

Fraxinus

Handsome and fast-growing, the ashes are large-scale forest trees found in the lowlands of the North Temperate Zones. They are used ornamentally as shade trees in large landscapes. In autumn, leaf color often turns a spectacular yellow; some varieties turn claret red. Of the native ashes, 16 species grow to tree size—at least one species for every region.

The most widely distributed species is the adaptable 50- to 60-foot green ash (*Fraxinus pennsylvanica*), which grows wild over a wide region—from the Canadian provinces all the way to northern Florida and westward to the Mississippi River Valley and Texas. A shapely tree with good yellow autumn color, it is a popular ornamental in the central and western states, Zones 3–9. It tolerates cold, heat, dry winds, and wet or dry soil that has a high pH. The most desirable cultivars are those advertised as

White ash (*Fraxinus americana* 'Autumn Purple') in fall

seedless and disease-resistant with good autumnal color.

In the Northeast, 'Autumn Purple' and 'Autumn Glory', cultivars of the 80- to 100-foot white ash (*F. americana*), make handsome lawn trees. The fall color is purple-red to red in the North but less intensely colorful in warmer regions. The 40- to 50-foot claret ash (*F. angustifolia* 'Raywood') also colors red to plum-purple in fall. Along the Pacific Coast, the big dense Oregon ash (*F. latifolia*), hardy in Zones 6 or 7–9, is an important street tree. The flowering, or manna, ash (*F. ornus*), planted in European gardens in Zones 5 or 6–9 for its showy panicles of fragrant flowers, isn't often seen here.

Culture: the ashes transplant readily in spring or early fall. They thrive in deep, well-drained soils but tolerate moist soils as long as the exposure has full sun. When young, ash trees require sustained moisture, but they tolerate drought once they become established.

Flowering ash (*Fraxinus ornus*)

FEATURED PROFILE
Green Ash

Botanical Name: *Fraxinus pennsylvanica* **Family:** Oleaceae
Type of Plant: large deciduous shade tree **Uses:** adaptable landscape specimen; shade; good yellow autumn color **Native Range:** Canada to N. FL, and W. to TX **Hardiness:** USDA Zones 3–9 **Height:** 50 to 60'
Growth Rate: fast **Form & Habit:** pyramidal when young, upright spreading at maturity **Bloom Period:** April **Flowers:** green and reddish purple **Fruits:** winged nutlet **Foliage:** dark green changing to yellow in fall **Soil & pH:** adaptable; tolerates high pH **Light & Moisture:** adaptable **Pruning Seasons:** during dormancy

Green ash (*Fraxinus pennsylvanica*) in fall

Ginkgo
also called "Maidenhair Tree"
Ginkgo biloba

Ginkgo (*Ginkgo biloba*)

The maidenhair tree (*Ginkgo biloba*) is the sole survivor of an ancient line of conifers native to southeastern China. But this extraordinary tree is unlike any other living conifer. Fossil records show that it was growing 150 million years ago, and botanists believe that it may be a link between modern conifers and the primitive tree-ferns and cycads that preceded them in the line of evolution. It differs from modern conifers in that its "cones" look like small golden plums; and instead of having needles, like other conifers, it has leaves, flat and fan-shaped, with rounded lobes. Gingkos are long lived and have been planted for centuries. A gingko in Korea is documented to be 1,100 years old. The strain we grow was introduced from China, but geologists have found that eons ago it thrived on this continent as well. A mature ginkgo is a tall, stately, handsome tree best suited to a large property. The tree's irregular horizontal branching forms a rounded crown near the top of the tall straight trunk. In autumn, the leaves turn a luminous yellow-gold. Because it tolerates pollution, salt, smoke, dust, and drought, it has been planted in tree

Ginkgo (*Ginkgo biloba*) in fall

boxes in major cities, where its growth is limited to 30 or 40 feet and the foliage is sparse. On the grounds of Capitol Hill in Washington, D.C., there are majestic 100-foot specimens.

Purchase only a male ginkgo plant, preferably a grafted cultivar. The female produces quantities of messy, foul-smelling plumlike fruits, though the edible nut they contain is the reason ginkgoes are cultivated in the Far East. There are several good male cultivars: 'Autumn Gold' has a handsome broad-headed form, and 'Princeton Sentry' has a columnar shape; both have beautiful fall foliage. 'Mayfield' is another narrow columnar type. 'Magyar', 50 to 60 feet tall, can withstand severe urban conditions, such as smoke, dust, and pollution. For small formal spaces, 25- to 40-foot tall 'Saratoga' has rich fall color.

Culture: the ginkgo transplants easily in spring or fall to sandy, deeply dug, moist but well-drained soil, pH 5.5 to 7.5. It requires full sun.

FEATURED PROFILE
Ginkgo, or Maidenhair Tree

Botanical Name: *Ginkgo biloba* **Family:** Gingkoaceae **Type of Plant:** tall deciduous conifer **Uses:** street and park tree; landscape specimen; fall color **Native Range:** eastern China **Hardiness:** USDA Zones 3–8 or 9 **Height:** 20 to 40', rarely to 100' **Growth Rate:** medium to slow **Form & Habit:** pyramidal when young; long, straight trunk topped by wide-spreading branches at maturity **Bloom Period:** March–April **Flowers:** male and female flowers on different trees; green male flowers on cylindrical 1" catkins; female flowers on 1½ to 2" greenish ovules **Fruits:** plum-shaped, tan to orange naked seed 1 to 1½" long; messy and malodorous **Foliage:** 2 to 3" long; bright green in summer, changing to bright yellow **Soil & pH:** well-drained; pH 5.5 to 7.5 **Light & Moisture:** full sun; sustained moisture when young **Pruning Seasons:** spring

Ginkgo (*Ginkgo biloba*) in fall

Kentucky Coffee Tree

Gymnocladus diocia

The Kentucky coffee tree (*Gymnocladus dioica*), a 60- to 75-foot almost tropical-looking plant, has an exceptional tolerance for city pollution, drought, and alkaline soils. This makes it a popular choice for open urban landscapes. Bold picturesque branching and highly textured scaly bark are striking winter assets. The leaves emerge late

Kentucky coffee tree
(*Gymnocladus dioica*)

in spring, pinkish at first, and then change in summer to blue-green and in fall to a warm yellow. In mid- to late spring, the female tree bears 8- to 12-inch panicles of greenish white flowers that have a lovely roselike fragrance. They are followed by thick brownish black seedpods 5 to 10 inches long that persist in winter and contain several large seeds embedded in a sweet pulp. Pioneers made a poor substitute for coffee from the roasted seeds. Because the male trees do not develop the messy fruit, they are the preferred ornamental.

The Kentucky coffee tree is native to midwestern and eastern North America, Zones 3 or 4–8. It's one of only two species that remain of a genus that flourished in Europe 50 to 70 million years ago. It grows at a moderate rate and usually lives for less than a century.

Culture: the Kentucky coffee tree transplants readily in spring and fall. It does best in full sun and in deep rich, moist soil, but it is adaptable to drought, pollution, and alkalinity.

Kentucky coffee tree (*Gymnocladus dioica*)

FEATURED PROFILE

Kentucky coffee tree
(*Gymnocladus dioica*)

Kentucky Coffee Tree

Botanical Name: *Gymnocladus dioica* **Family:** Leguminosae **Type of Plant:** tall deciduous tree **Uses:** fragrant spring flowers; shade; winter interest **Native Range:** NY and PA to MN, NB, OK, and TN **Hardiness:** USDA Zones 3 or 4–8 **Height:** 60 to 75' **Growth Rate:** medium **Form & Habit:** tall, open-branched with rounded crown **Bloom Period:** late spring **Flowers:** green-white panicles on male and female trees; female tree bears fragrant panicles 8 to 12" long, 3 to 4" wide **Fruits:** thick brownish black seedpods 5 to 10" long, 1 to 1½" wide **Foliage:** 36" long, 24" wide, composed of 3 to 7 pairs of dark green leaflets; fall color in some trees is a good yellow **Soil & pH:** rich, deep soil; pH adaptable **Light & Moisture:** full sun; tolerates drought **Pruning Seasons:** winter or early spring

The Silverbells

Halesia

Silverbells are at their most spectacular in spring, when thousands of pure white, snowdrop-like blooms dangle from their branches. From April to early May, before the leaves appear, the silverbell is smothered with clusters of white flowers that flutter in the breeze. The attractive ½-inch, four-winged seedpods that follow change from green to light brown and persist as the foliage turns yellow or yellow-green in fall. They bloom well in shady moist sites and give a springtime lift to woodland borders. They are lovely naturalized on a hillside or beside a stream. In a landscaped garden they show up best in front of a background of dark evergreens. Silverbells aren't particularly noticeable once out of bloom.

The 30- to 40-foot-tall Carolina silverbell (*Halesia tetraptera*) grows wild in Zones 4–8, from West Virginia to Florida and westward to eastern Texas. The mountain silverbell (*H. monticola*) is bigger than its Carolina cousin. Hardy only to Zone 5, it is native to mountainous areas above 3,000 feet but does well in cities; 'Rosea' is a pink-flowered form. Both have a graceful shape, pruned as trees or as multistemmed shrubs.

Culture: transplant a container-grown or balled-and-burlapped tree in early spring or fall. Silverbells thrive in rich, moist but well-drained soil that is slightly acid with a pH range of 5.0 to 6.0. They succeed in partial shade or full sun. These trees bloom on year-old wood: pruning should be undertaken immediately after the flowers go by.

Carolina silverbell (*Halesia tetraptera*) in spring

Carolina silverbell (*Halesia tetraptera*)

Carolina silverbell (*Halesia tetraptera*)

FEATURED PROFILE
Carolina Silverbell

Botanical Name: *Halesia tetraptera* **Family:** Styracaceae **Type of Plant:** deciduous flowering tree **Uses:** spring flowers; naturalize in moist, shaded site **Native Range:** WV to FL and eastern TX **Hardiness:** USDA Zones 4–8 Height: 30 to 40' in cultivation; in the wild to 80' **Growth Rate:** medium **Form & Habit:** low-branching or multistemmed tree **Bloom Period:** early spring, April to early May **Flowers:** clusters of pendulous bell-shaped white flowers ½ to ¾" long; borne on year-old wood **Fruits:** persistent, 4-winged brown 2" seedpod **Foliage:** 2 to 4" long; elliptical; green changing to yellow-green **Soil & pH:** moist; pH 5.0 to 6.0 **Light & Moisture:** full sun or light shade; sustained moisture **Pruning Seasons:** immediately after flowering

The Hollies

Ilex

The hollies are widely variable attractive, broad-leaved evergreen or deciduous trees and shrubs of great value in the home landscape. The leaves of some species resemble the typical holly on your Christmas card: shiny dark green, undulating, and edged with spines. The leaves of other species are as small and smooth as boxwood foliage. The berries may be red, orange, yellow, or blue-black. Female trees provide the best display of berries when growing near a suitable male pollinator. The hardiest tree hollies can be grown as far north as Zone 4, with protection from the wind. A black plastic wrap or burlap works fine, although neither is very attractive.

American holly
(*Ilex opaca*)

Native American holly (*Ilex opaca*) grows wild in the East and is the most tolerant of our wide range of climates. It is hardy from Zones 5–9 and grows to a handsome 40- to 50-foot pyramidal tree. Its bright red or yellow berries mature in October and last through the winter. There are over 1,000 varieties of American holly. In the South, from Zones 6–9, a good alternative to American holly is Foster holly #2 (*I. x attenuata*), a narrow tree about 25 feet tall with small spiky leaves and berries.

But English holly is the most beautiful tree holly. It grows best in the Northwest in Zones 6–9. Showy, 35 feet, and pyramidal, English holly (*I. aquifolium*) has shiny leaves and brilliant-colored fruits that have come to symbolize Christmas. Two striking variegated forms are white-edged 'Argentea-marginata' and yellow-edged 'Aureo-marginata'.

A popular home landscape plant on the West Coast is *I. aquipernyi*, a bright-berried cross of *I. aquifolium* and the species *I. pernyi*. The female clone, 'San Jose', has brilliant red fruit and small glossy leaves. It reaches 20 to 25 feet and requires no pollinator. In the South, the 15- to 25-foot *I. a.* 'Nellie R. Stevens' is widely planted. It can be pollinated by any nearby male, such as the large male clone 'Edward J. Stevens'.

English holly (*Ilex aquifolium*)

There are shrubby hollies for almost every landscape purpose and climate. For mixed shrub borders in Zones 3 or 4–8, try compact cultivars of the native inkberry (*I. glabra*) and the leaf-losing winterberry (*I. verticillata*). For a handsome hedge in Zones 4 or 5–8, plant cultivars of the shearable Japanese holly (*I. crenata*); in Zones 7 or 8–10, try Yaupon holly (*I. vomitoria*).

Culture: transplant young container-grown or balled-and-burlapped trees in early spring or early fall. The hollies do best in moist, well-drained somewhat acid soil and partial sun. Protect from drought and wind.

Variegated English holly (*Ilex aquifolium* 'Aureo-marginata')

FEATURED PROFILE
Variegated English Holly

Botanical Name: *Ilex aquifolium* 'Aureo-marginata' **Family:** Aquifoliaceae **Type of Plant:** red-berried, broad-leaved evergreen; female plant **Uses:** lawn specimen, shrub border, tall hedge **Genus Range:** southern and western Europe, northern Africa, western Asia **Hardiness:** USDA Zones 6–9 **Height:** 20 to 35' **Growth Rate:** medium **Form & Habit:** pyramidal **Bloom Period:** May **Flowers:** slightly fragrant, dull white **Fruits:** shiny ¼" round red berries **Foliage:** spiny, undulating, shiny, dark green, edged creamy white **Soil & pH:** well-drained, somewhat acid **Light & Moisture:** full to partial sun; sustained moisture **Pollinator:** male English holly, such as 'Monvila' **Pruning Seasons:** after flowering, or harvest berry-laden branches in December

The Junipers

Juniperus

The junipers are enduring evergreen trees, shrubs, and ground covers with needlelike or scalelike leaves that may be gray-blue, green-blue, or light green tipped with gold. Winter cold gives many junipers a purple cast. The cones of the male plants are yellow and resemble catkins; female "cones" are small round blue berries. A few handsome juniper trees make long-lasting landscape plants; however, some are susceptible to blight, so plant only blight-resistant cultivars recommended by a reliable local nursery.

The 50- to 60-foot Chinese juniper (*Juniperus chinensis*), a handsome, long-lived species, has been much hybridized. It can adapt almost anywhere in Zones 3–9. A cultivar for the Midwest is the broadly pyramidal 'Keteleeri', which has green foliage and blue fruits. 'Spartan', a fast-growing, densely branched form, reaches 15 to 20 feet high and about 5 feet wide. 'Kaizuka' (also known as 'Torulosa' and commonly called "Hollywood juniper")

Rocky Mountain juniper
(*Juniperus scopulorum*
'Tolleson's Blue Weeping')

Rocky Mountain juniper
(*Juniperus scopulorum*
'Tolleson's Blue Weeping')

reaches 20 to 30 feet and has a naturally twisted form popular along the California coast. The 15-foot 'Kaizuka Variegated' is a mottled yellow.

Native junipers should be used according to their region because they don't usually do well outside of their area of origin. Rocky Mountain juniper (*J. scopulorum*) grows best in gardens from British Columbia to California in Zones 3–7. It is a narrow pyramidal tree, 30 to 40 feet tall, with several colorful cultivars. 'Blue Heaven' and 'Gray Gleam' are smaller varieties named for the color of their foliage. 'Skyrocket' is a narrow 20-foot tree.

Chinese juniper (*Juniperus chinensis*)

Hollywood juniper
(*Juniperus chinensis* 'Kaizuka') twisted form

Chinese juniper
(*Juniperus chinensis*
'Keteleeri')

FEATURED PROFILE

Hollywood Juniper

Botanical Name: *Juniperus chinensis* 'Kaizuka' **Type of Plant:** picturesque evergreen tree **Family:** Cupressaceae **Genus Range:** China, Japan, Mongolia **Hardiness:** USDA Zones 5–9 **Height:** 20 to 30' **Growth Rate:** fast **Form & Habit:** twisted stylized form, irregularly branched **Uses:** accent plant **Flowers:** inconspicuous orange-yellow **Fruits:** cones **Foliage:** scalelike, vivid green **Soil & pH:** well-drained; pH 5.5 to 6.5 **Light & Moisture:** full sun; tolerates drought **Pruning Seasons:** during dormancy

Chinese juniper (*Juniperus chinensis* 'Pfitzeriana Compacta')

Chinese juniper (*Juniperus chinensis* variety *sargentii*)

Singleseed juniper
(*Juniperus squamata* 'Blue Star')

'Tolleson's Blue Weeping', a silvery blue weeping juniper, reaches about 20 feet tall.

The best juniper for midwestern and eastern states, Zones 2–9, is the native Eastern red cedar (*J. virginiana*). A dense 40- to 50-foot tree, there are both pyramidal and columnar forms. The cultivar 'Burkii', which is about 30 feet tall, has a good blue color that is tinted purple in winter. The hardy 'Canaertii' is yellow-green in spring and dark green in winter. 'Grey Owl' has soft silvery gray foliage.

There are excellent ground covers among the cultivars of the blue-green Sargent juniper (*J. c.* variety *sargentii*), hardy to Zones 3 or 4–9. These are mounding plants 2 to 3 feet tall that spread 8 to 10 feet. 'Glauca' has feathery blue-green leaves.

The assymetrically branched 5- to 10-foot Pfitzer cultivars are especially graceful and are available in several sizes and hues. The new branch tips of 'Pfitzerana Aurea' are tipped with gold. 'Hetzii Glauca' has frosty blue foliage. Gray-green 'Pfitzeriana Compacta' grows to about 3 feet. Blue-green 'Sea Spray' stays under 1 foot tall.

Shore juniper (*J. conferta*) is a vigorous trailing plant 1 to 1½ feet high with dense bluish green foliage. It flourishes in sandy soils and harsh seaside conditions in Zones 5–9. 'Blue Pacific' has exceptional winter color; 'Emerald Sea' is hardier and a little taller.

Creeping juniper (*J. horizontalis*), hardy in Zones 3–9, stays well under a foot high and spreads 8 to 12 inches per year. It has intense silver-blue foliage that takes on a purple cast in winter. In southern California, it is outstanding among the prostrate junipers. Six-inch-tall 'Wiltonii' is one of the finest trailing junipers.

The 2- to 3-foot single-seed juniper (*J. squamata* 'Blue Star') is used in Zones 4–7 in rock gardens and as striking, defining low border plants.

Culture: a spreading root system makes container-grown junipers easy to transplant in spring or fall. Most species thrive in moist soil with some coarse sand added and prefer pH 5.0 to 6.5. They require full sun.

Eastern red cedar
(*Juniperus virginiana* 'Grey Owl')
female "cones"

Eastern red cedar
(*J. virginiana* 'Grey Owl')

Golden-Rain Tree
also called "Varnish Tree"

Koelreuteria

Flame tree
(*Koelreuteria bipinnata*)
papery seed capsules

Golden-rain trees are small to midsize shade trees that from early- to midsummer bear huge showy 12- to 15-inch-long panicles of ½-inch yellow flowers. They are followed later in the summer by segmented papery capsules that change from green, to gold-buff, and then to a vivid cinnamon brown. These persist for a time, looking like cascades of tiny Chinese lanterns. In autumn, the feathery graceful foliage turns an attractive yellow. The golden-rain tree grows fast and resists most pests and diseases. At maturity, it reaches 30 to 40 feet and under good conditions develops a broad, almost flat, head. The common name given for the genus is golden-rain tree, not to be confused with the laburnums, which are commonly called "golden-chain tree." (See opposite page.)

In the eastern states, in Zones 6–9, the golden-rain tree (*Koelreuteria paniculata*) is featured on lawns and patios and as specimens in large properties. It may succeed in Zone 5 with protection. In warm Zones 7–9, a more heat-tolerant species, *K. bipinnata*, is planted. Called the "flame tree" or the "Chinese rain tree," it also grows to 30 or 40 feet but has a more rounded crown. The flowers are yellow and fragrant and appear two to three weeks later than the flowers of the golden-rain tree. The decorative capsules are a soft salmon pink and retain their color after drying.

Culture: both species transplant easily in early spring or fall and adapt to a wide range of soils. Tolerant of wind, pollution, drought, heat, and soil alkalinity, they flower most fully in full sun but succeed in light shade.

Golden-rain tree
(*Koelreuteria paniculata*)

FEATURED PROFILE
Golden-Rain, or Varnish, Tree

Botanical Name: *Koelreuteria paniculata* **Family:** Sapindaceae **Type of Plant:** deciduous flowering tree **Uses:** featured specimen **Native Range:** China, Japan, Korea **Hardiness:** USDA Zones 5 or 6–9 **Height:** 30 to 40' **Growth Rate:** moderate to slow **Form & Habit:** spreading, rounded **Bloom Period:** early to midsummer **Flowers:** 12 to 15' panicles of tiny yellow flowers **Fruits:** lanternlike papery capsules changing from green to gold-buff to cinnamon brown **Foliage:** feathery; purplish, changing to green, and then to yellow **Soil & pH:** soil tolerant; prefers pH range of 6.0 to 7.5 **Light & Moisture:** full sun or light shade; tolerates drought **Pruning Seasons:** during dormancy

Golden-rain tree (*Koelreuteria paniculata* 'September')

The Laburnums

Laburnum

For two weeks in May when it is in bloom, the laburnum, or golden-chain tree, is a dazzling horticultural ornament. It develops into a small tree 20 to 30 feet tall, and when in bloom it suggests a tree-wisteria streaming with broad chains of fragrant bright yellow pealike flowers about ¾ inch long. Then it becomes a pretty tree with airy blue-green foliage for the balance of the growing season. The seedpods that follow in October are not particularly ornamental, and they are poisonous. A dramatic use of the golden-chain tree is the famous laburnum walk created by British writer and gardener Rosemary Verey, who trained two rows of laburnums to meet overhead on metal arches. (See far right.)

The Waterer hybrid (*Laburnum* x *watereri*) is the most beautiful of the three European species in the genus. The cultivar 'Vossii' is an outstanding variety with dense flower chains as long as 24 inches. It is hardy in Zones 5–7. A similar but hardier species called "Scotch laburnum" (*Laburnum alpinum*) tolerates winters in Zone 4 with

Golden-chain tree (*Laburnum* x *watereri*)

some protection. It bears 10- to 15-inch-long racemes of golden flowers that last longer than the Waterer hybrid's but are not quite as showy.

In a small garden, laburnum is sometimes planted as a lawn specimen. Where there is space, a more satisfying plan is to group two or three laburnums with columnar evergreen trees and low flowering shrubs, such as evergreen azaleas or daphne, that are interesting when the golden chains have gone by. In regions outside laburnum's winter hardiness range, it may be grown as a container plant and wintered in a greenhouse.

Culture: transplant a young container-grown or balled-and-burlapped plant in early spring into moist but well-drained soil. Laburnum tolerates a range of soils but not wet feet. It does best with protection from noonday sun.

Scotch laburnum (*Laburnum alpinum*) flower panicle

Waterer hybrid laburnum (*Laburnum* x *watereri* 'Vossii') Rosemary Verey's famous laburnum walk

Waterer hybrid laburnum (*Laburnum* x *watereri* 'Vossii')

FEATURED PROFILE
Waterer Laburnum, or Golden-Chain Tree

Botanical Name: *Laburnum* x *watereri* 'Vossii' **Family:** Leguminosae **Type of Plant:** small deciduous flowering tree **Uses:** midspring flowers; specimen plant **Genus Range:** southeast Europe and western Asia **Hardiness:** USDA Zones 5–7 **Height:** 20 to 30' **Growth Rate:** medium **Form & Habit:** small tree; rounded crown **Bloom Period:** May, early June **Flowers:** bright yellow, ¾" long, borne on pendulous racemes to 24" long **Fruits:** unimpressive seedpods **Foliage:** composed of 3 leaflets 1 to 3" long; bright blue-green in summer; fall color unremarkable **Soil & pH:** well-drained; pH 5.0 to 6.5 **Light & Moisture:** dappled shade with protection from noon sun; sustained moisture **Pruning Seasons:** prune after floweringx

The Crape Myrtles

Lagerstroemia indica

Crape myrtle (*Lagerstroemia indica* 'Natchez')

The crape myrtles are the southern-belle equivalent of the northern lilac: small summer-flowering trees and large shrubs with lilaclike flowerheads grace the tip of each new branch in midsummer. The flowers last for four to six weeks or longer, in colors that range through melting shades of raspberry, pink, melon, and mauve. There are white forms, but they do not have the sparkling purity of white lilacs. Some crape myrtles also have beautifully decorative mottled bark. The new leaves in spring are yellow-bronze. In fall, they turn golden yellow, orange, and pink-red; the foliage of white-flowered varieties turns yellow in the fall; the leaves of pink and red types show more orange and red.

Crape myrtle
(*Lagerstroemia indica* 'Natchez')

Hardy only in Zones 7–9, the species from South and East Asia that were once prevalent in the American South and Southeast are prone to mildew. But beautiful new mildew- and disease-resistant hybrids are becoming available, developed by the late Dr. Donald Egolf of the United States National Arboretum. Most have exfoliating cinnamon bark and sinuous, almost muscular trunks. Egolf's larger introductions grow quickly to 15 or 20 feet and may be trained to a single trunk or pruned to encourage several trunks. Because crape myrtles bloom on new growth, they also may be cut almost to the ground when dormant. This will maintain a flowering shrubby form. Some outstanding Egolf hybrids named for Native American tribes are pink 'Potomac', medium pink 'Seminole', and white 'Natchez'. Dr. Egolf's 7- to 9-foot semidwarf introductions are easier to prune and make beautiful flowering hedges and back-of-the-border plants. Examples are white 'Acoma', medium pink 'Hopi', clear pink 'Pecos', and dark lavender 'Zuni'.

Culture: transplant a container-grown or balled-and-burlapped crape myrtle in spring to moist, heavy loam or clay soil in the acid range, pH 5.0 to 6.5. Because crape myrtles bloom on new growth, severe pruning before the leaves appear in early spring encourages flowering and controls height. A plant that appears to have been killed by winter cold will often send up branches that will flower.

Crape myrtle (*Lagerstroemia indica* 'Seminole')

FEATURED PROFILE
Crape Myrtle

Botanical Name: *Lagerstroemia indica* 'Seminole' **Family:** Lythraceae **Type of Plant:** small deciduous flowering tree or shrub **Uses:** showy midsummer flowers; fall color; colorful bark; lawn specimen; shrub border **Genus Range:** tropical Asia to Australia **Hardiness:** USDA Zones 7–9 **Height:** 15 to 20' **Growth Rate:** fast **Form & Habit:** upright with rounded crown **Bloom Period:** midsummer **Flowers:** long-lasting clusters of clear pink flowers with crinkled petals **Fruits:** 6-valved capsule **Foliage:** bronze; then green; then golden yellow **Soil & pH:** heavy loam and clay; pH 5.0 to 6.5 **Light & Moisture:** full sun, dappled shade; sustained moisture **Pruning Seasons:** prune severely every spring before leaves appear

The Larches

Larix

Larches are tall deciduous conifers native to cool mountainous regions in the Northern Hemisphere. These handsome trees with droopy branches provide stunning beauty in autumn, when the needle-shaped leaves turn a beautiful golden orange—and then drop. The fall color, spectacular against a backdrop of evergreens, is the tree's major asset. Its short, narrow needles have two white bands on the underside and grow in clusters. The reddish brown peeling bark (once used for tanning leather) and attractive cones that mature the first year are winter assets. The beautiful and fast-growing Japanese larch (*Larix kaempferi*) is among the most ornamental larches for Zones 5–7. It is lovely in the spring, when its soft, fresh sea green foliage emerges on pendulous branches, as well as in the fall, when the leaves turn yellow-gold. Its interesting scaly bark peels in long strips, showing

European larch (*Larix decidua*) leaves

red underneath. With a height of 70 to 90 feet and a spread of 25 to 50 feet, this tree is best suited to large landscapes. In cooler Zone 4, slow-growing golden larch (*Pseudolarix kaempferi*), which is a related tree from a different genus, also works well for large gardens. This beautiful Chinese plant grows 30 to 40 feet in cultivation and 120 feet in the wild. It has few pests, but finding a good location for it can be hard because it grows nearly as wide as it does high. Until recently, the hardy European larch (*L. decidua*) was planted extensively in Zones 2–6 of the Northeast, but other conifers less susceptible to pests are replacing it.

Culture: transplant a dormant container-grown or balled-and-burlapped Japanese larch easily in the early spring and thrives in moist but well-drained soil. Like other larches, it does not tolerate shade, pollution, or drought but will succeed in shallow and acid soils.

European larch (*Larix decidua*)

European larch (*Larix decidua*)

Japanese Larch (*Larix kaempferi*)

FEATURED PROFILE
Japanese Larch

Botanical Name: *Larix kaempferi* **Family:** Pinaceae **Type of Plant:** tall deciduous conifer **Uses:** colorful spring and fall foliage; landscape specimen; woodland feature **Native Range:** cold mountainous regions in Japan **Hardiness:** USDA Zones 5–7 **Height:** 70 to 90' **Growth Rate:** medium to fast **Form & Habit:** open, pyramidal, with slender drooping branches **Fruits:** cones 1" long or longer; male and female on the same tree; mature the first year **Foliage:** flat 1 to 1¼" long, soft sea green needles with 2 white bands on the underside; green in spring and summer; golden in autumn before falling **Soil & pH:** well-drained; pH adaptable **Light & Moisture:** full sun; sustained moisture **Pruning Seasons:** midsummer

American Sweet Gum

Liquidambar styraciflua

American sweet gum
(*Liquidambar styraciflua*)

American sweet gum
(*Liquidambar styraciflua*) in fall

The American sweet gum (*Liquidambar styraciflua*), a big, handsome shade tree, stages a spectacular fall show. The large, glossy, five-point star-shaped leaves are an attractive deep green in summer. In cold weather, they turn purple, red, and a true yellow and persist for weeks—even months.

In moist soil, the tree grows rapidly, 2 to 3 feet a year, to reach 60 to 75 feet. Its spread equals two-thirds its height. The grayish brown bark is interestingly corky. These are its assets; some consider the fruit a liability. Prickly, woody seedballs develop from male and female flowers that grow in clusters. The fruit later litters the ground and can damage a lawn mower and prick bare feet.

American sweet gum—the tree's sap really is sweet and gummy—thrives from southern Connecticut to the Gulf states and is outstanding in California, where it is called liquidamber. It's an excellent choice for a large open landscape with acid moist soil. Aside from the need to remove the prickly fruit before mowing, the tree makes a superb lawn feature. In the Southeast, sweet gum tends to spread through abandoned fields, pushing out other desirable species. The fast-growing cultivar *L. s.* 'Moraine' colors a rich red and can stand more cold than the species, which is hardy in Zones 5 or 6–9.

Culture: plant a young, dormant, container-grown or balled-and-burlapped tree in early spring. Handle the rootball with extreme care—even under the best of circumstances, sweet gum will need time to adjust. The plant does best in moist, slightly acid soil, pH 5.5 to 6.5. It thrives in full sun and tolerates partial shade but not pollution.

FEATURED PROFILE
American Sweet Gum

Botanical Name: *Liquidambar styraciflua* **Family:** Hamamelidaceae **Type of Plant:** large deciduous shade tree **Uses:** beautiful foliage; brilliant fall color; shade; lawn specimen **Native Range:** eastern U.S., CT to NY, FL, S. to OH, W. to TX and Mexico **Hardiness:** USDA Zones 5 or 6–9 **Height:** 60 to 75' in cultivation; 80 to 120' in the wild **Growth Rate:** medium to fast **Form & Habit:** neat pyramid in youth; rounding at maturity **Bloom Period:** April or May, when the leaves emerge **Flowers:** inconspicuous **Fruits:** tough, round, prickly woody capsule 1 to 1½" in diameter **Foliage:** star-shaped 4 to 7½" wide; finely serrated; deep glossy green in summer; changing to brilliant red, purple, yellow in fall **Soil & pH:** moist; pH 5.5 to 6.5 **Light & Moisture:** full sun or dappled shade; sustained moisture **Pruning Seasons:** winter

American sweet gum (*Liquidambar styraciflua*) prickly seedballs

The Tulip Trees

Liriodendron

Only two species of tulip tree are known in the world: the native tulip poplar (*Liriodendron tulipifera*), which grows wild from the southern Canadian border by the Great Lakes, from Massachusetts to Florida and westward to Wisconsin and Mississippi; and the Chinese tulip tree (*L. chinense*), a smaller tree not found in many North American nurseries.

The tulip poplar is the tallest native hardwood in North America. A majestic shade tree that is tolerant of city conditions, it turns a rich canary yellow in fall. The leaves look like a maple leaf squared across the tip and are a good blue-green in summer. In late May or early June, the tree bears large, chartreuse-green tuliplike blooms that are touched at the base with bright orange. The handsome flowers are borne so high up in the crown that they may be hard to see, except by bees that swarm to their rich nectar. The seeds in the conelike fruits, which resemble those of the large magnolias, attract finches and cardinals. Soft gray bark and a trunk that rises straight up until branching into an oval canopy complete the picture of a perfect specimen for parks and large landscapes. In cultivation, the tulip tree grows 70 to 90 feet. In the wild, it reaches 150 to 190 feet. Variegated, columnar, and dwarf forms have been developed. 'Palo Alto', 'Burgundy', and 'Festival' are California selections.

The showiest cultivar is 'Aureo-marginatum', with leaves that are outlined in yellow.

Culture: the tulip tree needs care in transplanting. Choose a young container-grown or balled-and-burlapped tree, and set it out in late winter or early spring in rich deep moist loam that is slightly acid, in the pH 5.5 to 6.5 range. The tulip tree requires full sun.

Tulip poplar (*Liriodendron tulipifera*)

FEATURED PROFILE
Tulip Tree, or Yellow Poplar

Botanical Name: *Liriodendron tulipifera* **Family:** Magnoliaceae **Type of Plant:** large deciduous shade tree **Uses:** tall shade; landscape specimen; spring flowers; fall color **Native Range:** MA to WI, S. to FL, and MS **Hardiness:** USDA Zones 4–9 **Height:** 70 to 90' in cultivation; 150 to 190' in the wild **Growth Rate:** fast **Form & Habit:** pyramidal in youth; oval to rounded crown at maturity **Bloom Period:** May to June **Flowers:** large, tuliplike; chartreuse with an orange band; borne high in the branches **Fruits:** persistent 2 to 3" cone, turning brown in fall **Foliage:** 3 to 8" long and wide, 2- to 4-lobed, with a squared top; in summer, bright green; in fall, yellow or golden yellow **Soil & pH:** well-drained; pH 5.5 to 6.5 **Light & Moisture:** full sun or dappled shade; sustained moisture **Pruning Seasons:** winter

Tulip poplar (*Liriodendron tulipifera*)

The Magnolias

Magnolia

Sweetbay magnolia (*Magnolia virginiana*)

'Galaxy' (*Magnolia liliiflora* x *M. sprengeri* 'Diva')

Magnolias are the oldest form of woody flowering plant on earth. Although some are native to Asia, many gorgeous magnolias are native to North America. All are grown for their spring and summer flowers, which are the largest—up to 1 foot wide—of any group of hardy plants in the North Temperate range.

Evergreen magnolias are native to warm, temperate, and semitropical regions; they sometimes do well as far north as Zone 6. Resembling water lilies, the flowers of the evergreens appear sporadically in summer, and their large, oblong, glossy stiff leaves are almost indestructible. The famous magnolia of southern plantations is the majestic 80-foot southern, or bull bay, magnolia (*Magnolia grandiflora*). It bears huge, fragrant flowers and has beautiful 12-inch leaves with cinnamon brown undersides. It is planted in large landscapes in Zone 7 and southward. If you live farther north, search for smaller cultivars that

Saucer magnolia (*Magnolia* x *soulangeana* 'Jane')

withstand winters in Zones 6 and 7. Slow-growing, compact 'Little Gem' grows to 25 feet, and 'Saint Mary', which bears large fragrant flowers, reaches 20 feet. They are good choices for smaller landscapes. The sweetbay, or swamp, magnolia (*M. virginiana*) reaches 60 feet in warm regions. Creamy white lemon-scented water lilylike flowers appear sporadically from late spring on. The 3- to 5-inch dark green leaves are silvery on the undersides. The sweetbay can survive as far north as Zone 5 in a protected spot, but there it rarely exceeds 20 feet and may lose its leaves in winter. In some species, the conelike magnolia fruits are quite decorative.

Deciduous magnolias do better than the evergreens in cold-winter zones. They have softer, smaller leaves than the evergreens, and their flowers, often with drooping, strap-shaped petals, appear in late winter or early spring, before the leaves emerge. In April, the beautiful 20- to 25-foot *M.* x *loebneri* 'Merrill' blankets itself with multi-petaled, slightly fragrant white flowers as far north as Zone 3. A common sight in Zone 4 in early spring is the 10- to 20-foot star magnolia (*M. stellata*) literally covered by slightly fragrant white flowers with multiple strap-shaped drooping petals. The saucer, or Chinese, magnolia

Southern magnolia
(*Magnolia grandiflora*)

Saucer magnolia (*Magnolia* x *soulangeana*)

(*M.* x *soulangeana*) has flowers that are purplish on the outside and cream-to-white on the inside. A 20- to 30-foot tree, it succeeds up to Zone 6. Some good-looking shrubby cultivars hardy in Zone 5 have been introduced by the National Arboretum and bear feminine names, such as pink-flowered 'Susan' and reddish purple 'Betty'.

Deciduous magnolias grow best in a cool location; buds lured out early in a warm microclimate are often lost to late winter cold snaps. 'Galaxy', a United States National Arboretum cultivar, escapes most late frosts because it blooms later than most. Its saucer-shaped, pink-red flowers open to a paler shade; it grows to 40 feet.

Culture: transplant container-grown magnolias in early spring or fall. Most species require rich, well-drained soil, not dry, and a pH range of 5.0 to 6.5. Most succeed in full sun but tolerate some shade. Magnolias look best without pruning.

FEATURED PROFILE
Star Magnolia

Botanical Name: *Magnolia stellata* **Family:** Magnoliaceae **Type of Plant:** small, usually deciduous, early flowering tree **Uses:** lawn specimen, shrub border **Native Range:** Japan **Hardiness:** USDA Zones 4 or 5–8 **Height:** 10 to 20' **Growth Rate:** slow **Form & Habit:** dense, upright **Bloom Period:** late winter, early spring **Flowers:** white, large, somewhat fragrant, many-petaled **Fruits:** clusters of follicles **Foliage:** light green **Soil & pH:** rich, well-drained but not dry; pH 5.0 to 6.5 **Light & Moisture:** full sun or dappled shade; sustained moisture

Star magnolia
(*Magnolia stellata*)

The Crabapples

Malus

The ornamental crabapple is one of the most valued spring-flowering ornamental fruit trees. It makes up a class of apple tree that bears fruit smaller than 2 inches. It is a small, usually spreading plant that covers itself in spring with exquisite, sometimes fragrant, single or double apple blossoms that range from pure white to scarlet. In fall it bears showy scarlet, yellow, or orange fruits that persist for months and are enjoyed by birds.

As members of the rose family, crabapples are susceptible to the problems that affect roses and to fire blight, scab, and cedar-apple rust. Enlist a responsible local nursery in your search for one of the many new disease-resistant hybrids. Two beautiful resistant trees are the picturesque 20-foot tea crab (*Malus hupehensis*) with its long, 25-foot wandlike branches, fragrant flowers, and greenish yellow-red fruits; and the 18-foot Japanese flowering crabapple (*M. floribunda*) with 25-foot branches that present a lovely silhouette in winter. Its deep pink-to-red buds open white; the fruits are yellow-red. This species does fairly well in the South. Both are hardy in Zones 4–7. The diminutive size of 'Tina', a 5-foot cultivar of *M. sargentii*, makes it a favorite for small gardens in Zones 4–8. Its long-lasting red flower buds open white. Persistent glossy red fruits follow.

Crabapple
(*Malus sargentii*)

Crabapple
(*Malus* 'Snow Cloud')

Crabapple
(*Malus* 'Dorothea')

The Garden Club of America recommends these cultivars for their beauty and disease resistance: red-flowered 'Adams'; 'Donald Wyman', a magnificent showy crab with soft pink buds and white flowers; and shrubby 'Mary Potter' and 'Professor Sprenger', a shapely 20-foot tree, both of which have pink buds that open white. All are hardy in Zones 5–7 or 8.

Culture: a young container-grown or balled-and-burlapped crabapple transplants easily in early spring or fall. Crabs do best in heavy loamy soil, pH 5.0 to 6.5. Complete pruning before early June. Keep crabapples at least 500 feet from red cedar to avoid a problem with red cedar galls.

FEATURED PROFILE
Flowering Crabapple

Botanical Name: *Malus* 'Donald Wyman' **Family:** Rosaceae **Type of Plant:** small deciduous flowering tree **Uses:** showy spring flowers; colorful persistent fall fruit; lawn specimen; shrub border; small shade tree **Genus Range:** Europe, Asia **Hardiness:** USDA Zones 4–8 **Height:** to 20' **Growth Rate:** medium **Form & Habit:** rounded **Bloom Period:** spring **Flowers:** soft pink buds open to white flowers **Fruits:** bright red pome **Foliage:** glossy green foliage **Soil & pH:** well-drained; pH 5.0 to 7.0 **Light & Moisture:** full sun; sustained moisture **Pruning Seasons:** after flowering

Crabapple (*Malus* 'Donald Wyman')

Black Gum
also called "Black Tupelo," "Sour Gum," or "Pepperidge"

Nyssa sylvatica

Straight and symmetrical, the black gum (*Nyssa sylvatica*) is a native eastern shade tree with fall color that consistently rivals that of the best red maples, even in the South. The glossy, leathery leaves are green in summer and change to glowing yellow in September, and then change again to orange, scarlet, and purple. Winter reveals a pyramidal structure, slightly drooping lower branches, and dark charcoal gray bark broken into thick blocky ridges. Bees produce a flavorful honey from the nectar-rich greenish white flowers that appear in spring. Bears and other wildlife like the fruits.

Black gum (*Nyssa sylvatica*) berries in fall

In cultivation, black gum reaches 30 to 50 feet, but it grows much taller in the wild, especially near water. The name *Nyssa* is derived from the Greek word for "water nymph." A tree of the lowlands, black gum is found in abandoned fields, in dry ridges, and near cold wet swamps throughout eastern North America, from Maine to southern Ontario, and from Florida to eastern Texas. It is best featured in a large landscape or near a stream or pond. Black gum tolerates air pollution.

Culture: black gum's long taproot makes transplanting difficult. Choose a thriving young container-grown plant, and set it out in early spring in full or partial sun. It will do best in moist but well-drained soil with a slightly acid pH, 5.5 to 6.5, but it can tolerate heavy clay soils. At the northern end of its hardiness range, protect young trees against winter winds with a burlap screen. Prune in late autumn, if required.

Black gum (*Nyssa sylvatica*)

FEATURED PROFILE
Black Gum, Black Tupelo, Sour Gum, or Pepperidge

Botanical Name: *Nyssa sylvatica* **Family:** Nyssaceae **Type of Plant:** midsize deciduous shade tree **Uses:** shade; nectar for bees; fall color; naturalizing **Native Range:** eastern North America **Hardiness:** USDA Zones 4–9 **Height:** 30 to 50' in cultivation; to 100' in the wild **Growth Rate:** slow to medium **Form & Habit:** pyramidal in youth; dense horizontal branching **Bloom Period:** spring **Flowers:** inconspicuous clusters, greenish white ½" or less **Fruits:** inconspicuous bluish black berrylike drupe ½" or less across **Foliage:** pointed oval 2 to 5" long; in summer shiny dark green; in fall yellow, orange, scarlet, and purple **Soil & pH:** well-drained; pH 5.5 to 6.5 **Light & Moisture:** full sun or partial shade; sustained moisture **Pruning Seasons:** late autumn

Black gum (*Nyssa sylvatica*) in fall

Sourwood
also called "Sorrel Tree"
Oxydendrum arboreum

Sourwood (*Oxydendrum arboreum*) fruit in fall

Sourwood (*Oxydendrum arboreum*) in fall

Sourwood (*Oxydendrum arboreum*) is a graceful native flowering shade tree. Its celebrated fall color display begins before that of the dogwoods and rivals the black gum and red maple for color. Yet the sourwood is a year-round ornamental. The finely textured foliage emerges glossy emerald green in spring. It turns rich green in summer, when it's almost obscured by long drooping clusters of fragrant, pretty, bell-shaped creamy white flowers. They resemble the lily-of-the-valley, hence the nickname, "lily-of-the-valley tree." Bees harvest the flower nectar and produce a honey that's commercially available. In fall the leaves turn plum red, pink, lavender, and yellow and are enhanced by profuse creamy tan fruit clusters. Deeply furrowed bark is an attractive winter feature. The tree's "sour" name refers to the acid-tasting sap.

Hardy in Zones 5–9, the sourwood grows wild along banks and streams from coastal southeastern Pennsylvania to southern Illinois, Florida, and Louisiana. It naturalizes without objection and will reward the efforts made to establish it in the home landscape. A slow-growing tree, sourwood growth is slowest at the northern part of its range, where trees rarely top 20 feet; farther south, a sourwood may eventually reach 75 feet.

Culture: select a young container-grown plant at a reliable nursery, and handle the transplanting with care. Sourwood requires lean, or relatively infertile, soil that is moist but well-drained and acid, pH 5.0 to 6.5; it does best in full sun. It tolerates dry soil and some shade but not pollution.

FEATURED PROFILE
Sourwood, or Sorrel Tree

Botanical Name: *Oxydendrum arboreum*
Family: Ericaceae **Type of Plant:** small to midsize deciduous tree **Uses:** shade; summer flowers; early fall color **Native Habitat:** PA to FL, W. to IN and LA **Hardiness:** USDA Zones 5 or 6–9 **Height:** 20 to 50' in cultivation; to 75' in the wild **Growth Rate:** slow **Form & Habit:** pyramidal with rounded top; slightly drooping branches **Bloom Period:** mid July **Flowers:** fragrant white bell-shaped flowers in pendulous clusters 6 to 10" long **Fruits:** conspicuous 5-angled dry capsules **Foliage:** oblong leaves 4 to 7" long; in summer lustrous dark green; in fall brilliant yellow, pink, lavender, scarlet to deep purplish red **Soil & pH:** well-drained; pH 5.0 to 6.5 **Light & Moisture:** full sun to dappled shade; sustained moisture **Pruning Seasons:** rarely needed

Sourwood (*Oxydendrum arboreum*)

Cork Tree
also called "Amur Cork Tree"

Phellodendron amurense

The cork tree (*Phellodendron amurense*) is a beautiful midsize shade tree that acquires something of the monumental presence of an oak as it matures. It is striking in the winter landscape. In cultivation, it grows 25 to 40 feet and develops a short massive trunk, broad spreading branches, an open rounded crown, and extraordinary, deeply furrowed corky gray-brown bark. The leaves—glossy, leathery, and dark green in summer—turn a handsome deep or bronzed yellow in fall. Inconspicuous clusters of yellow blooms appear in late spring. When the leaves fall, the female tree's crown is covered with branched clusters of ½-inch blue-black fruits that shrivel through the season until they resemble dried berries. The fruits are attractive but messy. Nurseries stock a nonfruiting male cultivar, 'Macho'. A handsome tree with highly textured bark, it has a more open crown than the species.

The phellodendrons are Asian trees found in the wild only in northeastern China and Japan. The cork tree, the only species popularly grown in North America, is hardy in Zones 4–7. It succeeds in cities but is most impressive growing in an open, airy landscape.

Culture: a young container-grown or balled-and-burlapped cork tree transplants readily in early spring or fall and adapts to many types of soil, acid and alkaline, pH 5.5 to 7.5. The phellodendrons tolerate drought but do best with sustained moisture and full sun.

Cork tree (*Phellodendron amurense*) in fall

Cork tree (*Phellodendron amurense*)

Female cork tree (*Phellodendron amurense*)

FEATURED PROFILE
Cork, or Amur Cork, Tree

Botanical Name: *Phellodendron amurense* **Family:** Rutaceae **Type of Plant:** small to midsize deciduous tree **Uses:** light shade; winter interest; great presence **Native Habitat:** northern China, Manchuria, Japan **Hardiness:** USDA Zones 4–7 **Height:** 25 to 40' in cultivation **Growth Rate:** medium **Form & Habit:** short thick massive trunk; spreading rounded crown **Bloom Period:** May–June, **Flowers:** inconspicuous yellowish green flowers borne in 2 to 3½" panicles **Fruits:** persistent, berrylike, ½ to ⅜" diameter, borne on female trees **Foliage:** composed of 5 to 13 oval- to lance-shaped leaflets 2½ to 4½" long; in summer lustrous dark green; in fall yellow to bronze yellow **Soil & pH:** tolerant of many types of soil; pH 5.5 to 7.5 **Light & Moisture:** full sun, tolerates drought **Pruning Seasons:** winter

The Spruces

Picea

A dwarf Norway spruce (*Picea abies*)

S pruces are among the most popular of all conifers. These noble trees exude a pungent pitch that was used in ancient times for caulking ships; the name *Picea* derives from the Latin word for "pitch." Other trademarks of the spruce clan are long life, leathery tan-colored cones, and short, rigid, sharp-pointed needles ranging in color from dark to light green, yellow, and blue. Some spruces lose their lower branches as they mature. Of the 40 species growing in the Northern Hemisphere, five are tree size and grace the home garden as foundation plants, as screens, and as green winter backdrops for deciduous shrubs and trees. The trees reach 40 to 60 feet in cultivation. There are shrubby spruces available too.

The most planted is the Norway spruce (*Picea abies*). It withstands a goodly range of temperatures, surviving winters in Zone 2 and summers in Zone 7, and it does well in both sun and shade. Its rapid growth rate makes it an ideal tall screen or windbreak. The tree's leafy new shoots are commercially harvested and used to flavor spruce beer. Equally hardy and easy to grow, the white spruce (*P. glauca*) is used for windbreaks in the Midwest and along the northern lake shores. Both species need growing room, eventually reaching 60 feet with a 20- to 30-foot spread.

The slow-growing Oriental spruce (*P. orientalis*) is a beautiful, graceful species with exfoliating bark. A symmetrical plant used in large formal landscapes in Zones 4–7, it thrives in the Midwest. For a small property, the slow-growing bright green 15- to 20-foot cultivar 'Gracilis' works well.

The elegance of the tall, slow-growing, narrow Serbian spruce (*P. omorika*), hardy in Zones 4–7, makes it an outstanding specimen on a large property. Its short cascading branches droop and then curve upward to give it an imposing, up-reaching appearance. In large northeastern

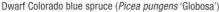

Norway spruce (*Picea abies*)

Dwarf Colorado blue spruce (*Picea pungens* 'Globosa')

Dwarf Alberta spruce
(*Picea glauca* variety *albertiana* 'Conica')

White spruce (*Picea glauca*)

Dwarf spruce (*Picea* 'Montgomery')

Hoopsii blue spruce
(*Picea pungens* 'Hoopsii')

landscapes it is often planted with groups of deciduous trees and other conifers. It is one of the few spruces with flat needles resembling those of the hemlock. It tolerates alkaline soils, pH 5.0 to 7.0, another unusual attribute.

The bluest spruce is the tall, symmetrical, and formal-looking Colorado blue (*P. pungens* 'Glauca'). A native of the higher Rocky Mountains, it is hardy in Zones 3–8 but is not at its best in warm regions. The soft silvery blue-gray foliage turns silver-gray to blue-green as the tree matures. It grows slowly to 30 to 50 feet and can live 600 to 800 years. The cultivar 'Foxtail' has greater heat tolerance.

Attractive shrub-size spruces have been developed for use in rock gardens and as accent plants. Of the dwarf Norway spruce cultivars, 'Little Gem' stays under 2 feet in Zones 3–7, and 'Nidiformis' stays under 3 feet. 'Conica', also known as the "dwarf Alberta spruce", assumes a perfect cone shape with soft, dense light green needles in

Zones 3–8. A slow grower, it reaches 10 to 12 feet in 25 to 30 years. Conical 'Nana', hardy to Zones 4–7, is a slow-growing 7- to 9-foot blue-green dwarf of the Serbian spruce. 'Fat Albert', a dwarf of the Colorado blue spruce, makes a wonderful Christmas tree, just 10 to 15 feet fully grown. 'Globosa', a slow-growing flat-topped cultivar, stops growing at 3 to 5 feet.

Culture: spruces tend to have a shallow root system that spreads. You can easily transplant young balled-and-burlapped or container plants in early spring or fall. They do best in open, airy settings and in moist but well-drained, humusy soil. They usually require acid soil, pH 5.0 to 6.0, and full sun.

FEATURED PROFILE
Serbian Spruce

Botanical Name: *Picea omorika* **Family:** Pinaceae **Type of Plant:** evergreen conifer **Uses:** background; winter color; screening; windbreak **Native Range:** S.E. Europe **Hardiness:** USDA Zones 4–7 **Height:** 50 to 60' in cultivation **Growth Rate:** slow **Form & Habit:** graceful, beautiful columnar form with pendulous branches **Fruits:** purple oblong cones, ripening to cinnamon brown **Foliage:** flat dark green needles with white undersides **Soil & pH:** well-drained, humusy; pH 5.0 to 6.0 **Light & Moisture:** full sun; moist soil

Serbian spruce (*Picea omorika*)

The Pines

Pinus

Austrian pine (*Pinus nigra*)

Swiss stone pine (*Pinus cembra*)

The pines are easily distinguished from other conifers by their needles, which are thin, soft, and from 2 to 5 inches to almost 1 foot long and grow in bundles of two to five. This diverse group of 90 species found from the Arctic Circle to Central America, Europe, Asia, North Africa, and Malaysia can be long-lived. Some bristlecone pine (*Pinus aristata*) specimens native to the Southwest are 4,000 to 5,000 years old—probably the oldest trees alive. They are sometimes confused with another antique tree species, the ancient pine (*P. longaeva*), which grows in the Northwest. Most ornamental pines are considered easier to grow than either the spruces or the firs, but only a few ornamental species tolerate city conditions.

The most attractive pine is the eastern white (*P. strobus*), a native of the United States and Canada. Hardy in Zones 2–8, it is straight trunked and regal with long soft bluish green needles and attractive 6- to 8-inch cones. This species has lovely color and texture and grows rapidly to 50 to 80 feet in cultivation. It makes a good hedge and windbreak, a first-rate screen, and an excellent specimen plant. The drooping branches of 'Pendula' sweep the ground attractively. The branch tips of 'Fastigiata', a beautiful columnar form, point skyward.

Of the pines that tolerate cities, only the beautiful lacebark pine (*P. bungeana*) has exfoliating bark. The young tree's bark is a striking mosaic of opalescent green, white, and brown. As the tree matures, the patches fade and the trunk becomes a beautiful chalky white. Plant a lacebark where its bark can be appreciated—on a raised terrace or at a corner of a building, for example. This multistemmed species grows 30 to 50 feet tall and is hardy in Zones 4 or 5–8. Heavy snow and ice can inflict damage. The Austrian pine (*P. nigra*) manages life in town as well and survives in a range of soils, including soil with a high pH. It also tolerates heat and drought. The deep green needles are stiffer than those of most other pines. A pyramidal tree, 50 to 60 feet tall in cultivation, it becomes more interesting with age and is hardy in Zones 4–7.

Some pines can withstand the salt and storms of seaside life—among them the Austrian pine and, in Zones 5 or 6–8, the Japanese black pine (*P. thunbergii*), a 30-foot tree with dark green needles and rugged scaly bark. One of the most appealing of the salt-tolerant group is the bluegreen Swiss stone pine (*P. cembra*). It is handsome, narrow, dense, and slow growing. Hardy in Zones 4–8, it grows 35 to 40 feet tall.

Japanese black pine (*Pinus thunbergii*)

Mountain pine (*Pinus mugo*)

Weeping eastern white pine (*Pinus strobus* 'Pendula')

Planted in naturalized gardens, two native species make excellent subjects in regions similar to their original climate. One is the Mexican pinyon pine (*P. cembroides*) that grows in California, Arizona, and Mexico. The tree's seeds are sold in gourmet food shops as pine nuts. It thrives in Zones 4 or 5 and does well in dry soil. The other is the beautiful gnarled limber pine (*P. flexilis*), which grows in Zones 4–7 and tolerates high winds and cold. Look for these two native species in local nurseries.

Eastern white pine (*Pinus strobus*)

Bristlecone pine (*Pinus aristata*)

Dwarf pines add texture and color to rock gardens, low borders, patio containers, and shrub groups. The best-known dwarfs are cultivars of the 2- to 6-foot mountain pine (*P. mugo*), Zones 2 or 3–7. They become attractive little bundles of dark green needles that do well near coastlines. Rounded 'Mops' grows 1 to 2 inches a year to about 3 feet. The dwarf blue Scots pine (*P. sylvestris* 'Glauca Nana'), a midsize form, slowly reaches 6 to 8 feet in Zones 3–7. The Tanyosho pine 'Umbraculifera Compacta' is a 12-foot cultivar of the Japanese red pine (*P. densiflora*), which grows in Zones 4 or 5–7. It has a picturesque umbrellalike crown and attractive scaly orange bark.

Culture: transplant a young container-grown pine in early spring. Pines tolerate many soils but thrive in well-drained, sandy, somewhat acid soil, pH 5.0 to 6.0. To encourage density or to change the shape, cut back the new candles by half in June when the tree is fully grown.

Lacebark pine (*Pinus bungeana*)

FEATURED PROFILE
White, or Colorado, Fir

Botanical Name: *Abies concolor* 'Candicans' **Family:** Pinaceae **Type of Plant:** tall evergreen conifer **Uses:** lawn and park specimen; winter color **Genus Range:** CO, CA, NM **Hardiness:** USDA Zones 3–7 **Height:** 30 to 50' in cultivation; to 100' in the wild **Growth Rate:** slow to medium **Form & Habit:** pyramidal **Flowers:** inconspicuous **Fruits:** green-purple cones 3 to 6" long **Foliage:** 2 to 3" long; silvery bluish green needles usually with two white bands on the underside **Soil & pH:** deep, rich, well-drained, sandy loam; slightly acid **Light & Moisture:** full sun; sustained moisture but tolerates drought

The Flowering Plums, Cherries and Almonds

Prunus

Purpleleaf sand cherry
(*Prunus* x *cistena*)

Myrobalan plum
(*Prunus cerasifera* 'Thundercloud')

The well-loved ornamentals of the genus *Prunus* that are known as flowering fruit trees are bred for their flowers, unlike the cherry, apricot, plum, and peach trees of the genus, which are grown for their fruit. The dwarfed fruits of the ornamentals are eaten eagerly by birds and leave little mess. These typically small to midsize trees tolerate city conditions if given space and good care. *Prunus* is a member of the rose family, however, and is subject to problems that plague America's favorite flower, so be sure to plant only resistant cultivars guaranteed by responsible, preferably local, nurseries. The flowering plum is the earliest of the ornamental *Prunus* to bloom—and the hardiest. In March or April, the branches are covered with small single pink or white blossoms—in most varieties before the leaves appear. The purple-leaf plums make dramatic specimens. A cultivar of the purple Myrobalan plum (*Prunus cerasifera*), 18-foot pink-flow-

Kwanzan cherry
(*Prunus serrulata* 'Kwanzan')

ered 'Thundercloud', retains its deep rich color throughout the growing season in Zones 5–8. The 30-foot cold- and heat-tolerant 'Krauter Vesuvius' is popular in California. Purpleleaf sand cherry (*P.* x *cistena*), which can reach 7 feet, is often grown as a hedge plant in the Midwest, Zones 4–8. The foliage retains its rich color all summer, and the fragrant pink-white flowers open after the leaves appear. *Cistena* means "baby" in the Sioux language.

Next come the flowering cherries, blooming in April and May. In a garden with space for just one type of *Prunus,* a weeping cherry is often the choice. Weeping *P. subhirtella* 'Pendula' blooms early and bears single pink flowers. 'Pendula Plena Rosea', the 25- to 30-foot double-flowered weeping Japanese cherry, becomes a vast pink umbrella in late April. With some protection, it will succeed as far north as Zone 4. 'Autumnalis', a double weeping pink that grows to 30 feet tall, blooms sporadically on warm days in the fall and blooms again lavishly the following spring. The durable Higan, or rosebud, cherries, upright varieties of *P. subhirtella,* live 30 to 50 years.

Kwanzan cherry (*Prunus serrulata* 'Kwanzan')

Yoshino cherry (*Prunus yedoensis*)

Flowering almond
(*Prunus glandulosa*)

The Japanese cherry trees that flower each March at the Tidal Basin in Washington, D.C., are the 40- to 50-foot Yoshino cherries (*P. yedoensis*). Though hardy in Zones 5–8, and Washington, D.C., is in Zone 7, the spring show is sometimes blasted by a late winter storm. The finest cultivar is 'Akebono', a pink-flowered fragrant plant that prefers somewhat acid soil and adapts to partial sun. 'Shidare Yoshino' is a weeping form. 'Ivensii' has fragrant white flowers on weeping branches. The hybrid *P.* 'Snowfozam', a beautiful white weeping cherry just 12 feet tall, is hardy in Zone 4.

Some cherries have colorful fall foliage. The leaves of the Sargent cherry (*P. sargentii*) turn bronze, orange, and red in the fall, harmonizing with the excellent cinnamon and chestnut brown bark. This long-lived upright tree grows to 50 feet and has spreading branches that bear showy clusters of single deep pink blooms in early spring. It is hardy to Zone 4. The handsome columnar cultivar 'Columnaris' is used for street planting.

The most popular double-flowered cherry is *P. serrulata* 'Kwanzan', a superb long-lived vase-shaped tree that reaches 20 feet tall and spreads almost as wide. Masses of pink double flowers hang in clusters on its branches. The flowers appear as the bronzy young leaves begin to open. 'Amanogawa', a columnar cultivar hardy in Zones 5–9, bears double pale pink flowers.

The durable dwarf flowering almond (*P. glandulosa*), a low-growing form often used as a miniature in containers and as a shrub, grows in Zones 4–8. Just 4 to 5 feet tall, it bears white or pink double flowers in April or May. The fruiting almond (*Amygdalus communis*) is unrelated. See page 227 for species used for hedges and screening.

Culture: transplant *Prunus* varieties as young container-grown or balled-and-burlapped plants in early spring or early fall. They do best in well-drained sandy loam with a pH of 6.0 to 7.5. They flower most fully in full sun but tolerate some shade. Prune after the flowers are finished.

Weeping Higan cherry (*Prunus subhirtella* 'Pendula')

FEATURED PROFILE
Weeping Higan Cherry

Botanical Name: *Prunus subhirtella* 'Pendula Plena Rosea' **Family:** Rosaceae **Type of Plant:** small deciduous flowering tree **Uses:** showy spring flowers; lawn specimen; light shade **Genus Range:** Japan **Hardiness:** USDA Zones 4 or 5–8 or 9 **Height:** 25 to 30' **Growth Rate:** slow to medium **Form & Habit:** spreading weeping branches **Bloom Period:** spring **Flowers:** clusters of deep pink buds open to pale pink persistent double flowers **Fruits:** small black fruits **Foliage:** pale green, changing to bright gold in fall **Soil & pH:** well-drained sandy loam; pH 6.0 to 7.5 **Light & Moisture:** full sun; medium to dry soil **Pruning Seasons:** right after flowering

Weeping Higan cherry
(*Prunus subhirtella* 'Pendula Plena Rosea')

Callery Pear
also called "Flowering Pear"

Pyrus calleryana

Bradford pear
(*Pyrus calleryana* 'Bradford')

Bradford pear (*Pyrus calleryana* 'Bradford')

The flowering pears are the ornamental varieties bred for improved flowers: the dwarfed fruits are useful only to birds. Pear trees grown for their fruit belong to the species *Pyrus communis.*

Most ornamental pears are cultivars of the callery pear (*Pyrus calleryana*); the best known of the cultivars is the Bradford pear (*P.* x 'Bradford'). Large for a flowering fruit tree, this cultivar in early to mid-spring covers itself with showy clusters of small white blossoms. The glossy dense foliage turns an attractive wine red in fall and persists into November. The small fruits are russet. Tolerant of urban conditions and resistant to the fireblight that plagues pears, the Bradford pear was once planted extensively as a street tree and park specimen. However, the Bradford pear has an enormous genetic flaw. Unless pruned aggressively when young to remove many of its closely grouped branches along a relatively short length of trunk, the excessive weight of branches in the wind or under heavy snow can split the tree. Some Bradfords can reach maturity without splitting, but the close branching of most Bradfords leaves them more likely to self-destruct before completing their second decade.

Several new cultivars avoid this problem. 'Capital', a 32-foot

These photos compare the unfortunate, and usually fatal, close branching of the Bradford pear, at left, and the more open structure of the Redspire cultivar, at right.

United States National Arboretum introduction, has a columnar form suited to narrow sites. The leaves turn a coppery color in fall and last through the season. It thrives in Zones 5–6, but farther south fireblight can become a problem. Other improved callery pear cultivars are 'Cleveland Select', 'Redspire', and the narrow 'Whitehouse'.

The callery pear is large for a small city garden but perfect for the average suburban landscape. Enlist the help of a local nursery in finding a plant that is disease resistant in your area.

The lovely Ussurian pear (*P. ussuriensis*) is the hardiest of the *Pyrus* species and the least susceptible to fireblight. Hardy in Zones 3 or 4–6, it is a spreading tree 30 to 40 feet tall that bears pink-tinged flower buds opening to white, followed by fruits 1 to 1½ inches in diameter. The fruits are faintly sweet but messy.

Culture: in early spring transplant a container-grown or balled-and-burlapped pear to well-drained loamy soil. Pears bloom in full sun or partial shade; they tolerate drought and adapt to pH.

Callery pear (*Pyrus calleryana* 'Autumn Blaze') fruit

Bradford pear (*Pyrus calleryana* 'Bradford') in spring and fall (inset)

Callery pear (*Pyrus calleryana* 'Capital')

FEATURED PROFILE
Callery, or Flowering, Pear

Botanical Name: *Pyrus calleryana* 'Redspire' **Family:** Rosaceae **Type of Plant:** midsize deciduous flowering tree **Uses:** showy spring flowers; fall color; street tree; lawn specimen **Genus Range:** China **Hardiness:** USDA Zones 4 or 5–8 **Height:** 30 to 35' **Growth Rate:** medium **Form & Habit:** narrow, pyramidal **Bloom Period:** early spring **Flowers:** large clusters of white flowers **Foliage:** green, then crimson and purple in fall **Soil & pH:** well-drained; pH 5.0 to 6.5 **Light & Moisture:** full sun or dappled shade; medium moisture **Pruning Seasons:** after flowering

Callery pear
(*Pyrus calleryana* 'Redspire')

The Oaks

Quercus

The oaks are magnificent long-lived spreading shade trees native to temperate regions where they are important sources of hardwood. Symmetrical and beautiful in youth, massive and grand as they mature, the ornamental species are among the most popular of all landscaping trees. Most grow to be over 50 feet tall. The nutty fruit of the oak is the hard-shelled acorn, a favorite food for wildlife. The majority of ornamental oaks are native to North America. They may have originated in Mexico, where they are evergreen; species in the South tend to be evergreen. Northern species are deciduous, and the fall foliage can be brilliant.

White oak (*Quercus alba*)

Swamp white oak (*Quercus bicolor*) fruit (acorn)

The most widely planted oak is the 60- to 70-foot beautiful deciduous red oak (*Quercus rubra*), because it transplants easily and grows fast. It is native to northeastern and central North America and is hardy well beyond those boundaries, through Zones 3 or 4–7. The young foliage is a bronze red, and in fall the leaves often turn stunning shades of scarlet-maroon.

The graceful pin, or swamp, oak (*Q. palustris*) has lower branches that reach down to the earth. It needs plenty of space to accommodate its wide-spreading middle and lower branches, and it quickly reaches 75 feet. The finely cut foliage turns brilliant red in autumn. Hardy in Zones 4–8 or 9, it makes an excellent specimen in large landscapes where the ground is moist and somewhat acid. It is native to the central and mideastern United States For wet spots farther south, the 80-foot Shumard oak (*Q. shumardii*) makes a good alternative. Hardy in Zones 5–8, it often turns a spectacular red-orange in fall.

For urban landscapes in the Southeast, Zones 5–10, try pollution-tolerant willow oak (*Q. phellos*). Unlike most oaks, it has willowlike leaves that in fall turn yellow and then russet. Fast growing, it can ascend 2 feet per year to reach up to 70 feet in cultivation, and it tolerates even poorly drained clay soil.

The live oak (*Q. virginiana*), a Southern favorite, also has willowlike leaves. A massive, long-lived tree 50 to 80 feet tall, it develops huge, wide-spreading horizontal branches and drops its foliage only in spring, before new growth begins. The live oak is at the top of its northern range in Zone 7 and is most impressive in Louisiana and southward. Its warm-weather counterpart in the hills and valleys of coastal California is the 50- to 70-foot native California live oak (*Q. agrifolia*), hardy in Zones 8–9. It has hollylike evergreen leaves and a picturesque spreading form.

The majestic white oak (*Q. alba*) is native to the eastern United States in Zones 3–8. It reaches 150 feet in the

Bur oak
(*Quercus macrocarpa*)

White oak
(*Quercus alba*) in fall

Pin oak (*Quercus palustris*), left, and scarlet oak
(*Quercus coccinea*), right, in fall

Sawtooth oak
(*Quercus acutissima*)

Live oak (*Quercus virginiana*)

wild but only about 70 feet in cultivation. The wide-spreading branches resist splitting, creating an eye-catching silhouette. The foliage tends toward blue-green in summer; in fall it ranges from brown to wine red and remains on the tree most of the winter. Because of production difficulties the white oak is offered by only a few nurseries that specialize in native plants.

The 70- to 80-foot tall bur, or mossycup, oak (*Q. macrocarpa*), looks magnificent growing in open fields and parks in the Midwest. Hardy in Zones 3–8, it's a picturesque shade tree with corky branches. It is hard to transplant, but once established it tolerates urban conditions and adapts to soil, thriving in dry or wet alkaline soil. In cold, wet sites in Zones 3–8, the 50- to 60-foot swamp white oak (*Q. bicolor*) naturalizes well. A timber tree native to eastern and central North America, it is characterized by flaking bark.

One of the few oaks that remain lower than 50 feet, the 35- to 40-foot sawtooth oak (*Q. acutissima*) is a good choice for a smaller property in Zones 5–8. It's fast growing, with narrow glossy serrated leaves that appear early in spring. In late fall the leaves turn yellow to rich brown and persist into winter.

The legendary English oak (*Q. robur*) is 40 to 60 feet tall and wide with an open broad head and a short mas-

sive trunk. It is hardy as far north as Zone 5 and probably 4. This oak has poor fall color, and its young foliage can poison cattle. A columnar form of the English oak, the 60-foot 'Fastigiata', is excellent where a vertical plant is needed.

Culture: transplant a young dormant container-grown or balled-and-burlapped oak to well-drained slightly acid soil, handling the rootball with care. Oaks adapt to various soils and do best in full sun.

FEATURED PROFILE
Red Oak

Botanical Name: *Quercus rubra* **Family:** Fagaceae **Type of Plant:** large deciduous shade tree **Uses:** for lawns, large landscapes, and street use **Native Range:** Nova Scotia to PA, W. to MN and IA **Hardiness:** USDA Zones 3 or 4–7 **Height:** 60 to 70' **Growth Rate:** fast **Form & Habit:** rounded **Fruits:** acorns **Foliage:** bronze-red; then scarlet and maroon **Soil & pH:** well-drained; slightly acid; avoid high pH **Light & Moisture:** full sun; medium-dry soil **Pruning Seasons:** during dormancy

Red oak (*Quercus rubra*) in fall

The Willows

Salix

Babylon weeping willow
(*Salix babylonica*)

The willows are moisture-loving trees and shrubs with flexible whiplike branches and long lance-shaped leaves. Fast growing, the willows are planted along stream banks to hold the soil and in suburban yards to create airy screening. But besides their graceful forms and useful affinity for water, willows provide seasonal interest. They leaf out early in spring, and in fall the foliage of many species turns to shimmering gold.

The trees called weeping willows epitomize the grace of pendulous plants, especially when reflected in the water of a pond or lake with wind sweeping through the branches. Weeping willows bear male or female flowers, in some cases while the plant is in leaf. Some shrubby male willows present elongated clusters, or catkins, called "pussy willows." The native pussy willow (*Salix discolor*), which grows wild from Newfoundland to British Columbia and south through Zone 8, bears attractive flower buds early in the season. The pussy willow sold in florist's shops is the goat willow (*S. caprea*). It bears velvety silvery gray catkins and is hardy in Zones 4–8.

Native pussy willow
(*Salix discolor*)

The beautiful Babylon weeping willow (*Salix babylonica*) grows 30 to 40 feet and has reddish brown branches that sweep the ground. The Swedish botanist Linnaeus, who named it in the eighteenth century, thought it originated in Babylon, but later research showed it was native to China, having reached the Middle East along caravan routes. It is hardy in Zones 6–8.

North of Zone 6, the best weeping willows to plant are the 50- to 70-foot *S. alba* 'Tristis', also known as 'Chrysocoma' (*S.* x *sepulcralis*), and the golden willow (*S. alba* variety *vitellina*), with showy bright yellow-orange twigs in winter. The twigs of the cultivar 'Britzensis' are a gorgeous dark orange. In early spring these trees are enveloped in a golden haze. *S. alba* variety *sericea* has leaves that are silvery on the undersides; they flicker airily when swept by a breeze. These willows are hardy in Zones 4–9.

Culture: the willows root easily in spring, even in dryish soil, but to flourish they need sustained moisture. They are best planted well away from water pipes, which they invade. They are most beautiful growing in full sun but tolerate partial shade and a wide range of soils, from pH 5.5 to 7.5. Research has shown that nematode damage is responsible for the inadequate root system that often causes willows to topple in a storm: look for introductions of long-lived willows in coming years.

Golden weeping willow (*Salix alba* 'Tristis') in fall

FEATURED PROFILE
Golden Weeping Willow

Botanical Name: *Salix alba* 'Tristis' **Family:** Salicaceae **Type of Plant:** graceful weeping deciduous tree **Uses:** in or near any wet site; lawn specimen **Genus Range:** S. Europe, central Asia, China **Hardiness:** USDA Zones 4–9 **Height:** 50 to 70' **Growth Rate:** fast
Form & Habit: rounded crown; branches sweep the ground **Bloom Period:** early spring
Flowers: golden catkins **Fruits:** capsule **Foliage:** lustrous green turning to gold in fall
Soil & pH: well-drained; pH 5.5 to 7.5 **Light & Moisture:** full sun or dappled shade; sustained moisture **Pruning Seasons:** summer or fall

The Sophoras

Sophora (also called *Styphnolobium*)

The two sophoras pictured here are both prized, trouble-free trees with lovely pealike flowers. The larger of the two, and the later to bloom, is the beautiful Japanese pagoda tree (*Sophora japonica*, now also known as *Styphnolobium japonicum*).

For several weeks in July or August, the pagoda tree is covered with showy, foot-long upright panicles of creamy white fragrant pealike flowers. The fruit develops in October in drooping clusters of yellow-green winged seedpods that look like showers of chartreuse beads and are as attractive as the flowers. The species begins to bloom at 10 to 25 years of age, but the cultivar 'Regent', a glossy-leaved, gray-barked introduction, blooms at 6 to 8 years. Hardy in Zone 4, it rapidly reaches 40 to 50 feet and develops a large spreading oval crown that provides good shade. Its tolerance of drought, heat, and city conditions makes the pagoda a popular tree for city parks. For landscapes that are small, the narrow cultivar 'Princeton Upright' is a better choice. A weeping form, 'Pendula', seldom flowers but is attractive nonetheless.

The native Southwestern evergreen species is known as the mescal bean, or Texas mountain laurel (*S. secundiflora*). In dry areas of Zone 8 it makes a good ornamental

Mescal bean
(*Sophora secundiflora*)

Japanese pagoda tree (*Sophora japonica*)

small tree or tall shrub 25 to 35 feet tall. As new leaves appear in March and April, it bears fragrant grape-scented violet-blue flowers. The fruit is a dry seedpod 1 to 7 inches long. Its red seeds contain poisonous alkaloids with narcotic properties.

Culture: plant a young dormant container-grown or balled-and-burlapped Japanese pagoda or mescal bean tree in midspring. Both do best in full sun but tolerate partial shade. They prefer well-drained loamy soil but succeed in a wide range of soil conditions.

FEATURED PROFILE
Weeping Japanese Pagoda, or Chinese Scholar Tree

Botanical Name: *Sophora japonica* 'Pendula' **Family:** Leguminosae **Type of Plant:** deciduous shade tree **Uses:** accent plant; beautiful fruit in fall **Genus Range:** China, Korea **Hardiness:** USDA Zones 4–7 or 8 **Height:** 40 to 50' **Growth Rate:** fast **Form & Habit:** upright, wide-spreading, broadly rounded crown **Bloom Period:** several weeks in July and August **Flowers:** slightly scented ½" creamy yellow to greenish white pealike flowers in broad terminal panicles to 12" long **Fruits:** yellow-green winged seedpods 2 to 4" long that look like strings of beads **Foliage:** medium to dark green 6 to 10" long branchlets, composed of 7 to 17 leaflets 1 to 2" long **Soil & pH:** well-drained; pH adaptable **Light & Moisture:** full sun or dappled shade; sustained moisture **Pruning Seasons:** fall

Weeping Japanese pagoda tree (*Sophora japonica* 'Pendula')

The Mountain Ashes

Sorbus

European mountain ash (*Sorbus aucuparia*)

Mountain ash foliage is bright green in spring, glossy dark green in summer, and yellow, orange, red, and luminous brown in fall—a perfect foil for the bright red-to-orange fruits that are the tree's crowning glory. The berries are also eaten by wildlife when other foods are scarce. However, the mountain ash is a member of the rose family, susceptible to borers, fireblight, and other problems, especially when stressed, as in polluted areas.

Ashes do best naturalized in open ground, on a slope or ridge. Before buying, ask a responsible local nursery to recommend a cultivar that resists these problems.

In Zones 3–6 of the Northeast, the mountain ash least susceptible to borers is *Sorbus alnifolia,* a 40- to 50-foot Korean species. In May it bears masses of flat white flower clusters. The scarlet-orange fruits are ¼ to ⅜ inch in diameter. This species has simple rather than the compound leaves more typical of the genus. The smooth dark gray bark, rather like that of the European beech, provides a lovely color accent in winter.

In frigid Zone 2 the European species *S. aucuparia* is the hardiest mountain ash. Known as the rowan tree, the 45-foot tree was introduced to North America in Colonial times in the belief that it warded off evil spirits. It has naturalized in the North and spread all the way to Alaska. The fruits are bright red; the foliage is colorful in fall. But because the plant is susceptible to fireblight where summers are hot, it is recommended only for cold climates in and north of Zone 6.

Culture: transplant a young container-grown or balled-and-burlapped tree in early spring to well-drained loamy soil in full sun. It can stand wet conditions for a time but does not do well in urban settings. Almost all species do best in somewhat alkaline soil but tolerate pH 5.0 to 7.0.

European mountain ash (*Sorbus aucuparia*)

FEATURED PROFILE
Golden Weeping Willow

Botanical Name: *Salix alba* 'Tristis' **Family:** Salicaceae **Type of Plant:** graceful weeping deciduous tree **Uses:** in or near any wet site; lawn specimen **Genus Range:** S. Europe, central Asia, China **Hardiness:** USDA Zones 4–9 **Height:** 50 to 70' **Growth Rate:** fast **Form & Habit:** rounded crown; branches sweep the ground **Bloom Period:** early spring **Flowers:** golden catkins **Fruits:** capsule **Foliage:** lustrous green turning to gold in fall **Soil & pH:** well-drained; pH 5.5 to 7.5 **Light & Moisture:** full sun or dappled shade; sustained moisture **Pruning Seasons:** summer or fall

Korean mountain ash (*Sorbus alnifolia*) in fall

The Stewartias

Stewartia

The stewartias are small trees and tall shrubs that bear camellialike flowers in late summer when little else blooms. A few shrubby species are native to warm regions of the United States, but the ornamentals are Asian imports with foliage that turns vivid orange and orange-red in fall. Smooth bark that sheds in patterns of gray, orange, and brownish red adds to their winter appeal. The stewartias grow into lovely lawn specimens and have only one drawback: they can be difficult to transplant.

The Japanese stewartia (*Stewartia pseudocamellia*) has the most colorful bark but also the smallest flowers of the group. It is a beautiful small to midsize tree 30 to 40 feet tall with flowers that resemble camellias. The 2½-inch white cup-shaped blooms have a mass of orange anthers at the center and open in July. The leaves emerge purple-bronze. In summer they turn green; with cold weather, the leaves turn yellow, purple-orange, and bronze-red. As the branches reach 2 to 3 inches thick, the bark sheds in striking patterns of cinnamon, red-gray, and orange. The plant is hardy to Zones 4 or 5–7.

Better suited to a small garden—and to summer heat—is the 20- to 30-foot Korean stewartia (*S. koreana*), which thrives in Zones 5–7. The flowers are larger and flatter than those of the Japanese stewartia, and they have a wavy margin. The leaves turn red and purple in fall, and the bark flakes to show soft silvery patches streaked with cinnamon and orange-brown.

Culture: transplant a dormant young container-grown stewartia in early spring to well-drained, moist, humusy soil that is acid, pH 4.5 to 5.5. Once planted, the trees do not like to be moved. Stewartias will succeed in full sun but tolerate some shade at the southern end of their hardiness zones. They require sustained moisture, especially the first year or two after transplanting.

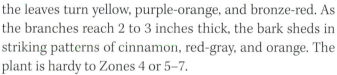

Korean stewartia
(*Stewartia koreana*)

Korean stewartia
(*Stewartia koreana*) in fall

Japanese stewartia (*Stewartia pseudocamellia*) in July

FEATURED PROFILE

Weeping Japanese Pagoda, or Chinese Scholar, Tree

Botanical Name: *Sophora japonica* 'Pendula' **Family:** Leguminosae **Type of Plant:** deciduous shade tree **Uses:** accent plant; beautiful fruit in fall **Genus Range:** China, Korea **Hardiness:** USDA Zones 4–7 or 8 **Height:** 40 to 50' **Growth Rate:** fast **Form & Habit:** upright, wide-spreading, broadly rounded crown **Bloom Period:** several weeks in July and August **Flowers:** slightly scented ½" creamy yellow to greenish white pealike flowers in broad terminal panicles to 12" long **Fruits:** yellow-green winged seedpods 2 to 4" long that look like strings of beads **Foliage:** medium to dark green 6 to 10" long branchlets, composed of 7 to 17 leaflets 1 to 2" long **Soil & pH:** well-drained; pH adaptable **Light & Moisture:** full sun or dappled shade; sustained moisture **Pruning Seasons:** fall

Japanese stewartia (*Stewartia pseudocamellia*)

The Snowbells

Styrax

Both of these ornamental snowbells from Japan produce lovely flowers in late spring after most other flowering trees have gone by. In June, the leafy horizontal branches of the Japanese snowbell (*Styrax japonicum*) are hung with clusters of slightly scented, drooping, yellow-centered bell-shaped white flowers. As the flowers mature, the petals arch backward, revealing the colorful centers. The tree in full bloom is breathtaking. The flowers are followed by ½-inch gray or greenish white egg-shaped fruits. The glossy summer leaves are rich green; in fall they turn yellowish or red. This little tree or tall shrub for Zones 5–8 reaches 20 to 30 feet at maturity and develops a wide-spreading crown that casts light shade. Its smooth gray-brown bark and curious structure lend interest to the winter landscape. The Japanese snowbell looks lovely in partial shade as a patio or shrub border. There are weeping cultivars, such as the 12-foot 'Pendula', and

pink varieties, such as 'Pink Chimes', with clear pink flowers.

Fragrant snowbell (*S. obassia*) flowers are much more fragrant than those of the Japanese snowbell. But this tree is not as popular as the Japanese snowbell, because its flowers are partly hidden by leaves, which do not color in fall. It blooms earlier than the Japanese snowbell, shortly after the dogwoods.

Japanese snowbell (*Styrax japonicum*)

Culture: set out a young container-grown or balled-and-burlapped plant in early spring, and provide winter protection from sweeping winds for the first few years. The Japanese snowbells do best in moist, well-drained, somewhat acid soil rich in organic matter, but also tolerate clay. They bloom most fully in a sunny site but tolerate some shade.

Fragrant snowbell
(*Styrax obassia*)

FEATURED PROFILE
Japanese Snowbell

Botanical Name: *Styrax japonicum* **Family:** Styracaceae **Type of Plant:** small deciduous flowering tree **Uses:** lovely summer flowers; light shade; lawn specimen; shrub border **Native Range:** China, Japan **Hardiness:** USDA Zones 5 or 6–8 **Height:** 20 to 30' **Growth Rate:** slow to medium **Form & Habit:** wide-branching broad crown **Bloom Period:** late spring **Flowers:** clusters of bell-shaped, drooping, slightly fragrant yellow-centered white flowers **Fruits:** small oval drupe **Foliage:** glossy rich green, rarely turning yellow and red in fall **Soil & pH:** well-drained, humusy, somewhat acid soil **Light & Moisture:** full sun or dappled shade; sustained moisture **Pruning Seasons:** winter

Japanese snowbell (*Styrax japonicum*)

The Arborvitaes

Thuja

American arborvitae (*Thuja occidentalis* 'Emerald')

The arborvitae is one of the most beautiful of the small to midsize evergreens. Typically symmetrical, dense, and pyramidal in form, it has graceful frondlike foliage that is aromatic when crushed. This slow-growing, long-lived plant withstands repeated shearing. Arborvitaes make good vertical accent plants as backdrops for deciduous trees and flowering shrubs. They can reach 40 to 60 feet but more often stop at 12 to 15 feet. They can be grown as trees or shrubs, and dwarf forms are available. Choose established cultivars known to maintain good winter color.

In Zones 2–7 or 8, the columnar American arborvitae (*Thuja occidentalis*) can reach 40 to 60 feet but more often stays below 25 feet. It tolerates limestone soils, unusual for an arborvitae; it's most often found in moist, eastern wild woods. The 10- to 15-foot 'Emerald' holds its brilliant color in winter and has considerable heat tolerance, as does 15-foot 'Techny'.

The 18- to 25-foot Oriental arborvitae (*T. orientalis*, now known as *Platycladus orientalis*) is widely planted on the West Coast and in the Southeast and Southwest in Zones 6–9. It is a small tree with foliage arranged in vertical planes with the edges facing out. When young, the leaves are grass green; they mature to a darker green. Among the numerous cultivars that are available you will find 'Baker', with its bright green foliage and a tolerance for dry areas; 8-foot 'Blue Cone', a pyramidal green tree with a blue cast; and 'Fruitlandii', which has deep green foliage and an upright conical form.

The cinnamon-color barked Western, or giant, arborvitae (*T. plicata*), Zones 5–7, has beautiful foliage that resists turning brown in cold northern winters. A fast-growing tree found from northern California to Alaska, it can reach 200 feet in the wild but rarely tops 30 to 50 feet in the garden. It thrives in wet places and where the air is moist but doesn't tolerate salt spray. Several cultivars have good yellow color, among them 'Zebrina', and 'Stoneham Gold'.

Culture: container-grown and balled-and-burlapped plants transplant easily in early spring and fall. Most arborvitae do best in fertile, moist but well-drained, somewhat acid soil and full sun. They can adapt to some shade but will then lose the dense texture that is their greatest asset.

Western, or giant, arborvitae (*Thuja plicata*)

FEATURED PROFILE
American Arborvtae

Botanical Name: *Thuja occidentalis* 'Emerald' **Family:** Cupressaceae
Type of Plant: midsize evergreen conifer **Uses:** windbreaks; screening; hedges; formal landscape specimen **Genus Range:** eastern U.S.
Hardiness: USDA Zones 2 or 3–7 or 8 **Height:** 10 to 15' **Growth Rate:** slow **Form & Habit:** narrow, densely branched pyramid **Flowers:** inconspicuous **Fruits:** light brown cones **Foliage:** rich emerald green year-round **Soil & pH:** well-drained, fertile, somewhat acid soil but tolerates limestone soil **Light & Moisture:** full sun; sustained moisture
Pruning Seasons: before spring growth

American arborvitae (*Thuja occidentalis* 'Emerald')

The Lindens
also called "Basswoods"
Tilia

Littleleaf linden (*Tilia cordata*)

Slow-growing, massive, easy to maintain, and tolerant of urban environments, the lindens make excellent shade trees in towns and cities. In late spring or early summer, clusters of inconspicuous cream-color flowers appear. In some linden species, the flowers yield an oil used in perfumery; bees produce a superb honey from the flower nectar. Pea-size tan-gray nutlets follow the flowers and are messy. The heart-shaped leaves turn a beautiful golden yellow in autumn; as the trees mature, the smooth light gray bark becomes interestingly furrowed. In the lumber industry, the lindens are known as "basswood." Native species are widely distributed, but they are absent from western North America.

Littleleaf linden (*Tilia cordata*)

The littleleaf linden (*Tilia cordata*), often featured in formal European landscapes, is used as a street and park tree in Zones 3–7. A slow-growing 60- to 70-foot European tree with dainty leaves and fragrant flowers, the species tolerates urban pollution. 'Greenspire', a popular cultivar, succeeds as far south as Zone 8. It grows somewhat faster than the species, and its straight trunk is well suited to avenues and allées.

Perhaps the most beautiful is the Crimean, or Caucasian lime, linden (*T.* x *euchlora*), hardy in Zones 3–7. Less massive than the littleleaf linden, the Crimean is a good size for residential landscaping. Fragrant flowers appear in July. The leaves are a glossy dark green; the branches sweep the ground.

The most colorful is the 40- to 60-foot silver linden (*T. tomentosa*), native to Europe and western Asia, and hardy in Zones 4–7. The leaves, dark green on top with silvery backs, look exquisite ruffled by a breeze. This linden grows medium fast and makes a handsome windbreak or tall screen. The smooth, light gray bark resembles that of the beech. The cultivar 'Sterling Silver' has fine foliage and tends to resist Japanese beetles and gypsy moths. It also tolerates heat and drought.

Culture: container-grown or balled-and-burlapped lindens transplant easily in early spring to fertile, well-drained, moist soil, pH 5.0 to 7.0. They require full sun.

Silver linden (*Tilia tomentosa*)

FEATURED PROFILE
Silver Linden, or Silver Lime

Botanical Name: *Tilia tomentosa* **Family:** Tiliaceae **Type of Plant:** tall deciduous shade tree with inconspicuous scented flowers in spring **Uses:** urban lawn specimen, street tree **Native Range:** S.E. Europe, W. Asia **Hardiness:** USDA Zones 4–7 **Height:** 40 to 60' **Growth Rate:** medium **Form & Habit:** pyramidal; then upright and oval **Bloom Period:** June, early July **Flowers:** sweetly fragrant, yellowish white **Fruits:** egg-shaped **Foliage:** heart-shaped and lustrous dark green with silvery backs **Soil & pH:** fertile; well-drained; adaptable, pH 5.0 to 7.0 **Light & Moisture:** full sun; sustained moisture **Pruning Seasons:** late winter

The Hemlocks

Tsuga

Native to both coasts of North America, where there is abundant water year-round, hemlocks are among the most graceful of the narrow-leaved evergreens for the home landscape. The species with the greatest diversity of forms is the Canadian hemlock (*Tsuga canadensis*). Easy to transplant and tolerant of shearing, the Canadian hemlock's natural form is a graceful pyramid with slightly drooping branches. The short, dark green, flat, aromatic needles have two white bands on the undersides. The needles persist for up to eight years, so the tree is always full. The fruits are pretty little coppery brown cones ½ to 1 inch long. The cinnamon-brown bark becomes in time attractively ridged and furrowed. Birds like to nest in hemlocks.

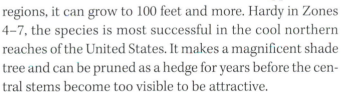

Carolina hemlock
(*Tsuga caroliniana*)

Slow-growing and long-lived, this species reaches 40 to 70 feet in cultivation; in the wild in its native midwestern, northeastern, and Appalachian regions, it can grow to 100 feet and more. Hardy in Zones 4–7, the species is most successful in the cool northern reaches of the United States. It makes a magnificent shade tree and can be pruned as a hedge for years before the central stems become too visible to be attractive.

There are a few smaller forms. Use the cultivar 'Monler' for low hedges and screening. It grows into a dense column 6 to 10 feet tall and 2 feet wide. 'Pendula', the weeping Canadian hemlock, is a dark green prostrate form that takes decades to grow to 5 feet tall. This tree thrives in shade and looks attractive spilling over a rocky formation.

Canadian hemlock
(*Tsuga canadensis* 'Pendula')
weeping form

The 45- to 65-foot Carolina hemlock (*T. caroliniana*) is considered a better choice in the South and in urban environments. Native from southwestern Virginia to northern Georgia, it's also a good shore tree.

Culture: shallow-rooted, hemlock transplants easily in early spring or fall. It thrives in well-drained humusy soil, pH 5.0 to 6.5. In warm regions, hemlock does best in partial shade; in the North it succeeds in full sun. Light pruning of new growth is acceptable after the main growth spurt and throughout the growing season but not after the plant becomes dormant. Hemlocks on the East Coast are dying from infestations of the wooly adelgid. As a preventative, apply dormant oil in late winter and insecticidal soaps in June and October.

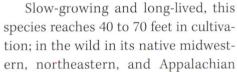

Canadian hemlock
(*Tsuga canadensis*)
fruits (cones)

Canadian hemlock (*Tsuga canadensis*)

FEATURED PROFILE
Canadian, or Eastern, Hemlock

Botanical Name: *Tsuga canadensis* **Family:** Pinaceae **Type of Plant:** tall aromatic evergreen conifer **Uses:** shade; lawn specimen; tall screen; sheared hedge **Native Range:** Nova Scotia to MN; AL; GA **Hardiness:** USDA Zones 3–7 **Height:** 40 to 70' in cultivation; may exceed 100' in the wild **Growth Rate:** fast **Form & Habit:** pyramidal tree; pendulous when mature **Flowers:** inconspicuous, male and female on same tree **Fruits:** cones ½ to 1"; male cone is yellowish; female is green and leathery **Foliage:** aromatic needles ¼ to ⅔" long; lustrous dark green on top; two whitish bands on the undersides; new growth light yellow-green changing to dark green **Soil & pH:** well-drained; pH 5.0 to 6.5 **Light & Moisture:** partial shade or full sun; sustained moisture **Pruning Seasons:** after main spurt of growth

Chinese Elm
also called "Lacebark Elm"

Ulmus parvifolia

Chinese elm (*Ulmus parvifolia*)

Chinese elm (*Ulmus parvifolia*)

The tall, stately American elm (*Ulmus americana*) once dominated street plantings and the countryside but has been all but wiped out by Dutch elm disease introduced from Europe in 1930. The disease-resistant 40- to 50-foot Chinese, or lacebark, elm (*U. parvifolia*) makes an excellent substitute. The cultivar 'Allee' ('Emer 11') is one of several introductions with a structure that closely resembles that of the American elm. It grows fast to 50 feet and has a beautiful round-top habit. The leaves are dark green, and the trunk and branches have attractive gray-orange bark that exfoliates in lacy patches. Adaptable to many types of soils and climates, it succeeds from the Atlantic to the Pacific coasts, Zones 4 or 5–9. Local nurseries may have other options.

Culture: the Chinese elm transplants easily in early fall or early spring and thrives in fertile, moist but well-drained soil. It adapts to extremes of pH and tolerates urban environments.

American elm (*Ulmus americana*)

Weeping Chinese elm (*Ulmus parvifolia* 'Sempervirens')

FEATURED PROFILE
Chinese, or Lacebark, Elm

Botanical Name: *Ulmus parvifolia* **Family:** Ulmaceae **Type of Plant:** tall deciduous shade tree **Uses:** street or specimen tree; shade; winter interest **Native Range:** northern and central China, Korea, and Japan **Hardiness:** USDA Zones 5–9 **Height:** 40 to 50' in cultivation **Growth Rate:** medium to fast **Form & Habit:** vase-shaped; round-headed with arching branches at maturity **Bloom Period:** August–September **Flowers:** inconspicuous clusters **Fruits:** ⅓" samaras that ripen September–October **Foliage:** elliptical, ¾ to 2½" long; in summer lustrous dark green; yellowish or reddish purple in fall **Soil & pH:** adapts to soil and pH **Light & Moisture:** sun or shade; averse to excessively wet soil **Pruning Seasons:** late fall or early winter

Chinese elm (*Ulmus parvifolia*)

Japanese Zelkova
also called "Saw Leaf Zelkova"

Zelkova serrata

Japanese zelkova
(*Zelkova serrata*)

The zelkovas are Asian trees that resemble elms and thrive under conditions that elms also prefer. The Japanese zelkova (*Zelkova serrata*) is a tall majestic shade tree with interesting bark and elmlike foliage and structure. A mature Japanese zelkova is a magnificent tree. The cultivar 'Village Green' is one of several that are highly resistant to pests and to the dreaded Dutch elm disease. This cultivar has a straight trunk and a vaselike shape. It grows quickly—about 2 to 3 feet a year—to a height of 50 to 80 feet, with an equivalent spread. It has large dark green leaves that resemble those of the elm and turn yellow-brown or rusty red in the fall. The bark is brown and smooth, and with age it becomes gray and exfoliates, revealing the cinnamon brown interior. Zelkova tolerates some urban pollution.

Japanese zelkova
(*Zelkova serrata* 'Village Green') in fall

Japanese zelkova (*Zelkova serrata*)

Culture: zelkova transplants easily in early spring and in the fall before Indian summer. Protection from winter winds and cold is highly recommended until the plant is well established. It thrives in deeply worked soil that is moist but well-drained. Zelkova tolerates drought and is adaptable to varied pH; it does best in full sun or light shade.

FEATURED PROFILE
Japanese, or Saw Leaf, Zelkova

Botanical Name: *Zelkova serrata* **Family:** Ulmaceae **Type of Plant:** tall deciduous shade tree, massive at maturity **Uses:** street tree; landscape specimen; fall color **Native Range:** Japan, Korea **Hardiness:** USDA Zones 3 or 4–9 **Height:** 50 to 80' **Growth Rate:** medium to fast in youth **Form & Habit:** low-branched and vase-shaped **Bloom Period:** April, with the leaves **Flowers:** insignificant **Fruits:** $\frac{1}{8}$" drupe in fall **Foliage:** pointed oval 2 to 5" long; serrated; in summer dark green; in fall yellow-brown to rust red **Soil & pH:** well-drained, deeply worked loam; pH adaptable **Light & Moisture:** full sun or light shade; sustained moisture; tolerates drought when established **Pruning Seasons:** fall

Japanese zelkova
(*Zelkova serrata* 'Green Vase')

PART 3

All about Shrubs

This section will help you choose shrubs to complement the trees, hedges, and other elements of your home landscape. You will find many options wherever you live. The ones listed here belong to 44 major shrub groups called "genera" (plural for "genus").

You'll find shrub genera listed alphabetically by scientific name. So if you know the genus name, you can simply turn to it alphabetically. But if you don't know the scientific name for mountain laurel, which is *Kalmia*, you can find the mountain laurel page by checking the Table of Contents or the Index. In addition, many common names are listed on page 155, where you'll also find shrubs that can be trained as hedges.

Main Facts and Key Details

It's easy to tell the difference between trees and shrubs. The difference rests primarily in their growth habits. Shrubs have many stems and often have branches that are leafy nearly to the ground. Trees have either one trunk with lateral branches extending out from it, or one or several trunks bare of limbs for some distance above the ground, and topped by a leafy crown.

Shrub Basics

Trees tend to be taller than shrubs, although a large shrub can be taller than a small tree. For example, an upright Japanese maple, profiled in this section of the book, may reach 25 feet tall, while a miniature crape myrtle, profiled in "All about Trees," may grow no more than 3 feet tall. Many other genera of woody plants—for example, dogwoods, hollies, and junipers—have both tree and shrub species. But while some species of woody plants are always trees and others are always shrubs, many woody species can develop into either shrubs or small trees, depending on where and how they are grown. Some small trees take on a shrubby habit in parts of their range, and can be guided by pruning to develop either form.

With pruning, even some of the shrubbiest shrubs can be trained into treelike shapes called "standards" and have their lower branches removed in a process called "limbing up" to create a treelike form.

Shrubs, because of their smaller size and bushy shape, have a vital role in the garden, serving as the framework that connects the verticals of the trees and the horizontal lines of ground covers and flower borders and offering an immense variety of form, color, and texture. Enduring from year to year, shrubs provide interest in all seasons and usually need little maintenance. In a traditional herbaceous border, shrubs are the permanent backdrop for showy annuals and perennials. But a simple combination of shrubs and ground covers—a green garden—can be attractive and requires minimal upkeep.

Shrubs may be grouped according to their use in landscape design: the flowering shrubs, those grown for their foliage, and those that have interest in fall and winter. Each group includes both evergreen and deciduous plants, large and small, in many forms, as shown on the opposite page.

FLOWERING SHRUBS

The flowering shrubs are an important source of color all year. From the time the forsythias bloom golden in early spring, at least one of the flowering shrubs is in bloom through fall. Some flower all summer long. Small buttercuplike blooms cover the compact, nearly indestructible potentilla from June until frost. Pink spirea, yellow St. John's wort, and many hybrid roses bloom from summer into fall. Starting in midsummer, hydrangeas open big blue, pink, or cream pompoms, and the graceful sprays of the butterfly

Azaleas are popular in regions with acid soil. If your soil tends toward neutral, you'll need to add leaf mulches or apply sulfur to increase acidity.

bush are a magnet for butterflies from late summer to mid-fall. The sprays of white nandina florets become bright red fruits in late fall and winter.

Shrubs with fragrant flowers, including the mock oranges, the winter honeysuckle, and the fragrant viburnums, can perfume a whole garden. The fragrance of roses is usually more intimate, inviting you to press your nose into the velvety petals. Yet a few, such as the beautiful green-eyed white 'Madame Hardy' and David Austin's 'Graham Thomas', scent the air around them.

The flowering broad-leaved evergreen shrubs aren't as numerous, but they are beautiful in bloom, and their foliage is a great asset the rest of the year. Among the earliest evergreens to bloom, winter daphne bears fragrant flowers in February, and the foliage of the cultivar 'Aureo-marginata' is edged with gold. Spring-blooming mountain laurels, pieris, rhododendrons, and azaleas thrive in moist, acid, well-drained humusy soil. Clethra blooms in late summer and is fragrant. There are spring- and fall-blooming camellias bred for increasing cold hardiness. The fragrant flowers of late-blooming holly olive (page 224) still scent the air in November in the mid-Atlantic region and the Pacific Northwest.

Shrub Forms

Although the terms illustrated below are helpful in describing shrub forms, plants that qualify as shrubs in various growing or pruned conditions can look vastly different, as illustrated by the Japanese maple, left, and the multicolored group of Scotch heathers, above.

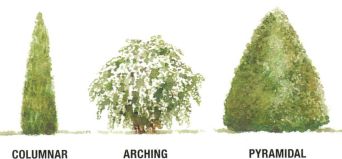

| COLUMNAR | ARCHING | PYRAMIDAL | ROUNDED | SPRAWLING, OR PROSTRATE |

FOLIAGE SHRUBS

As dazzling as the flowering shrubs are, ornamental foliage shrubs create a greater effect. Of these, the evergreens, especially the needle-leaved and scale-leaved conifers, contribute the most to the landscape, adding year-round color to the garden plan. Many are dwarf or slow-growing forms of coniferous trees. The rich green, hummocky mugo pine is a sturdy anchor for sunny corners. Columnar junipers and the showy dwarf blue spruce 'Fat Albert' add ever-present texture and color. The aroma of their foliage is a bonus.

The yellow, red, and purple foliage of some of the broad-leaved evergreens—among them yellow-speckled gold-dust tree (below right), purplish leucothoe, and red-tinged Oregon grape holly—also add year-round splashes of color. But their greens, like those of the conifers, are the mainstay of the garden. Boxwood, evergreen cotoneasters, and daphne have fine green foliage that softens a too-vivid color scheme.

Deciduous foliage shrubs excel at providing stunning fall color, in some cases matching even the brilliant sugar maple. Smoke trees and viburnums turn yellow, red, and purple when the weather cools. Perhaps the flashiest autumn foliage appears on the Japanese maples, many of which are red from early spring onward and in autumn rival the red maple's crimson. The leaves of some cultivars, such as beautiful 'Osakazuki', are yellow to light green in summer and turn a stunning fluorescent red in fall. You can also find season-long foliage color among cultivars of deciduous shrubs, such as barberry and Scotch heather. Shrubs with variegated foliage—winter daphne and weigela—lighten a mass of darker greens.

PLACING A SHRUB

Besides supplying the framework for the garden, shrubs can screen unwanted sights, define property boundaries, provide a backdrop for flower gardens, guide the eye, and set the overall tone of a garden. When allowed to assume their natural habit, shrubs can make essential contributions to naturalistic and informal gardens. Carefully pruned or neatly sheared into idealized or geometric shapes, shrubs add interest to formal designs. Shrubs can also be massed for screening or retaining soil on slopes, combined with other plants in mixed borders, or planted as focal points or specimen plants.

Plan for color and texture, as well as form, in your design, and keep in mind the changing scene through the seasons. The choices will seem nearly infinite. Your decisions should be based more on the shrubs' combinations

WINTER INTEREST

In the winter garden, the twiggy shapes and colorful stems of leafless shrubs can be an important presence. The bright red stems of the shrubby Tartarian and red-osier dogwoods and the yellow of yellow-stemmed dogwood are striking and decorative (pages 100–101). The leafless stems of others have distinctive shapes, perhaps none more fascinating than Harry Lauder's walking stick. (See page 102.)

Berries also add color to the winter scene. Red is supplied by viburnums, cotoneasters, and pyracantha. Species and cultivars of some of these shrubs have orange or yellow berries, as well as blue, white, or shiny black ones. If allowed to develop, the fruits of the rugosa rose and many other roses become red hips. All these shrubs provide birds with welcome meals throughout autumn and winter.

Protecting Plants. More plants are damaged or killed in winter than in any other season. They may freeze during a severe cold spell, suffer broken branches from snow and ice, or dry out from winter winds. You can gain protection from drying winds by wrapping evergreen shrubs with burlap, as shown, or by spraying them with antitranspirants.

You'd need a clogged paint sprayer to imitate the speckled variegation of the gold-dust tree, described on page 164.

with one another than with their relation to the perennials, annuals, vines, and bulbs. Because shrubs are such prominent and permanent fixtures, they deserve precedence over the smaller, more ephemeral plants. Certain foliage colors are particularly useful. Green adds weight and stability, while blue-green and gray tone down potentially clashing colors and are good foils for white, pink, purple, or blue. Yellow adds a splash of brightness to a dark corner, while maroon and purple almost vibrate next to acid green.

Shrubs are generally undemanding, provided you get them off to a good start and do not crowd them. Choose shrubs according to their expected height and spread, and give new ones room to grow; fill in the gaps around them with shade-tolerant annuals, such as impatiens and caladiums. It would be a waste of effort to place a wide-spreading shrub, such as a forsythia, in a tight space, where you would eventually need to hack it back and ruin its shape.

In selecting your shrubs, attend to their soil, moisture, and light requirements as well. Remember to account for the encroaching shade of growing trees, and select adaptable species to plant near them.

Pests and diseases usually cause the worst problems when a shrub is under stress. A susceptible shrub squeezed into an airless corner invites an infestation of whiteflies, which love hot, airless spots. A rose in a damp, shady place is much more susceptible to mildew and blackspot than a rose in sun. Rather than struggle with sprays and powders, select disease-resistant varieties, plant them where they grow best, and tend them well.

Once you have chosen the right plant for the right spot, examine the plant carefully before you buy. Like trees, shrubs are sold balled-and-burlapped, bare-root, or in containers. The sidebar below explains what to look for in selecting a container plant. For consumer guidance on root systems in general, see page 26.

Guidelines for Selecting Container Shrubs

Poor-quality plants have one or more of these problems:

- Bent, broken, or dried-out shoots
- Missing or discolored foliage
- Container only partially filled with soil; soil dry
- Container too small for plant
- One or more thick roots coiling near soil surface
- One or more thick roots emerging from drains

Healthy plants meet these tests:

- Plant size appropriate for container
- Small, if any, roots emerging from drain holes
- Soil within 1 inch of rim; soil moist
- Symmetrical, uniform shape with good foliage color and vigor

Planting Shrubs

Experts agree on the value of matching plants to the soil they prefer. But roots of a woody plant placed in a hole amended with organic materials tend to remain content there, as if in a container. Thus it's usually better to place new plants in soil typical of that location.

However, amending the soil does make sense when you plant a group of shrubs with similar, particular soil requirements or a bed of shrubs combined with perennials and smaller plants. For example, rhododendrons, azaleas, and other members of the heath family thrive in a raised bed of well-drained, humus-rich, moist acidic soil; many less-fussy shrubs will prosper in the amended soil you have prepared for your mixed border, as long as you allow plenty of room for their roots to grow. Follow the instructions on soil preparation and planting, beginning on page 27. For information on watering, see page 36; fertilizing is discussed on pages 44–47.

When planting a bare-root shrub, such as this rose, spread the roots over a cone of firm, undisturbed soil, first ensuring that the crown is a couple of inches above ground level. A stick or shovel laid over the hole helps gauge proper crown height. Because roses have thorns, heavy garden gloves are recommended.

Spacer

If the stems of a woody plant emerge from the ground too close together, use a spacer to widen the angles between them, to keep them from touching.

---

how to

Prepare a Container Shrub for Planting

DIFFICULTY LEVEL: EASY

1 **Remove the plant** from the container. If it doesn't come easily with a little squeezing of the container or by tapping its rim against a firm object, cut the container away with a knife or scissors.

2 **Lay the plant on its side,** and cut slits on the roots and soil. If the roots have grown too long in an undersized container, they may be potbound, evidenced by circular, tangled, large roots that need to be addressed as shown on page 34.

3 **Use your hands** to spread the cut sections and tease the roots apart, essentially directing root ends in the spreading configuration in which you want them to grow. Place the plant in a hole as illustrated on page 34.

SHRUBS FOR EVERY SEASON AND REASON

When planning your landscape, also consider trees that have exceptional qualities, seasonal interest, and perhaps optional uses, such as trained hedges. **Note:** the plants are alphabetized by scientific name.

FOR FLOWERS
Glossy Abelia
    (*Abelia* x *grandiflora*), 160
Butterfly Bush (*Buddleia*), 165
Camellia (*Camellia*), 167
Summersweet (*Clethra*), 171
Daphne (*Daphne*), 174
Deutzia (*Deutzia*), 175
Heath (*Erica*), 176
Forsythia (*Forsythia*), 177
Fothergilla (*Fothergilla*), 178
Gardenia (*Gardenia*), 179
Woadwaxen (*Genista*), 181
Hydrangea (*Hydrangea*), 184
St. John's wort (*Hypericum*), 185
Mountain Laurel (*Kalmia latifolia*), 186
Japanese Kerria (*Kerria japonica*), 187
Beauty Bush (*Kolkwitzia amabilis*), 188
Crape Myrtle
    (*Lagerstroemia indica*), 118
Leucothoe (*Leucothoe*), 189
Mahonia (*Mahonia*), 190
Oleander (*Nerium oleander*), 223
Osmanthus (*Osmanthus*), 224
Mock Orange (*Philadelphus*), 192
Eastern Ninebark (*Physocarpus*), 193
Pieris, also known as
    Andromeda (*Pieris*), 194
Cinquefoil (*Potentilla*), 195
Azalea (*Rhododendron*), 196
Rhododendron (*Rhododendron*), 197
Rose (*Rosa*), 198, 229
Spirea (*Spiraea*), 230
Lilac (*Syringa*), 202
Viburnum (*Viburnum*), 203
Chaste Tree (*Vitex*), 204
Weigela (*Weigela*), 205

FOR FRUITS
Barberry (*Berberis*), 216
Flowering Quince (*Chaenomeles*), 169
Cotoneaster (*Cotoneaster*), 172
February Daphne
    (*Daphne mezereum*), 174
Holly (*Ilex*), 113
Mahonia (*Mahonia*), 190
Heavenly Bamboo (*Nandina*), 191
Firethorn (*Pyracantha*), 228
Rose (*Rosa*), 229
Rugosa Rose (*Rosa*), 229
Sweet Box (*Sarcococca*), 200
Japanese Skimmia

(*Skimmia japonica*), 201
Viburnum (*Viburnum*), 203

FOR EVERGREEN FOLIAGE
Gold-Dust Tree (*Aucuba japonica*), 164
Boxwood (*Buxus*), 218
Camellia (*Camellia*), 167
Cotoneaster (*Cotoneaster*), 172
Leyland Cypress (*Cupressocyparis*), 219
Dwarf Japanese Cedar
    (*Cryptomeria japonica*), 173
Daphne (*Daphne*), 174
Some Euonymus (*Euonymus*), 220
Gardenia (*Gardenia*), 179
Holly (*Ilex*), 113
Juniper (*Juniperus*), 114
Mountain Laurel (*Kalmia latifolia*), 186
Japanese Kerria (*Kerria japonica*), 187
Privet (*Ligustrum*), 221
Mahonia (*Mahonia*), 190
Heavenly Bamboo (*Nandina*), 191
Oleander (*Nerium oleander*), 223
Osmanthus (*Osmanthus*), 224
Christmas Berry (*Photinia*), 225
Pieris, also known as
    Andromeda (*Pieris*), 194
Spruce (*Picea*), 128
Pine (*Pinus*), 130
Podocarpus (*Podocarpus*), 226
Cherry Laurel
    (*Prunus laurocerasus*), 227
Firethorn (*Pyracantha*), 228
Some Azaleas (*Rhododendron*), 196
Rhododendron (*Rhododendron*), 197
Yew (*Taxus*), 231
Arborvitae (*Thuja*), 143
Hemlock (*Tsuga*), 145

FOR FALL COLOR
Japanese Maple (*Acer palmatum*), 162
Barberry (*Berberis*), 216
Scotch Heather (*Calluna vulgaris*), 166
Clethra (*Clethra*), 171
Dogwood (*Cornus*), 100
Smoke Tree (*Cotinus*), 103
Winged Euonymus (*Euonymus*), 220
Fothergilla (*Fothergilla*), 178
Witch Hazel (*Hamamelis*), 182
Crape Myrtle
    (*Lagerstroemia indica*), 118
Oakleaf Hydrangea (*Hydrangea*), 184

Firethorn (*Pyracantha*), 228
Spirea (*Spiraea*), 230
Viburnum (*Viburnum*), 203

FOR WINTER INTEREST
Barberry (*Berberis*), 216
Boxwood (*Buxus*), 218
Scotch Heather (*Calluna vulgaris*), 166
Camellia (*Camellia*), 167
Flowering Quince (*Chaenomeles*), 169
Clethra (*Clethra*), 171
Leyland Cypress
    (*Cupressocyparis leylandii*), 219
Daphne (*Daphne*), 174
Winged Euonymus and Wintercreeper
    (*Euonymus*), 220
Gardenia (*Gardenia*), 179
Salal and Wintergreen (*Gaultheria*), 180
Woadwaxen (*Genista*), 181
Witch Hazel (*Hamamelis*), 182
Japanese Kerria (*Kerria japonica*), 187
Beauty Bush (*Kolkwitzia amabilis*), 188
Honeysuckle (*Lonicera*), 222
Mahonia (*Mahonia*), 190
Nandina (*Nandina*), 191
Oleander (*Nerium oleander*), 223
Osmanthus (*Osmanthus*), 224
Pieris, also known as
    Andromeda (*Pieris*), 194
Christmas Berry (*Photinia*), 225
Eastern Ninebark
    (*Physocarpus opulifolius*), 193
Firethorn (*Pyracantha*), 228
Azalea (*Rhododendron*), 196
Rhododendron (*Rhododendron*), 197

ALSO USED AS HEDGES
Glossy Abelia (*Abelia* x *grandiflora*), 160
Gold-Dust Tree (*Aucuba japonica*), 164
Camellia (*Camellia*), 167
Ceanothus (*Ceanothus*), 168
Flowering Quince (*Chaenomeles*), 169
Cotoneaster (*Cotoneaster*), 172
Dwarf Japanese Cedar
    (*Cryptomeria japonica*), 173
Deutzia (*Deutzia*), 175
Forsythia (*Forsythia*), 177
Gardenia (*Gardenia*), 179
Hydrangea (*Hydrangea*), 184
Beauty Bush (*Kolkwitzia amabilis*), 188
Nandina (*Nandina*), 191
Lilac (*Syringa*), 202

Pruning Shrubs

Prune newly planted shrubs only to remove dead, diseased, or damaged wood. Once the shrubs are established, prune early to remove weak and crossed growth, and tip-prune straggly branches. Most mature shrubs need only light routine pruning to keep their shape, to open a congested framework, to take out dead wood, to encourage blooming, and to remove spent flowers. You can easily prune most shrubs with pruning shears, loppers, or hedge shears. For an informal, natural look, use pruning shears. Use loppers for tough, woody stems and branches. Use hedge shears to trim broad-leaved evergreens that have small leaves, such as boxwoods, and those deciduous shrubs that need regular trimming. See pages 214–215 for information on pruning hedges. Deadhead rhododendrons carefully by hand to avoid damaging adjacent leaf buds. See the "Shrub Profiles" section, beginning on page 160, for specific pruning needs of individual shrubs.

To make deciduous foliage shrubs denser and bushier, encourage new growth by cutting off half of each succulent new shoot when plants are in active growth. They will immediately begin to grow lateral shoots. When a shrub has reached the desired size, wait until the plant has completed its growth for the season, and then prune it, cutting back a little into the old wood.

Many flowering shrubs benefit from more drastic pruning to enhance their production of blooms. Shrubs that flower on new wood are cut back to a short woody framework. Potentilla, for instance, may be cut back to 1 foot in early spring every other year. Some other shrubs that bloom on new wood, like butterfly bush or peegee hydrangea, should be cut almost down to the ground to keep them within bounds or promote vigorous growth. Others can be cut back to the ground because their new stems are ornamental, for example, red-stemmed and yellow-stemmed dogwoods. This harsh treatment, called "coppicing," is shown on page 158.

Deciduous and evergreen shrubs that flower on old wood should be pruned right after they finish blooming. Roses that flower on new wood are treated specially. The techniques for pruning coniferous evergreen shrubs are the same as those used for evergreen trees. See page 85 for information on pruning conifers.

PINCHING BACK BROAD-LEAVED EVERGREENS

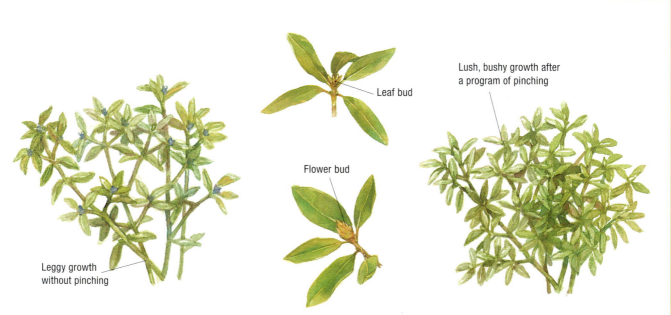

Lush, bushy growth after a program of pinching

Leaf bud

Flower bud

Leggy growth without pinching

You can avoid leggy growth (shown above left) on plants such as rhododendrons, stimulate lush branching growth (shown above right), and control plant size by pinching back end buds of new branches. In a phenomenon known as apical dominance, these end buds have been controlling hormonal flow and inhibiting growth of dormant side buds. Pinching (removal) of end buds sends chemical signals that stimulate growth of the side buds. Caution: avoid mistakenly pinching off the bigger, fatter flower buds.

Shrub Pruning Based on Location of Blooms

Pruning when Dormant. For plants that bloom on new wood (mostly summer bloomers, such as potentilla, abelia, and St. John's wort), prune when the plant is dormant. Prune all suckers, dead and broken wood, and taller older branches. Your goal is to remove about one-third of the old wood each year, gradually replacing all wood over several years.

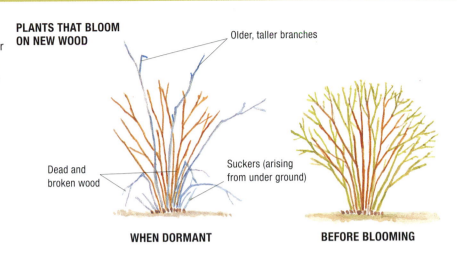

PLANTS THAT BLOOM ON NEW WOOD

Older, taller branches

Dead and broken wood

Suckers (arising from under ground)

WHEN DORMANT

BEFORE BLOOMING

Pruning after Flowering. Shrubs such as forsythia, lilac, and mock orange bloom on old wood (previous year's branches) in spring. After blooms have faded, prune out old, broken, and diseased wood. Then thin out about one-third of the taller older branches close to ground level.

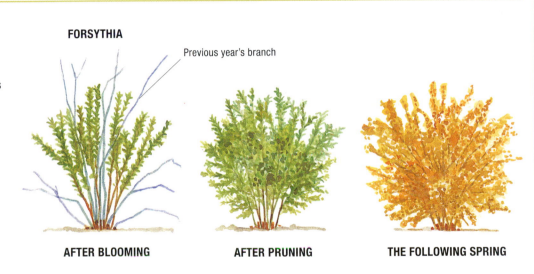

FORSYTHIA

Previous year's branch

AFTER BLOOMING

AFTER PRUNING

THE FOLLOWING SPRING

Hard Pruning after Flowering (vigorous grower). Fast-growing shrubs that flower on old wood (mostly late spring and summer), such as spirea and weigela, often have overcrowded branches that can result in fewer flowers the next year and leave the plant looking unkempt. After flowering, prune hard to just above the new shoots.

WEIGELA

OVERGROWN

HARD-PRUNED

THE FOLLOWING SUMMER

Renovating an Old Shrub

Old, neglected shrubs become overgrown, unproductive, and cluttered with dead wood and weak branches. Removing the old wood promotes the growth of vigorous new wood. Heavy pruning rejuvenates leggy azaleas, scraggly mock oranges, and many other deciduous shrubs. You need to remove defective stems, cut half the healthy stems to within 2 to 3 inches of the ground, and shorten the remaining stems by half their length to a healthy bud or shoot. Many deciduous shrubs (but not evergreen ones), including lilacs and some roses, respond with vigor when all the stems are pruned at once to about a foot from the ground. Thin the abundant new shoots the next dormant season. Note: this is not coppicing, shown below, which is done annually to selected plants. Heavy pruning is done when a shrub is overgrown.

Renovate broad-leaved evergreens, such as rhododendrons, in stages over two or three years because they grow poorly when the foliage is removed all at once. The first year, cut out defective growth and the oldest stems, and shorten the remaining old stems by half. The second year, cut back half the remaining old stems, and thin crowded new shoots. The third year, cut back the remaining old stems. For renovation purposes, prune deciduous shrubs when they are dormant and evergreens just as they begin growth in the spring.

Weak, crossing branches

Old branches

Cut blackened winter-damaged shoots back to healthy, white pith (at the center of the stem).

BEFORE   **AFTER**

Pruning Hybrid Tea and Grandiflora Roses. Every spring, remove old, weak, or damaged shoots; stems that are crossing or crowded; and stems that stick out too far and look asymmetric. In cold-winter climates, cut the canes to 12 inches tall. In mild-winter climates, cut to 20 inches.

DEADHEADING HYBRID TEA AND GRANDIFLORA ROSES

PRUNING HIPS

45° cut

Removing Spent Rose Flowers and Hips. Because roses look messy as they fade, cut them off by pruning the stem back to a five-leaflet leaf, above left. If you enjoy the ornamental and edible rose hips (fruits, above right), don't remove faded flowers. The red or orange hips add winter interest and can feed birds and people. Remove any remaining hips in early spring.

Coppicing. Some woody plants that have grown too large for their space can be cut back every year or two to within a few inches of the ground. This illustration shows red-osier dogwood. New sprouts from the substantial root system will spring forth and can be selectively pruned into new forms.

Special Effects

Training a Shrub Against a Wall. Some shrubs make good espalier plants. Many shrubs can be trained flat against a flat vertical surface.

Try quince, camellias, hollies, pyracanthas, roses, and other shrubs with flowers that develop along stems that tolerate the hard pruning necessary to train them. If you have a structure to support it, an espalier is an ideal feature in a small garden, and the results are quick. For more on espalier training, see page 84.

Training Evergreens as Topiary. The art of shaping plants, or topiary, has been practiced since the days of ancient Rome. Over the centuries, shrubs have been trained and carved into fantastic forms resembling animals, ships, or human figures. In the famous Ladew Gardens in Maryland, a shrubby huntsman and hounds seem to dash over hedges and across the lawns in pursuit of a fox, each fashioned of Japanese yew. You might want to start with something simpler: a geometric shape, perhaps a ball or a cone, made of yew, arborvitae, boxwood, or fast-growing evergreen privet. Training a shrub into a standard, or single-trunk, form is easy. But you need to create that central trunk early.

Espalier training makes pyracantha an especially striking feature, whether informal, above, or formal. Firethorn has a spectacular display of scarlet berries (inset).

This topiary rooster was fashioned from a boxwood. He's either riled up or due for another shearing.

Pruning shrubs with dense growth into decorative shapes, such as balls, is an art that only appears to be intimidating.

Glossy Abelia

Abelia x *grandiflora*

Glossy abelia (*Abelia* x *grandiflora*)

Native to Asia and Mexico, glossy abelia (*Abelia* x *grandiflora*) offers a great summer-long show of flowers. An arching, dense, semievergreen shrub with twiggy branches, it produces masses of small, slightly fragrant, funnel-shaped white flowers tinged with purple from summer until frost. In late fall, the dainty foliage turns purple-bronze. In cool regions, the leaves eventually drop; in southern gardens, they often remain through the winter. Even leafless, abelia's twiggy arching structure is attractive. Glossy abelia is used for massing and to cover banks and slopes. It also makes a good informal hedge. In Zone 5, abelia sometimes freezes but usually grows back.

The cultivar 'Francis Mason', suited to Zones 6–9, is a beautifully variegated dwarf 3 to 4 feet high and wide. The foliage blends green and a rich yellow, and colors most intensely growing in full sun. 'Prostrata', also for Zones 6–9, is a white-flowered form 2 to 3 feet high and 4 to 5 feet wide with foliage that turns burgundy-green in cold weather. 'Sherwood', which is a smaller, denser version, reaches about 3 feet at maturity.

A longtime garden favorite is the 3- to 6-foot hybrid abelia 'Edward Goucher', hardy in Zones 5 or 6–9, with orange-throated lilac-pink flowers. An excellent bank cover, 'Edward Goucher' makes an attractive informal hedge and is handsome enough to be a featured specimen.

Glossy abelia (*Abelia* x *grandiflora* 'Dwarf Purple')

Glossy abelia (*Abelia* x *grandiflora* 'Francis Mason')

Glossy abelia (*Abelia* x *grandiflora* 'Francis Mason' variegated)

Culture: abelias transplant easily in early fall and early spring, either as balled-and-burlapped or container-grown plants. Glossy abelia prefers well-drained, humusy, sandy soils in the acid range, pH 5.5 to 6.5, but it adapts to a range of pH. It flowers most prolifically when growing in a sunny, somewhat sheltered place but does well in light shade.

Glossy abelia (*Abelia* x *grandiflora* 'Edward Goucher')

FEATURED PROFILE
Glossy Abelia

Botanical Name: *Abelia* x *grandiflora* 'Edward Goucher' **Family:** Caprifoliaceae **Type of Plant:** semievergreen flowering shrub **Uses:** specimen, hedge, foundation planting **Genus Range:** Asia, Mexico **Hardiness:** USDA Zones 5 or 6–9 **Height:** 3 to 6' **Growth Rate:** medium-fast **Form & Habit:** upright, arching **Bloom Period:** mid-July to frost **Flowers:** clusters of 2 to 5 slightly fragrant tubular lilac-pink flowers ¾" long **Fruits:** insignificant **Foliage:** 2" long; shiny dark green in summer, bronze-plum in fall and winter **Soil & pH:** well-drained humusy sandy soil; pH 5.5 to 6.5 **Light & Moisture:** full sun for best color, but tolerates light shade; prefers sustained moisture but tolerates drought **Pruning Seasons:** late winter for flower production; after flowering to control growth

Japanese Maple

Acer palmatum

The Japanese maples (*Acer palmatum*) are a group of large deciduous shrubs and small trees with colorful, deeply cut, elegant, beautiful foliage. Smaller varieties grow 8 to 15 feet and have layered, often weeping branches. Worthy of featured positions as lawn specimens, these plants are hardy in Zones 5 or even 6–8, depending on the cultivar.

Japanese maple foliage colors are dazzling. Smaller cultivars usually retain their rich red foliage color throughout the season. The deep green leaves of the species *A. palmatum* turn a flaming orange-scarlet in autumn. The cultivar 'Bloodgood', a taller form, is red in spring and through the growing season. In fall, it turns rich scarlet. The leaves of 'Atropurpureum' are red in spring, reddish purple in summer, and a sensational yellow or coral red in fall.

The threadleaf Japanese maples, the *A. palmatum* Dissectum group, have smaller varieties with exquisitely cut leaves and a picturesque, often weeping, form that give them a refined appearance. 'Atropurpureum Dissectum' combines the lovely color of 'Atropurpureum' and the laciness of the Dissectum group.

Japanese maple
(*Acer palmatum* 'Bloodgood')

Japanese maple (*Acer palmatum* variety *dissectum*) in fall

The silken bark of 'Sango-kaku' ('Senkaki'), the coral-bark Japanese maple, is a brilliant coral red that intensifies in winter in Zones 6–8 or 9. The leaves start out reddish, become green in summer, and in fall turn orange-tinged gold. This small upright tree grows to 25 feet. 'Okushimo', a small vase-shaped tree, has yellow-gold foliage. The multicolored foliage of 'Orido Nishiki' combines bright pink, cream, and green, which blends to pink when seen from a distance.

Culture: Japanese maples require care in transplanting but rarely require pruning to develop a beautiful form. In early spring, set a container-grown plant in well-drained humusy soil in full sun. In warm regions a Japanese maple will benefit from noon shade. Biweekly watering is advisable during dry spells.

FEATURED PROFILE

Japnese Maple

Botanical Name: *Acer palmatum* **Family:** Aceraceae **Type of Plant:** deciduous shrub or small tree **Uses:** lawn specimen, in a shrub or mixed border **Native Range:** Korea, China, Japan **Hardiness:** USDA Zones 5 or 6–8 **Height:** 8 to 15' in cultivation; 40 to 50' in the wild **Growth Rate:** slow **Form & Habit:** rounded, somewhat pendulous layered branches **Bloom Period:** May or June **Flowers:** umbels of small purple florets **Fruits:** samaras ½" long, often turning red in fall **Foliage:** 2 to 5" long, deeply cut; color varies **Soil & pH:** well-drained, humusy, somewhat acid **Light & Moisture:** full sun for best color; sustained moisture **Pruning Seasons:** early spring

Japanese maple (*Acer palmatum* 'Shishio Improved')

The Serviceberries
also called "Shadblows"

Amelanchier

Saskatoon shadblow
(*Amelanchier alnifolia*)

Downy serviceberry
(*Amelanchier arborea*) in fall

In early spring, airy leafless serviceberry bushes light up sunny woodlands across North America with clusters of delicate ivory white flowers—at just the moment the shad fish start migrating up rivers along the Atlantic coast. The leaves follow the flowers; then the sweet red-to-purple fruits mature in early summer. Excellent for pie, these berries also attract songbirds, deer, chipmunks, squirrels, and bears. In fall, serviceberry foliage turns yellow, orange, and dark red. Plant these lovely shrubs and small-scale trees so that they naturalize in groups at the edge of a woodlands, or set them toward the back of an island of shrubs where their fall color can be appreciated. They accommodate to their site: in a garden they become full and sturdy; in a wild setting, in competition with other trees, they grow tall and slim.

The species of serviceberries native to north temperate woodlands and mountains will succeed in a variety of soils, from swamps to arid hillsides. The showiest hybrid of these species is *Amelanchier* x *grandiflora*, grown coast to coast in Zones 4–9. Good cultivars include 'Autumn Brilliance', an Illinois introduction; 'Autumn Sunset', which is exceptionally drought tolerant; and a Princeton Nurseries selection, 'Cumulus', which loads itself with flowers.

For warm regions in Zones 4–9, a better choice is *A. arborea*, a native of the Piedmont woods of Georgia. In the cool hill country and wet woodlands of Zones 4–8, try shadblow serviceberry (*A. canadensis*), found in bogs and swamps from New Brunswick to Texas. Some of the tastiest berries come from Saskatoon, or western, shadblow (*A. alnifolia*), in Zones 4–8. Native peoples of the Prairies used them to flavor pemmican, a winter staple made from buffalo meat and fat. This species has been developed for commercial fruit production.

Shadblow serviceberry
(*Amelanchier canadensis*)
in summer

Culture: serviceberries transplant easily in well-drained moist acid soil in full sun or partial shade. They are not particularly tolerant of air pollution.

Apple serviceberry (*Amelanchier* x *grandiflora*) in spring

FEATURED PROFILE
Apple Serviceberry

Botanical Name: *Amelanchier* x *grandiflora* **Family:** Rosaceae
Type of Plant: small deciduous flowering tree or shrub **Uses:** early spring flowers; shrub border; naturalizing **Native Range:** north temperate forests and mountain regions **Hardiness:** USDA Zones 4–9
Height: 15 to 25' in cultivation **Growth Rate:** medium **Form & Habit:** shrub or small tree, with rounded crown **Bloom Period:** March–April, before the leaves **Flowers:** delicate white clusters tinged pink in the bud **Fruits:** sweetish berrylike pome ripening to purple or black
Foliage: purplish in youth **Soil & pH:** well-drained; pH 5.0 to 6.5
Light & Moisture: full sun or dappled shade; sustained moisture

Gold-Dust Tree
also called "Japanese Laurel"

Aucuba japonica 'Variegata'

Gold-dust tree (*Aucuba japonica* 'Variegata')

The big, leathery, yellow-flecked bright green leaves of the gold-dust tree (*Aucuba japonica* 'Variegata') and its success in shade are this tall shrub's major assets. A beautifully marked cultivar of the all-green species, it was introduced from Japan in the late 1700s. This lush, handsome, broad-leaved evergreen shrub grows 6 to 9 feet high and develops multiple succulent stems that branch and leaf out, usually reaching all the way to the ground. Shoots that extend to the ground will eventually set new roots and produce new plants, which transplant readily in the fall. Hardy from Zones 6 or 7–10, aucuba tolerates droughts and urban situations and is pest- and disease-resistant. It survives under densely rooted trees where even grass won't grow. Use groups of aucuba to soften shaded walls and brighten dim corners, or as a

Gold-dust tree (*Aucuba japonica* 'Variegata')

background hedge for perennials or small flowering shrubs, such as azaleas. Gardeners in cold regions can grow gold-dust trees in tubs and use them as a screen or as background plants in patio and terrace gardens. It overwinters indoors successfully in a bright cool room.

Aucuba produces male and female flowers on separate plants. 'Variegata', a female plant, produces large, persistent red berries when pollinated by a male. Another cultivar, 'Maculata', is a male plant blotched with yellow-white. 'Mr. Goldstrike' has more gold than 'Variegata' and grows just 4 to 6 feet high.

Culture: a container-grown gold-dust tree transplants easily in early spring or late summer. It thrives in well-drained humusy soil with high organic content. It also survives droughts and adapts to pH, but it requires shade. Late winter and late summer are the best times to prune to control its sprawl and height.

FEATURED PROFILE
Gold-Dust Tree

Botanical Name: *Aucuba japonica* 'Variegata' **Family:** Cornaceae **Type of Plant:** variegated broad-leaved evergreen **Uses:** screen, hedge, background shrub for shade **Genus Range:** Japan **Hardiness:** USDA Zones 6 or 7–10 **Height:** 6 to 9' or higher **Growth Rate:** slow **Form & Habit:** upright, rounded **Bloom Period:** March–April **Flowers:** female flowers are borne in the axils of the leaves; male flowers, in upright terminal panicles 2 to 4" long **Fruits:** scarlet berry-like drupes on female plants; also, plant any male *Aucuba japonica* as pollinator **Foliage:** stiff, leathery, elliptical, 3 to 8" long, lustrous dark green on top flecked with yellow **Soil & pH:** well-drained, humusy, pH adaptable **Light & Moisture:** shade to deep shade; prefers sustained moisture but tolerates drought **Pruning Seasons:** early spring, summer

Gold-dust tree (*Aucuba japonica* 'Variegata')

Butterfly Bush
also called "Summer Lilac"

Buddleia

Alternate-leaf butterfly bush
(*Buddleia alternifolia*)

The buddleias are enduring deciduous flowering shrubs and small trees that attract butterflies with their fragrance. Most common is *Buddleia davidii*, hardy in Zones 5 or 6 to 9, which grows 6 to 8 feet in a single season and, from July until frost, shoots out slim arching canes that sweep the ground. In late summer, they are tipped with 4- to 10-inch spikes of orange-centered, lightly scented florets. The flowers' rich nectar attracts hummingbirds and bees as well as butterflies. The leaves are gray-green, narrow, 4 to 10 inches long and silvery on the underside. Among the beautiful widely available cultivars are 'White Bouquet', 'Pink Delight', and dark purple-violet 'Black Knight'. 'Harlequin' bears reddish purple flowers; its new foliage is edged with yellow that changes to creamy white.

Some less well-known buddleias can fit specific landscape needs. In a small garden, 4-foot dwarf cultivars of *B. davidii* variety *nanhoensis* (hardy in Zones 5–9) are charming, especially 'Mongo' and 'Monum'. 'Mongo' is also sold under the name of Petite Indigo, and 'Monum' as Petite Plum. Where a small weeping tree would be right, 12-foot alternate-leaf buddleia (*B. alternifolia*) will do the job. It has dainty foliage, and in midspring, clusters of slightly fragrant lilac-purple flowers. It is hardy in Zones 5 or 6–8 or 9. The cultivar 'Argentea' has silvery foliage. In warm regions (Zones 8–10), the 6- to 15-foot semievergreen fragrant orange ball tree (*B. globosa*) is popular.

Orange ball tree (*Buddleia globosa*)

Culture: buddleias transplant easily in early spring and fall to well-drained, fertile, neutral soil in full sun. Deadheading increases flowering. *B. davidii* may freeze to the ground in severe Zone 5 winters, but it usually regrows. It blooms on new wood. So to encourage vigorous new growth, prune it back in late winter to within a foot of the ground. *B. alternifolia* and its cultivars bloom on wood from the previous season. After flowering, remove older shoots, reducing the plant by one-third.

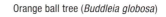

FEATURED PROFILE
Butterfly Bush, or Summer Lilac

Botanical Name: *Buddleia davidii* **Family:** Loganiaceae
Type of Plant: deciduous flowering shrub **Uses:** shrub and perennial borders, rose garden filler, wild garden
Native Range: western China **Hardiness:** USDA Zones 5 or 6–9 **Height:** 6 to 8' **Growth Rate:** fast **Form & Habit:** erect or arching, rounded **Bloom Period:** mid-July until frost **Flowers:** tiny fragrant florets, orange at the mouth, borne on flowering spikes 4 to 10" long **Fruits:** inconspicuous ¼- to ⅓"- long capsules **Foliage:** lance-shaped, gray- to blue-green, 4 to 10", dark green above, white-silver beneath, woolly **Soil & pH:** well-drained, fertile; neutral pH **Light & Moisture:** full sun; doesn't tolerate wet feet **Pruning Seasons:** late winter, early spring; deadhead to enhance flower production

Butterfly bush (*Buddleia davidii*)

Scotch Heather

Calluna vulgaris

Corbett red heather
(*Calluna vulgaris*
'Corbett Red')

Scotch heather (*Calluna vulgaris* 'Wickwar Flame', 'Red Wings',
'Silver Queen') in foreground

Scotch heather (*Calluna vulgaris*), a slow-growing little evergreen shrub, blooms in late summer on the moors of northern England, Scotland, and Europe. The species is a 3-foot plant with ascending branches covered with tiny, overlapping, dark green scalelike leaves. The flowers consist of dense clusters of small, pink-to-purple bell- or urn-shaped florets and cover the plant in a haze of color that attracts honeybees. In gardens, Scotch heather is used as an edging plant, in front of shrubs and in rock gardens, to give texture and substance to flowering borders. It also makes a good naturalized ground cover along roadsides and on slopes. It has been cultivated for so long in America that it grows wild in the Northeast. Indoors, heather is a long-lasting cut flower that is excellent for drying.

There are hundreds of cultivars of Scotch heather, blooming from summer through fall. 'Alba Plena', a lovely plant, bears double white flowers in September and October. 'County Wicklow', a beautiful old favorite with double true pink flowers, blooms in August. 'H. E. Beale' has silvery foliage and bears double silvery pink flowers in September and October. In late winter, the leafy tips of 'Spring Torch' are fiery red; the flowers are lavender-pink. 'Gold Haze' sports pale gold shoots year-round; in August and September, it bears white flowers. An ideal heather for rock gardens is 'Foxii Nana', a dense mound 6 inches tall.

Culture: Scotch heather requires care in transplanting. Set out a young container-grown plant in early spring in well-drained, lean, sandy, humusy soil, pH 6.0 or less. It flowers best in full sun, tolerates partial shade, and needs watering during droughts. To encourage the full, bushy growth that produces masses of flowers, cut back the tips of the lead branches after planting. Every year in late March or April, just as growth begins, cut back by half the vigorous growth from the previous season.

FEATURED PROFILE
Scotch-Heather

Botanical Name: *Calluna vulgaris* **Family:** Ericaceae **Type of Plant:** low evergreen flowering shrub **Uses:** edging, in flowering borders, as a ground cover **Native Range:** northern England, Europe, Asia Minor; naturalized in eastern North America **Hardiness:** USDA Zones 4 or 5–7 **Height:** 18 to 24" **Growth Rate:** slow **Form & Habit:** upright branching mat **Bloom Period:** August to October **Flowers:** 1 to 10" racemes of bell- or urn-shaped florets **Fruits:** insignificant capsules in October **Foliage:** closely packed, tiny scalelike evergreen leaves give the stems a squarish look **Soil & pH:** well-drained; pH 6.0 or less **Light & Moisture:** full sun for best flowering; tolerates partial shade; sustained moisture **Pruning Seasons:** before growth begins in winter; deadhead after flowering

Scotch heather (*Calluna vulgaris* 'Blazeaway')

The Camellias

Camellia

Sasanqua camellia (*Camellia sasanqua*)

Sasanqua camellia
(*Camellia sasanqua*)

Camellias are beautiful evergreen flowering shrubs and small trees from China and Japan. They have lustrous olive green foliage and bear beautiful, sometimes fragrant, many-petaled flowers. There are semidouble- and double-flowered varieties in white or in colors ranging from pink to rose, crimson, and purple-red, as well as bicolor blooms. In the warm South, the flowers open in late fall or winter; where winters are longer they bloom in early spring. Prized lawn specimens, camellias are used as flowering hedges and in shrub borders. In the North, camellias are greenhouse plants.

The most widely grown species is the rather formal-looking Japanese camellia (*Camellia japonica*). Cultivars grow 10 to 15 feet or taller. The flowers, as large as 5 inches across, appear in late winter and early spring. Plants are hardy in Zones 7–9, but when temperatures fall below 32°F, the frostbitten buds turn brown, ruining the flowers.

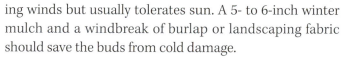

Japanese camellia fruit
(*Camellia japonica*)

The smaller, charming sasanqua camellia (*C. sasanqua*) is slightly less hardy than the Japanese camellia. In Zone 7, it needs protection from drying winds but usually tolerates sun. A 5- to 6-inch winter mulch and a windbreak of burlap or landscaping fabric should save the buds from cold damage.

The winter-hardy camellias introduced by the United States National Arboretum may withstand temperatures as low as -12°F. They have such names as 'Snow Flurry', 'Winter's Dream', 'Winter's Rose', 'Winter's Charm', 'Frost Queen', and 'Cinnamon Cindy'. Some are fragrant.

Culture: transplant camellias with care. Set out a young container-grown plant in early spring in well-drained, humusy, moist soil in the acid range. Camellias require protection from high noon sun and freezing winds. Deadheading improves flowering. Do not prune winter-killed shoots until you can see where the new buds will break. Annual pruning is usually not needed. However, you can improve the flowering of a plant that is getting straggly by shortening long shoots back to sturdy outward-facing sideshoots or buds. Rejuvenate an old plant by removing one-third of the older branches in early spring every year for three years.

FEATURED PROFILE
Japanese Camellia

Botanical Name: *Camellia japonica* **Family:** Theaceae **Type of Plant:** large broad-leaved evergreen flowering shrub **Uses:** specimen, massed, in shrub border **Native Range:** China, Japan **Hardiness:** USDA Zones 7 or 8–9 **Height:** 10 to 15' **Growth Rate:** slow **Form & Habit:** pyramidal **Bloom Period:** November to April **Flowers:** anemone or roselike, white, pink, red, and combinations **Fruits:** 1" woody capsules **Foliage:** leathery, deep green, evergreen, oval, serrated, 2 to 4" long **Soil & pH:** well-drained, humus-rich soil in the acid range **Light & Moisture:** partial shade; maintain moisture **Pruning Seasons:** after flowering

Japanese camellia (*Camellia japonica*)

Ceanothus
Ceanothus

Ceanothus are profusely flowering shrubs native to both coasts of North America, but these plants are especially popular in California. Some present their blue, purple, pink, or white flowers in clusters, and others produce lilaclike spikes. Evergreen species flower in the spring, deciduous types in summer.

The white-flowered species is known as New Jersey tea (*Ceanothus americanus*). The hardiest of the ceanothus, it grows wild in Zones 4–8 from eastern Canada to Manitoba and Texas. In Colonial times, its leaves were used as a substitute for tea. This attractive summer-blooming shrub is compact and dense but transplants with difficulty. It has given rise to better-flowering hybrids.

Hybrid ceanothus are widely grown along the West Coast, from British Columbia to southern California, and inland in warm dry regions of Zones 7–8. Known as blueblossom or California lilac, reaching 6 to 12 feet tall and usually evergreen, hybrid ceanothus are at-tractive in informal hedges and as specimens. Cultivars include 'Frosty Blue', with large bright blue flowers frosted with white; and 'Joyce Coulter', which is a low, mounding plant 2 to 4 feet high and 8 to 10 feet wide, with medium blue flowers. 'Julia Phelps', a 4- to 8-foot shrub that bears indigo-blue flowers, and 6- by 6-foot 'Concha', which bears dark blue flowers, are more tolerant of humidity than others.

California lilac
(*Ceanothus* 'Concha')

California lilac (*Ceanothus* x *pallidus* 'Marie Simon')

Wild lilac
(*Ceanothus griseus horizontalis* 'Yankee Point')

Nurseries in southern California offer evergreen cultivars of the cold-sensitive but lovely *C. thyrsiflorus*, hardy in Zones 8–9 or 10; it can grow to 21 feet. Some cultivars are somewhat hardier than the species. For example, 'Louis Edmunds' bears sky blue flowers and tolerates heavy soil and water. It reaches 6 to 19 feet. 'Snow Flurry', called "white California lilac," is smaller, growing 6 to 10 feet high. 'Victoria', bearing deep blue flowers in spring, responds well to shearing, is the hardiest, often succeeding in Zone 7.

Culture: ceanothus transplant easily in early fall or spring to well-drained soil with a neutral to alkaline pH. They do best in dry sunny sites—a lot of moisture is detrimental. To keep a ceanothus compact and to improve flowering, prune in April.

FEATURED PROFILE
California Lilac

Botanical Name: *Ceanothus thyrsiflorus* 'Victoria' **Family:** Rhamnaceae **Type of Plant:** broad-leaved evergreen flowering shrub
Uses: soft, informal hedge, screen, windbreak for coastal gardens
Genus Range: western U.S. **Hardiness:** USDA Zones 7–9
Height: 9' **Growth Rate:** medium **Form & Habit:** upright grower, tall and wide **Bloom Period:** flowers in spring **Flowers:** deep blue in clusters **Fruits:** 3-lobed capsule **Foliage:** long oval, dark green **Soil & pH:** well-drained or dryish; neutral to alkaline **Light & Moisture:** full sun; let soil dry between waterings **Pruning Seasons:** early spring to keep compact

Wild lilac
(*Ceanothus thyrsiflorus*)

The Flowering Quinces

Chaenomeles

Flowering quince
(*Chaenomeles* x *superba* 'Rowallane')

F ew spring-flowering shrubs can match the beauty of flowering quince (*Chaenomeles*). These woody shrubs bloom almost before winter is over, usually before the leaves appear. The scarlet, coral, pink, or white flowers seem to sprout from the bark, like apple blossoms, and are followed in fall by hard, faintly aromatic, yellowish quince-like fruits about 2 inches long. New foliage is a red-rose-bronze that gradually turns to glossy rich green on branches that develop an elegant asymmetrical sprawl. These shrubs are attractive in an informal hedge and make handsome specimens and espaliers. Branches can be forced into bloom and are beautiful in bouquets.

A smaller less cold-tolerant species, a Japanese flowering quince (*C. japonica*), has been popular in the West since the nineteenth century, when it was called "fairy fire." It is hardy in Zones 5–8. Modern cultivars produce striking flowers—some roselike, some semidouble, some anemone-flowered. 'Cameo' bears masses of large, double, pink-peach flowers over a long period. 'Jet Trail', a 3-foot white-flowered cultivar hardy to Zone 4, and 'Texas Scarlet' with fiery red flowers, are offered by Midwest and West Coast nurseries.

A cross between *C. japonica* and *C. speciosa* produced *C.* x *superba*, which bears exceptionally large flowers, though it is smaller than the species and more suitable for the front of a shrub border, as a hedge, and as an edger. In warm regions, it can bloom in the fall. It is hardy in Zones 5–8.

Flowering quince
(*Chaenomeles speciosa*)

Culture: you can transplant a flowering quince in loamy soil, pH 5.5 to 7.0 in spring or fall. It thrives in full sun. Quince flowers on the previous season's wood and on a system of spurs. When the blooms fade and before May, remove older canes and suckers to keep the center open. Then as new wood hardens in summer, remove branches that cross or that are badly positioned. Finally, after the leaves fall, take the main branches back by two or three buds.

FEATURED PROFILE
Flowering Quince

Botanical Name: *Chaenomeles speciosa* **Family:** Rosaceae **Type of Plant:** deciduous flowering shrub **Uses:** specimen planting, informal hedge **Native Range:** China, eastern Asia **Hardiness:** USDA Zones 4 or 5–8 **Height:** 5 to 10' **Growth Rate:** 1' per year **Form & Habit:** spreading, rounded **Bloom Period:** early spring **Flowers:** white, pink, coral, scarlet; bowl-shaped 1 to 1½" across, 5 petals, many stamens **Fruits:** hard yellow-green pomes in the fall that persist until frost **Foliage:** 1½ to 3" long; oval to oblong; sharply serrated; bronze when new; then glossy rich green **Soil & pH:** loamy soil; pH 5.5 to 7.0 **Light & Moisture:** full sun; maintain moisture, but tolerates some drought **Pruning Seasons:** after flowering

Flowering quince (*Chaenomeles speciosa*)

The Rock Roses

Cistus

Rock rose (*Cistus* x *purpureus*)

Rock rose (*Cistus* x *purpureus*)

The rock roses are handsome, low-growing, mostly evergreen shrubs from the Mediterranean. They are beautiful in flower, handsome the rest of the year, and truly rugged. For several weeks in June and July they produce masses of wide-open showy flowers that each last just one day. Their capacity to withstand alkaline soils and strong winds has made them enduring favorites on both coasts and in regions of the South where summer humidity is low and frost is rare or light.

The species with the largest flowers is gum rock rose, or ladanum (*Cistus ladanifer*), a 3- to 5-foot shrub also known as gum ladanum and brown-eyed rock-rose. The flowers are 4 inches wide, single, and white, and each petal has a maroon-red splotch at its base. The leaves are aromatic and sticky, dark green above and whitish beneath. For Zones 8–9, a less cold-tolerant hybrid, the orchid rock rose (*C.* x *purpureus*) bears rose-purple flowers spotted maroon at the base; its narrow leaves are a rich green. The dwarf pink rock rose (*C.* x *skanbergii*), a neat, low-growing hybrid, performs beautifully in sunny dry areas and will naturalize in near-desert conditions in Zones 8–9.

Culture: the rock roses transplant with some difficulty. In early spring before growth begins, plant a young container-grown rock rose in well-drained light soil that is somewhat alkaline. It needs full sun and withstands considerable drought. Prune to remove tips damaged by winter as the buds break in spring. Do not take the cuts back into older wood. No other pruning should be necessary.

Gum rock rose (*Cistus ladanifer*)

Rock rose (*Cistus* x *skanbergii*)

Gum rock rose (*Cistus ladanifer*)

The Clethras
also called "Summersweet" or "Sweet Pepper Bush"

Clethra

Clethra's deliciously fragrant white blooms are an asset in the summer garden. A deciduous shrub 3 to 8 feet tall and native to the eastern United States, summersweet (*Clethra alnifolia*) naturalizes readily in shady damp places and coastal gardens. It is valuable in the home garden for its dense, rather shiny green foliage, which turns yellow-orange in the fall, and its interesting shrubby silhouette during the winter.

In July and August, summersweet's generous crop of flowers in fuzzy little panicles is so fragrant that just a few shrubs can perfume a whole garden. Bees love them. Cultivars expand the range of sizes and flower colors. 'Rosea' is a small pink-flowered variety. 'Ruby Spice' bears deep rose-colored, fragrant flowers that fairly cover a plant 6 to 8 feet tall. 'Pink Spire' has glossy foliage, and the pink-rose buds open to a soft pink. The compact 'Hummingbird', a low-growing mounded form, bears masses of delightfully fragrant white flowers.

Summersweet (*Clethra alnifolia*)

Japanese clethra (*Clethra barbinervis*)

In the South, the similar woolly summersweet (*C. tomentosa*) is popular. It flowers in September and is suited to Zones 5–8 or 9. For the large garden, there's the 30-foot Japanese clethra (*C. barbinervis*), which grows in Zones 5 or 6–8 and bears 4- to 6-inch racemes of somewhat fragrant white flowers. They are followed by lasting fruits in the fall, when the leaves turn red to yellow.

Culture: a balled-and-burlapped or container-grown summersweet will transplant fairly easily to rich, moist, well-drained soil. Clethra tolerates pH 4.5 to 7.0 and succeeds in either full sun or partial shade. In winter, cut bare older branches back to ground level.

FEATURED PROFILE
Clethra, Summersweet, or Sweet Pepper Bush

Botanical Name: *Clethra alnifolia* **Family:** Clethraceae **Type of Plant:** deciduous fragrant flowering shrub **Uses:** massing in a garden, naturalizing, coastal gardens **Native Range:** eastern U.S. **Hardiness:** USDA Zones 3–8 **Height:** 3 to 8' **Growth Rate:** slow **Form & Habit:** upright, round-topped **Bloom Period:** July–August **Flowers:** white, sweetly fragrant, ½" across, borne on upright racemes 2 to 6" long **Fruits:** dry capsules persisting through winter **Foliage:** oblong 1¾ to 4" long, ¾ to 2" wide, sharply serrated, somewhat shiny on both sides **Soil & pH:** rich, well-drained; pH 4.5 to 7.0 **Light & Moisture:** full sun or partial shade; does best in moist soil **Pruning Seasons:** early spring

Summersweet (*Clethra alnifolia*)

The Cotoneasters

Cotoneaster

Bearberry cotoneaster (*Cotoneaster dammeri* 'Skogholm')

Willowleaf cotoneaster (*Cotoneaster salicifolius*)

The cotoneasters are refined evergreen or semievergreen shrubs with finely textured foliage, a charming sprawl, dainty pink or white flowers in spring, and attractive red or black fruits in fall. They range in height from the 10- to 15-foot- willowleaf cotoneaster (*Cotoneaster salicifolius*), which is hardy in Zones 6–8, to low-growing plants used as ground covers or to edge walls. Low-growing plants include creeping cotoneaster (*C. adpressus*), reaching 1 to 1½ feet in height in Zones 5–7, and bearberry cotoneaster (*C. dammeri*), which grows in Zones 7–8 in a tiered mound that can spread 6 feet or wider.

The most widely planted species is the midsize rockspray cotoneaster (*C. horizontalis*), a broad upright semievergreen that grows into a tiered mound 3 to 5 feet high. It bears light pink flowers and masses of red fruits. In fall the leaves turn scarlet-orange and last into winter. The leaves of a variegated cultivar, 'Variegatus', turn rosy red in autumn.

Two species accept shearing and shaping and make good hedges and screens. The rounded 6- to 10-foot hedge cotoneaster (*C. lucidus*), hardy in Zones 6–8, bears pinkish flowers and sports red-to-yellow foliage in the fall. Spreading cotoneaster (*C. divaricatus*), a fast-growing pink-

Creeping cotoneaster (*Cotoneaster adpressus*)

flowered shrub 5 to 6 feet tall, has glowing reddish purple fall foliage in Zones 4–7.

Culture: a young container-grown cotoneaster transplants fairly easily in early spring to a sunny site and almost any soil that is moist and well drained, acid or alkaline. It does not tolerate wet feet, but once established it handles some drought. Cotoneaster blooms on old wood. Minimal pruning is needed, best undertaken when the berry display is over. To grow rockspray cotoneaster against a wall, secure a few widely separated main branches on the surface and allow them to develop their side branchlets. Keep an informal hedge in bounds with light selective pruning during the growing season. Lightly shear a formal hedge as needed.

FEATURED PROFILE
Rockspray Cotoneaster

Botanical Name: *Cotoneaster horizontalis* **Family:** Rosaceae **Type of Plant:** spreading, flowering, fruiting, almost evergreen shrub **Uses:** ground cover, screening, massing, espalier **Native Range:** western China **Hardiness:** USDA Zones 4 or 5–7 **Height:** 3 to 5' **Growth Rate:** slow to medium **Form & Habit:** tiered mound **Bloom Period:** May–June **Flowers:** small, pink, inconspicuous **Fruits:** spherical bright red fruit ¼" diameter **Foliage:** flat, ⅓ to ½" long, not quite as wide, lustrous dark green above **Soil & pH:** well-drained sandy soil or clay; tolerates salt when established; pH 6.0 to 7.0 **Light & Moisture:** full sun to high shade cast by tall trees; needs moisture but can handle drought once established **Pruning Seasons:** after fruiting

Rockspray cotoneaster (*Cotoneaster horizontalis*)

Japanese Cedar

Cryptomeria japonica

Japanese cedar (*Cryptomeria japonica* 'Benjamin Franklin')

Dwarf Japanese cedar (*Cryptomeria japonica* 'Globosa Nana') is a conical shrubby form of a beautiful Japanese evergreen tree. The densely whorled, flattish leaves, ½ to 1 inch long, become bluish as the shrub matures and turn rust red in cold weather. 'Globosa Nana' grows slowly to a height of 2 to 5 feet. It's an excellent evergreen for rock gardens

Dwarf Japanese cedar
(*Cryptomeria japonica* 'Globosa Nana')

Dwarf Japanese cedar (*Cryptomeria japonica* 'Globosa Nana')

and shrub borders and works well as a background plant in large perennial borders. It succeeds in seacoast gardens if protected from the worst of the wind. 'Elegans' grows to 15 feet, and in winter the foliage turns brownish red. 'Elegans' makes a good formal hedge if trimmed every August. 'Benjamin Franklin', a nondwarf cultivar with blue-green foliage, grows 30 to 40 feet tall.

Culture: a container-grown cryptomeria transplants well to moist, rich, well-worked light soil on the acid side, pH 6.0 to 6.7. It adapts to heavy clay soils. A site in full sun is best, but high shade is acceptable, and protection from strong winds is beneficial. The dwarf Japanese cedar does not usually need pruning.

FEATURED PROFILE
Dwarf Japanese Cedar

Botanical Name: *Cryptomeria japonica* 'Globosa Nana' **Family:** Taxodiaceae **Type of Plant:** dwarf evergreen shrub **Uses:** specimen planting, foundation plant, background for deciduous shrubs and for perennials **Genus Range:** China and Japan **Hardiness:** USDA Zones 5 or 6–8 or 9 **Height:** 2½ to 5' high, 2½ to 4½" wide **Growth Rate:** slow **Form & Habit:** compact, dome shaped, pyramidal **Fruits:** globular cones ½ to 1" long, dark brown **Foliage:** evergreen, persisting 4 to 5 years, ¼ to ¾" long, spirally arranged **Soil & pH:** rich, deeply dug, well-drained, moist, somewhat acid soil; pH 6.0 to 6.7. **Light & Moisture:** high shade; needs protection from wind; does best in moist soil **Pruning Seasons:** after growth is completed

Dwarf Japanese cedar (*Cryptomeria japonica* 'Globosa Nana')

The Daphnes

Daphne

Daphne (*Daphne* x *burkwoodii* 'Carol Mackie')

Rose daphne (*Daphne cneorum*)

The daphnes are low, wide, slow-growing semievergreen or evergreen shrubs that bear wonderfully fragrant flowers followed by brightly colored fleshy fruits. They are native to southern and western Asia. The hardiest daphne is the semievergreen cultivar *Daphne* x *burkwoodii* 'Somerset', hardy in Zones 4–8, a shrub 3 or 4 feet tall and 6 feet wide. Its shiny green foliage often persists into winter. In late spring, and often again in summer, it opens masses of star-shaped, delightfully fragrant pale pink flowers. In the coastal gardens of the Northwest, it blooms from midwinter to midspring. The leaves of the handsome cultivar 'Carol Mackie' are edged with a gold band. The February daphne (*D. mezereum* 'Bowles White') is as hardy and grows in Zones 4 or 5–8.

The rose daphne, or garland flower (*D. cneorum*), which originated in the mountains of central and southern Europe, is a dense foot-high evergreen used in rock gardens and as a

Variegated winter daphne (*Daphne odora* 'Aureomarginata')

ground cover and edger. The fragrant rosy flowers cover the plant in midspring and often reappear in summer. Rose daphne is hardy in Zones 5–8. 'Variegata' has cream-edged leaves. 'Pygmaea' is a prostrate form.

The most perfumed daphne and the easiest to grow is variegated winter daphne (*D. odora* 'Aureomarginata'). It succeeds only where winters are mild, in Zones 7–9, where it's evergreen and slowly reaches 4 to 5 feet. In early spring, deep crimson buds open to dense heads of fragrant white flowers.

Culture: the daphnes transplant with some difficulty. Set out a young container-grown daphne in early spring in well-drained humusy loam that has a neutral pH. A site in full sun will produce the most flowers. The daphnes generally do not require pruning, but if necessary, prune after flowering and before mid-July.

FEATURED PROFILE
Pacific Dogwood

Botanical Name: *Daphne* x *burkwoodii* **Family:** Thymelaeaceae **Type of Plant:** fragrant semievergreen flowering shrub **Uses:** specimen plant **Native Range:** Europe and North Africa **Hardiness:** USDA Zones 4–8 **Height:** 3 to 4' **Growth Rate:** slow **Form & Habit:** rounded, dense **Bloom Period:** midspring **Flowers:** dense terminal clusters of fragrant, creamy white flowers flushed pink, 2" wide **Fruits:** red berries in fall **Foliage:** oblong, 2" long, shiny green; remains on the plant through late fall **Soil & pH:** well-drained loam; neutral pH **Light & Moisture:** full sun for best flowering; best when neither wet nor too dry **Pruning Seasons:** after flowering, before mid-July

Daphne (*Daphne* x *burkwoodii* 'Somerset') in late spring

The Deutzias

Deutzia

Deutzia (*Deutzia crenata* 'Nikko')

The deutzias are beautiful deciduous flowering shrubs related to the mock oranges, but deutzias lack fragrance. The species available almost everywhere is slender deutzia (*Deutzia gracilis*). A graceful compact 2- to 4-foot shrub, hardy in Zones 4 or 5–8, it is covered in late April and early May with a froth of pure white flowers. In fall the foliage takes on hints of burgundy. It is lovely blooming at the front of a shrub border, in a rock garden, or in a low informal hedge. The foliage of the popular cultivar 'Nikko', a wide-spreading 1- to 2-foot dwarf, turns burgundy in the fall. Also attributed to *D. crenata*, 'Nikko' is hardy only to Zone 6. 'Rosea' has a profusion of pink bell-shaped flowers.

Deutzia (*Deutzia crenata* 'Nikko')

Other colorful cultivars may be harder to locate but are worth a search. Similar to 'Nikko' and growing in Zones 3 or 4–7, lemoine deutzia (*D.* x *lemoinei*) reaches 5 to 7 feet tall and is more cold-tolerant. The flowers of *D.* x *kalmiiflora*, hardy in Zones 5–8, are carmine on the outside and white within on gracefully branching 4- to 5-foot plants. *D. ningpoensis* is a 6-foot shrub with soft pink-white flowers, hardy in Zones 6–8. The foliage of *D. scabra* 'Aureo Variegata', hardy in Zones 5–8, is marbled lemon yellow.

Culture: a container-grown deutzia transplants fairly easily to well-drained humusy loam and grows well in almost any pH. The best flowering occurs in a site that gets full sun, but deutzia will do reasonably well in bright shade. When flowering is over, prune out damaged wood and cut a number of older branches to the ground to encourage new growth.

FEATURED PROFILE
Slender Deutzia

Botanical Name: *Deutzia gracilis* **Family:** Hydrangeaceae **Type of Plant:** deciduous flowering shrub **Uses:** in front of a shrub border or as an edger or hedge plant **Native Range:** Japan **Hardiness:** USDA Zones 4 or 5–8 **Height:** 2 to 4' **Growth Rate:** slow to medium **Form & Habit:** low, wide mound **Bloom Period:** late May **Flowers:** pure white ½ to ¾" across, borne in erect panicles **Fruits:** capsules **Foliage:** slim oval green leaves, 1 to 2½" long, somewhat serrated **Soil & pH:** well-drained, humusy; pH adaptable **Light & Moisture:** full sun or bright shade; sustained moisture **Pruning Seasons:** after flowering

Slender deutzia (*Deutzia gracilis*)

The Heaths

Erica

The heaths are low, wide-spreading evergreen shrubs, a foot or less in height, that rapidly form dense rounded mounds covered with fine needlelike foliage. From January through March, heaths produce clusters of tiny tubular flowers. They're most often seen fronting perennial borders, as naturalized ground cover, in neglected corner borders, and in rock gardens.

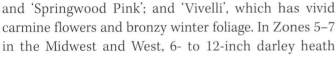

The most widely planted heaths are 12- to 18-inch Cornish heath (*Erica vagans*), and spring heath (*E. carnea*), both hardy in Zones 5–7. The Cornish heath cultivar 'Mrs. D. F. Maxwell' is among the hardiest—an outstanding, colorful plant with cherry red flowers from July through October. Spring heath, which resembles heather, begins blooming in January in warmer regions, in spring farther north, and continues blooming until May. Popular cultivars of spring heath include 'King George', a clear deep pink; 'Springwood White' and 'Springwood Pink'; and 'Vivelli', which has vivid carmine flowers and bronzy winter foliage. In Zones 5–7 in the Midwest and West, 6- to 12-inch darley heath

Spring heath (Erica carnea 'Vivelli')

Darley heath (*Erica* x *darleyensis*)

(*Calluna* x *darleyensis*) is widely available in cultivars with flowers in white, shades of pink, red, and reddish purple.

There are some larger heaths, 3 to 5 feet tall, such as *E. x erigena* 'Mediterranean Pink' and 'Irish Dusk' (Zones 7–9), which has salmon-colored flowers. They are hard to find, however.

Culture: the heaths transplant easily and flourish in well-drained, sandy, loamy, acid soil, pH 5.0 to 6.0, that includes lots of organic matter. They succeed in full or partial sun and do best when soil moisture is constant. Prune summer-flowering Cornish heath annually in March as soon as new growth begins; prune winter-flowering spring heath annually in spring as the flowers fade and new growth begins. When pruning the heaths, avoid cutting into old wood.

FEATURED PROFILE
Spring Heath

Botanical Name: *Erica carnea* **Family:** Ericaceae **Type of Plant:** evergreen, low, wide-spreading shrub **Uses:** ground cover, naturalizing, rock gardens, fronting perennial borders **Native Range:** Europe, temperate Africa, western and central Asia **Hardiness:** USDA Zones 5–7 **Height:** 12 to 18" **Growth Rate:** slow **Form & Habit:** low, wide-spreading, mounded **Bloom Period:** late winter, early spring **Flowers:** urn-shaped, to ¼" long, held in upright racemes 1 to 2" long **Foliage:** needlelike, lustrous green leaves ½" long **Soil & pH:** well-drained, sandy, loamy, acid soil; pH 5.0 to 6.0 **Light & Moisture:** full sun for best color; maintain moisture **Pruning Seasons:** as new growth begins

Spring heath (*Erica carnea* 'Springwood White')

The Forsythias

Forsythia

Forsythia is a rugged, beautiful, deciduous flowering shrub that covers its branches with small brilliant yellow flowers in late winter or early spring, even before the shrub's leaves appear. The flower buds that form over the summer are so ready to bloom by fall that a warm spell in winter will pop a few. The leaves turn orange-plum when the weather gets cold. Fast-growing, forsythia is used for screening, in informal hedges, as a tall ground cover and to prevent erosion on a slope. It can stand a lot of shearing and can be espaliered. Forsythia branches cut in late winter as the buds swell are easily forced into bloom in cool water indoors.

Forsythia (*Forsythia* x *intermedia* 'Beatrix Farrand')

Border forsythia (*Forsythia* x *intermedia* 'Spectabilis') is a favorite 8- to 10-foot, showy upright arching shrub for Zones 5–8. It has given rise to many popular cultivars, such as 'Lynwood', which bears bright yellow flowers; 'Spring Glory', an 8-footer with sulfur-yellow blooms; and 5- to 8-foot-tall 'Nana', which roots where it touches and makes a good ground cover. 'Gold Tide' stays under 20 inches and is excellent on slopes. The flower buds of

Forsythia (*Forsythia* x *intermedia* 'Spring Beauty')

'Meadowlark' and 'Northern Sun', suited to Zones 4–7, are especially cold resistant. In cold regions, such as northern Vermont, forsythia may only bloom to the height that was covered by snow during the coldest part of the winter. Thus the plant may have blooms from about 3 feet on down, but none above.

Weeping forsythia (*F. suspensa*) trails branches 20 to 30 feet long and is attractive growing over low walls in Zones 5 or 6–8, but it isn't a heavy bloomer.

Culture: whether a bare-root, balled-and-burlapped, or container-grown, forsythia transplants easily to well-drained loamy soil, pH 6.0 to 8.0, but tolerates most soils and some drought. The best flowering occurs in full sun. Forsythia flowers on growth made the previous season. Older twiggy branches that are blooming sparsely should be removed when the flowers fade. Allow upright forsythias to develop naturally.

Border forsythia (*Forsythia* x *intermedia* 'Spectabilis')

FEATURED PROFILE

Border Forsythia

Botanical Name: *Forsythia* x *intermedia* 'Spectabilis' **Family:** Oleaceae **Type of Plant:** deciduous flowering shrub **Uses:** specimen, shrub border, screen, hedge **Genus Range:** Europe **Hardiness:** USDA Zones 5–8 **Height:** 8 to 10' **Growth Rate:** fast **Form & Habit:** upright, arching **Bloom Period:** late winter to early spring **Flowers:** pale to bright yellow **Fruits:** insignificant brown capsules **Foliage:** 3 to 5" long, toothed toward the tip; bronze-plum in fall **Soil & pH:** well-drained; pH adaptable **Light & Moisture:** full sun for good bloom; handles some drought **Pruning Seasons:** after flowering

The Fothergillas

Fothergilla

Native to the Southeast, fothergillas are deciduous shrubs that are related to witch hazels. Similar to witch hazels, fothergillas bear flowers early in the season that consist mainly of stamens, and in fall their foliage turns beautiful colors. From April to early May, they bear honey-scented bottlebrush-type flower spikes. But while the flowers and the crinkly dark green foliage that follows are pleasant, the shrub's brilliant fall color is the main reason for its popularity. The leaves turn yellow-gold, orange, and scarlet, sometimes all at once. Fothergillas are good foundation plants and light up shrub borders of azaleas, rhododendrons, and evergreens.

The most widely planted species is the dwarf witch alder, or Alabama fothergilla (*Fothergilla gardenii*), a bushy shrub 2 to 4 feet tall and as wide or wider. It is hardy in Zones 5–8. Cultivars vary in growth habit and in summer and fall color. 'Jane Platt', a somewhat pendulous plant, has excellent fall color. 'Mount Airy', hardy in Zones 5–7, grows to 5 feet and bears a profusion of white flower spikes; it has consistent fall color.

Fast-growing *F. major,* known as "large fothergilla," has flowers and foliage similar to 'Mount Airy' but grows upright to 6 to 10 feet. It thrives in Zones 5–8.

Large fothergilla (*Fothergilla major*) in spring

Culture: fothergillas transplant fairly easily in early spring. Set out a young container-grown or balled-and-burlapped plant in moist, well-drained humusy soil. It will do best where the pH is under 6.0. Dwarf witch alder prefers full sun, but in hot regions it benefits from noon shade. Prune before growth starts in the spring by cutting back to the ground any old branches that are crowding others. Take care not to damage young shoots coming up from the base.

Dwarf witch alder
(*Fothergilla gardenii* 'Mount Airy')

FEATURED PROFILE
Dwarf Witch Alder, or Alabama Fothergilla

Botanical Name: *Fothergilla gardenii* **Family:** Hamamelidaceae **Type of Plant:** deciduous flowering shrub with colorful fall foliage **Uses:** foundation plant, specimen; in borders with rhododendrons **Native Range:** native from Virginia to Georgia **Hardiness:** USDA Zones 5–8 **Height:** 2 to 4' **Growth Rate:** slow **Form & Habit:** airy, open **Bloom Period:** April–May **Flowers:** white filaments, yellow anthers borne on upright 1 to 2" terminal spikes **Fruits:** insignificant capsules **Foliage:** rounded, 1 to 2" long, leathery and medium green in summer, turning brilliant yellow, orange, and crimson in fall **Soil & pH:** well-drained, humusy; under pH 6.0 **Light & Moisture:** full sun for best flowering and color; sustained moisture **Pruning Seasons:** before buds open in early spring

Dwarf witch alder (*Fothergilla gardenii*) in fall

Gardenia
also called "Cape Jasmine"

Gardenia jasminoides

The gardenia is an evergreen shrub 4 to 6 feet tall with waxy white flowers that are among the world's most fragrant. The flowers are borne in spring and summer and are set off by leathery, glossy bright green leaves about 4 inches long. Native to China, the gardenia has been treasured in America since Colonial times. Semishaded in frost-free Zones 8–11, it grows into a magnificent shrub. Where it isn't hardy, many gardeners grow it in a container outdoors in summer and overwinter it indoors. Gardenias will continue to form flower buds indoors where the plants can have full sun (placed near a sunny window) and cool temperatures of 60° to 70°F.

Gardenia jasminoides (also known as *G. augusta*), the most widely planted species, grows to about 6 feet. There are double flowered and dwarf cultivars. The cultivar 'Fortuniana' is double-flowered, as is the smaller 'August Beauty', which grows to about 5 feet and blooms over an extended period, from May through November. 'Aimee' is the first to bloom in spring. 'Radicans', a mounding miniature 6 to 12 inches tall and 2 to 3 feet wide, has small leaves and many small flowers. It makes a good ground cover. 'Radicans Variegata' has variegated foliage. 'White Gem' grows to about 2 feet and may be used as a low hedge.

Culture: a container-grown gardenia transplants easily in early spring or fall to fertile, well-drained, moist, humusy, acid soil—pH 5.0 to 6.5. Sustained moisture is necessary to keep the plant looking good. It succeeds in full sun and in bright or dappled shade. Deadheading encourages flowering. To keep the plant compact and bushy, cut back extra-long branches to the desired length when the blooms fade.

Gardenia (*Gardenia jasminoides* 'White Gem')

Gardenia (*Gardenia jasminoides*)

Gardenia (*Gardenia jasminoides*)

FEATURED PROFILE
Gardenia, or Cape Jasmine

Botanical Name: *Gardenia jasminoides* **Family:** Rubiaceae **Type of Plant:** fragrant, flowering broad-leaved evergreen shrub **Uses:** specimen, foundation plant, low shrub; greenhouse and house plant
Native Range: China **Hardiness:** USDA Zones 8–11 **Height:** 6' **Growth Rate:** medium **Form & Habit:** erect twiggy shrub **Bloom Period:** spring through November **Flowers:** waxy white, many-petaled, sometimes double; 3" across **Fruits:** insignificant **Foliage:** glossy evergreen lance-shaped leaves 4" long
Soil & pH: fertile, well-drained, humusy; pH 5.0 to 6.5. **Light & Moisture:** full sun; sustained moisture
Pruning Seasons: after flowers fade

Gardenia (*Gardenia jasminoides*)

Salal and Wintergreen

Gaultheria

Wintergreen (*Gaultheria procumbens*)   Salal (*Gaultheria shallon*)

The gaultherias are beautiful evergreen shrubs and ground covers that grow wild in North America and Asia. They belong to the heath family. In spring and summer, they bear heatherlike urn- or bell-shaped flowers.

The lustrous dark green 5-inch leaves of salal (*Gaultheria shallon*) make it the most conspicuous of the gaultherias. This West Coast native, hardy in Zones 6–8, is also called "lemon leaf" by florists, who use it in arrangements. An airy sprawling shrub that grows 1½ to 2 feet high, it carpets coastal forests with wide-spreading slim shoots. In spring and summer, salal produces loose clusters of small waxy white or pinkish urn-shaped flowers followed by edible purple-black fruits. It's an excellent tall ground cover for moist acid woodland soils, and it looks beautiful in front of evergreens. The 3-foot Chinese species (*G. veitchiana*), hardy in Zones 7–9, has lustrous leaves and white-to-blush pink bell-shaped flowers in midspring, followed by indigo blue berries.

An eastern cousin of salal is wintergreen, or checkerberry (*G. procumbens*). Native Americans made a tea of its minty tasting fruits to relieve rheumatism and fevers.

Wintergreen is a beautiful creeping ground cover less than a foot tall that grows wild in the Northeast woods and in gardens in Zones 3 or 4–8. It is planted in rock gardens and as ground cover beneath low-branched trees such as hemlocks and beeches.

Culture: gaultheria is most easily transplanted in early spring to soil that approximates its native site. Set out a young container-grown plant in a well-drained peaty bed in the acid range. Gaultheria does best in light shade but tolerates some direct sun. Keep the soil evenly moist. The gaultherias generally need minimal pruning.

Salal (*Gaultheria shallon*)

FEATURED PROFILE
Salal, or Shallon

Botanical Name: *Gaultheria shallon* **Family:** Ericaceae **Type of Plant:** low evergreen shrub **Uses:** tall ground cover **Native Range:** Alaska to California **Hardiness:** USDA Zones 6–8 **Height:** 1½ to 2' **Growth Rate:** medium **Form & Habit:** asymmetrical, airy, spreading **Bloom Period:** spring to summer **Flowers:** clusters of white to pinkish urn-shaped flowers ⅓" long **Fruits:** persistent purplish black berries **Foliage:** rounded, leathery, dark green to 5" long **Soil & pH:** well-drained, peaty, pH 5.5 to 6.5 **Light & Moisture:** partial shade, tolerates some direct sun; maintain moisture **Pruning Seasons:** after flowering

Woadwaxen

Genista tinctoria

The woadwaxen are low-growing deciduous and semi-evergreen shrubs native to Europe, Asia, and Africa. Members of the pea family, they resemble broom (*Cytisus*). In spring they are covered with masses of showy pealike yellow flowers, which are followed by dried pods. Their leaves are insignificant. In winter, genista stems remain green, adding an attractive touch of color to the garden. The genistas are useful edgers and look handsome in rock gardens. They thrive with little care on sunny slopes and, because they grow rapidly, they can be used to control erosion on dry infertile sandy slopes.

The hardiest species is woadwaxen, or dyer's greenwood (*Genista tinctoria*), which grows in Zones 4 or 5–7 and was once used to make dyes. An erect twiggy shrub about 3 feet high and wide, it has spiny stems and bright green leaves about an inch long. In June, it covers itself with clusters of bright yellow flowers; the shrub may bloom again if cut back after flowering. It has naturalized in parts of North America. 'Royal Gold' is a 2-foot cultivar. There are even shorter species. Silky-leaf woadwaxen (*G. pilosa*), hardy

Lydia woadwaxen (*Genista lydia* 'Primula')

Silky-leaf woadwaxen
(*Genista pilosa* 'Vancouver gold')

in Zones 5 or 6–7 or 8, grows slowly to about a foot high. It has small hairy leaves and, in spring and summer, it bears short clusters of yellow flowers. 'Vancouver Gold' is an especially floriferous cultivar. *G. lydia*, which has become popular in the West and Northeast, is a prostrate form about a foot high.

Lydia woadwaxen (*Genista lydia*)

Culture: genista transplants with difficulty and needs time to establish itself, though it is carefree once growing. Set out a young container-grown plant in early spring in well-drained infertile sandy soil that is rather dry. Genista thrives in soil in the alkaline range and requires full sun. It may rebloom sparsely if pruned back lightly after blooming, but the genistas look best when they develop naturally.

FEATURED PROFILE
Woadwaxen, or Dyer's Greenwood

Botanical Name: *Genista tinctoria* **Family:** Leguminosae **Type of Plant:** deciduous flowering shrub **Uses:** erosion control on slopes; rock garden; edger **Native Range:** Europe, western Asia, **Hardiness:** USDA Zones 4 or 5–7 **Height:** 3' **Growth Rate:** slow **Form & Habit:** erect, mounded, twiggy **Bloom Period:** June, with some repeat bloom **Flowers:** yellow, ½ to ¾" long, borne on upright racemes 1 to 3" long **Fruits:** insignificant pods **Foliage:** ½ to 1" long, rich green **Soil & pH:** well-drained, infertile dryish sandy soil; pH 6.5 to 7.5 **Light & Moisture:** full sun; handles drought **Pruning Seasons:** after flowering, but better left natural

Woadwaxen (*Genista tinctoria*)

The Witch Hazels

Hamamelis

Witch hazel (*Hamamelis virginiana*)

Chinese witch hazel
(*Hamamelis mollis* 'Pallida')

The witch hazels are small picturesque trees and tall shrubs that flower in cold seasons. In fall, they turn lovely shades of yellow, orange, and carmine red. The peculiar flowers consist of four twisted ribbonlike petals dangling on bare branches; they survive sudden drops in temperature by curling up. Witch hazel foliage resembles hazelnut foliage, though it is less glossy, hence the name. Successful in the light shade of deciduous woods in the East and Midwest, witch hazels are used in naturalized plantings, as specimens in small gardens, and for screenings, hedges, and container plants.

Of the species that flower in late fall, 15-foot native *Hamamelis virginiana* is the best choice for cold climates and for moist shaded sites in Zones 3–8 of eastern Canada and the United States. This shrub bears fragrant yellow flowers in November or December. The somewhat taller Chinese witch hazel (*H. mollis*) is the most fragrant species. In February or March, it produces large yellow flowers that have a reddish base. The fall color is a luminous yellow or orange-yellow. The Chinese witch hazel is hardy only as far north as Zone 6.

The most common witch hazels for garden culture are varieties of *H. x intermedia* that bloom between January and March. Depending on the variety, they bear wonderful soft yellow or bronze red fragrant flowers; the fall foliage is a rich yellow with red tints. Each has its own appeal: 'Arnold's Promise' has pure yellow flowers; the flowers of 'Jelena' are a beautiful copper. The fall

Chinese witch hazel
(*Hamamelis mollis*)

foliage of red-flowered 'Diane' is a rich orange-red. These cultivars reach heights of 10 to 20 feet, and the plants are hardy in Zone 5 with winter protection and in Zones 6–8.

Culture: set out a container-grown or balled-and-burlapped plant in early spring in well-drained, moist, somewhat acid loam. Witch hazels succeed in full sun at the northern end of their range; farther south they do better with midday shade.

FEATURED PROFILE
Witch Hazel

Botanical Name: *Hamamelis x intermedia* 'Jelena' **Family:** Hamamelidaceae **Type of Plant:** tall deciduous flowering shrub or small tree with colorful fall foliage **Uses:** scented flowers; lawn specimen; naturalizing; screening; hedges **Genus Range:** E. Asia and North America **Hardiness:** USDA Zones 5 or 6–8 **Height:** to 15' **Growth Rate:** medium-slow **Form & Habit:** large, spreading, open form **Bloom Period:** between January and mid March **Flowers:** bright yellow, wavy, straplike petals tinged with red **Fruits:** small capsules **Foliage:** medium green in summer; rich orange-red in fall **Soil & pH:** well-drained; pH range **5.5 to 6.5** **Light & Moisture:** full sun or light shade; best in moist soil

Witch hazel
(*Hamamelis x intermedia* 'Jelena')

Rose-of-Sharon
also called "Shrub Althea"

Hibiscus syriacus

Rose-of-Sharon
(*Hibiscus syriacus* 'Diana')

Rose-of-Sharon
(*Hibiscus syriacus* 'Aphrodite')

The old-fashioned hibiscus, called "rose-of-Sharon" and "shrub althea" (*Hibiscus syriacus*), has been grown in America since Colonial days and in Europe for 200 years before that. A tall shrub or small tree 8 to 12 feet high and almost as wide, it bears lots of short-lived flowers from July until the end of September. The trumpet-shaped blooms are 4 to 5 inches across and have ruffled petals that are crinkled on the margin. The usual colors are white, pink, crimson, and purple. Planted in a sheltered corner, shrub althea survives winters in Zones 5–8.

Chinese hibiscus (*Hibiscus rosa-sinensis*)

Rose-of-Sharon (*Hibiscus syriacus*)

Some outstanding hybrids introduced by the United States National Arboretum bloom over an even longer period. The flowers of 'Diana' are pure white; 'Helene' has white flowers with deep reddish purple eyes; the blooms of 'Minerva' are lavender-pink; and 'Aphrodite' bears deep rose pink flowers with showy dark red eyes. 'Red Heart' makes a handsome flowering hedge.

The tropical Chinese hibiscus (*H. rosa-sinensis*) is grown in Zones 10 and 11 in southern Florida and California and as an annual or houseplant in cool regions. A fast-growing handsome evergreen shrub 6 to 8 feet tall, Chinese hibiscus bears showy single or double 6-inch-wide trumpet-shaped flowers in red, pink, yellow, orange, or white, sometimes with a contrasting eye. Each flower lasts only one day but flowers appear just about year-round.

Culture: a young balled-and-burlapped or container-grown rose-of-Sharon transplants easily in early spring or fall to humusy well-drained soil, pH 5.5 to 7.0. It will flower most fully in a sunny site but tolerates bright shade. To encourage flowering, selectively prune older branches back to a strong outward facing bud in early spring before growth begins.

FEATURED PROFILE
Rose-of-Sharon, or "Shrub Althea"

Botanical Name: *Hibiscus syriacus* **Family:** Malvaceae **Type of Plant:** late-blooming deciduous flowering shrub or small tree **Uses:** specimen, shrub border, tall flowering hedge **Native Range:** China **Hardiness:** USDA Zones 5–8 **Height:** 8 to 12' **Growth Rate:** medium **Form & Habit:** erect, spreading **Bloom Period:** late June or July until frost **Flowers:** trumpet-shaped, 4 to 5" across, crinkled margins; white, pink, crimson, and purple, often with a contrasting eye **Fruits:** persistent capsules **Foliage:** 2 to 4" long; variously toothed and notched; leathery; dark green **Soil & pH:** humusy well-drained soil; pH 5.5 to 6.5 **Light & Moisture:** full sun for best flowering; needs moisture but handles some drought. **Pruning Seasons:** early spring before buds open

Rose-of-Sharon (*Hibiscus syriacus*)

Hydrangea

Hydrangea

Peegee hydrangea (*Hydrangea paniculata* 'Grandiflora')

The hydrangeas are fast-growing deciduous shrubs with canelike branches and large handsome leaves. The large flowerheads are composed of small flat florets.

The bigleaf (*Hydrangea macrophylla*) is an old-fashioned plant 3 to 6 feet tall that blooms in mid- to late summer in Zones 5–9. There are two types of bigleaf hydrangea flowers: the rounded hortensia, or mopheads, and the flattened lacecaps, which have both the opened and unopened (sterile) florets. Flowers come in cream, rose, or dark blue. The soil acidity determines the color of pink or blue blooms. Acid soil in the pH range of 5.0 to 5.5 results in a soft blue; soil pH of 6.0 to 6.5 or slightly higher produces pink flowers. There are also crimson varieties and miniatures. The leaves of 'Variegata' are edged with creamy white.

Lacecap hydrangea (*Hydrangea macrophylla* 'Blue Wave')

Hills of snow hydrangea (*H. arborescens* 'Grandiflora'), a hardy shrub for Zones 3–9, produces big clusters of creamy white florets. 'Annabelle' bears rounded 12-inch flowerheads.

A tall magnificent hydrangea valued for its foliage as well as its flowers is the native oakleaf hydrangea (*H. quercifolia*). Its white cone-shaped flowers open in early summer; the big, handsome, oak-shaped leaves turn red-purple in fall. It is hardy in Zones 5–9. 'Snowflake' and 'Snow Queen' are improved forms.

The peegee hydrangea (*H. paniculata* 'Grandiflora') is a treelike plant growing to about 20 feet tall that in late summer bears large cone-shaped heads of white flowers that age to rose, and then bronze. It serves well in dried-flower arrangements. It is hardy in Zones 4–8.

Culture: the hydrangeas transplant easily in early spring to well-drained humusy soil. *H. macrophylla* requires acid soil; color depends on the soil's pH, as described; the hills of snow and oakleaf hydrangeas are tolerant of varied pH. Hydrangeas bloom best in full sun or bright or dappled shade; in hot regions, noon shade is beneficial. Prune *H. macrophylla* and *H. quercifolia* to remove old weak branches in spring before growth begins. *H. arborescens* 'Grandiflora' flowers on new wood; so to maintain its vigor, cut out the oldest canes between late fall and early spring.

Bigleaf hydrangea (*Hydrangea macrophylla* 'All Summer Beauty')

Oakleaf hydrangea (*Hydrangea quercifolia* 'Snow Queen')

FEATURED PROFILE
Oakleaf Hydrangea

Botanical Name: *Hydrangea quercifolia* 'Snow Queen' **Family:** Hydrangeaceae **Type of Plant:** large flowering shrub **Uses:** background for flowering border; massing, featured specimen, flowering hedge **Genus Range:** S.E. U.S. **Hardiness:** Zones 5–9 **Height:** 6 to 8' **Growth Rate:** medium **Form & Habit:** tall, wide, upright with extensive branching **Bloom Period:** May to July **Flowers:** white, semidouble, 1" wide, in cone-shaped clusters up to 13" long, turning dusty rose with age **Foliage:** oaklike, to 9" long, and finely serrated; turning rose, claret, and burgundy in autumn **Soil & pH:** well-drained; tolerates clay but not salt; pH 4 to 7 **Light & Moisture:** full sun for best color but tolerates light shade; tolerates some drought, but does best with sustained moisture **Pruning Seasons:** during dormancy

St. John's wort

Hypericum

The hypericums are dwarf or slow-growing woody shrubs and ground covers with bright yellow flowers that resemble small single roses with conspicuous gold or red stamens. They bloom for as long as two months and are handsome carpeting the ground and fronting shrub borders. They're evergreen in the South and semievergreen in cooler regions.

The most widely grown species is broombrush, or shrubby St. John's wort (*Hypericum prolificum*), a small,

Shrubby St. John's wort
(*Hypericum prolificum*)

woody evergreen 3 to 5 feet tall that flowers all summer long in Zones 4–8. 'Hidcote', a hybrid that some experts attribute to *H. prolificum* and others to goldencup St. John's wort (*H. patulum*), is perhaps the most beautiful hypericum. Its mound of arching branches with blue-green foliage produces the largest flowers of any hypericum in June, and it blooms throughout the growing season. *H. kalmianum*, a smaller, hardier shrub with smaller flowers, can withstand temperatures to -40°F. So it is popular in northern gardens.

A smaller, variegated species for shrub borders and rock gardens in Zones 6–8 is goldflower (*H.* x *moserianum* 'Tricolor'). Two feet tall and globelike with arching red stems, 'Tricolor' has long-lasting gray-green foliage edged in pink-tinged creamy white. The dark gold flowers are set off by bright orange stamens. Blooming throughout the summer, 'Tricolor' is especially effective planted in groups.

Culture: the hypericums transplant easily in early spring to dry rocky soil, pH 6.5 to 7.0. They flower best in full sun but tolerate light shade. Less hardy species sometimes die to the ground in winter in the northern parts of their growing range, but they usually regrow and flower that year. Hypericums bloom on new growth, so pruning is best done in early spring. Remove all dead and weak thin growth, old seedheads, and damaged branch tips.

St. John's wort
(*Hypericum androsaemum*)

St. John's wort (*Hypericum* x *moserianum* 'Tricolor')

FEATURED PROFILE
Shrubby St. John's wort

Botanical Name: *Hypericum prolificum* **Family:** Hypericaceae
Type of Plant: low-growing flowering shrub **Uses:** shrub border, ground cover **Native Range:** NJ to GA, W. to IA **Hardiness:** USDA Zones 4–8 **Height:** 3 to 5' **Growth Rate:** slow **Form & Habit:** small, rounded, with erect stems **Bloom Period:** late June to July and August **Flowers:** bright yellow, ¾ to 1" across, borne in terminal cymes **Fruits:** inconspicuous dry 3-valved capsules **Foliage:** narrow, slim ovals 1 to 3" long, dark lustrous green **Soil & pH:** dry rocky soil; pH 6.5 to 7.0 **Light & Moisture:** full sun or partial shade; does best in dryish conditions **Pruning Seasons:** early spring

Shrubby St. John's wort (*Hypericum prolificum*)

Mountain Laurel

Kalmia latifolia

Mountain laurel
(*Kalmia latifolia* 'Elf')

Mountain laurel
(*Kalmia latifolia* 'Carousel')

Mountain laurel (*Kalmia latifolia* 'Ostbo Red')

Mountain laurel is an outstanding flowering broad-leaved evergreen native to temperate zones of North America. It has large handsome glossy leaves and in midspring bears large rounded heads of pink cup-shaped florets. Seven to 8 feet tall, mountain laurel (*Kalmia latifolia*) grows wild in light woodlands in Zones 4–7 or 8, from Connecticut to northern Florida. The pale pink flowers of the species are lovely, but the white, pink, or variegated flowers of the cultivars are far more exciting. One of the best is 'Ostbo Red', with bright red buds that open to a soft deep pink. 'Elf', a miniature slow-growing laurel, eventually reaches 4 to 6 feet tall; its light pink buds open to white. The flowers of 'Bullseye' and 'Fuscata' have white centers surrounded by bands of red. Like the rhododendron, mountain laurel does best in tall or dappled shade and where summers are cool. Every part of the plant is poisonous to people and livestock, but not to wildlife.

Sheep laurel, or lambkill (*K. angustifolia*), the 2- to 3-foot shrubby ground cover favored by Henry David Thoreau, is hardy in Zones 2–8. Its flowers are colored lavender-rose, and they are a little smaller than those of the mountain laurel. It's a good shrub for naturalizing, because in the wild it grows on rocky barrens and old pastures, often in semishade. There is also a white-flowered form.

Culture: kalmias transplant easily in early spring or fall to soil that is well-drained, humusy, fertile, and in the acid range—pH 4.5 to 6.5. To flower well, they need a half day of sun or bright shade all day. Remove flowerheads as they fade. Kalmias recover slowly from pruning, perhaps because it is unnecessary in healthy plants. To rejuvenate an old shrub, prune after flowering to remove one or two less-desirable branches over a period of three to five years.

FEATURED PROFILE
Mountain Laurel

Botanical Name: *Kalmia latifolia* **Family:** Ericaceae **Type of Plant:** broad-leaved evergreen flowering shrub **Uses:** specimen or shrub border for the shade **Native Range:** CT to N. FL **Hardiness:** USDA Zones 4–7 or 8 **Height:** 7 to 8' **Growth Rate:** slow **Form & Habit:** oval when young, open-branched later **Bloom Period:** May–June **Flowers:** ¾ to 1" across; pink buds open to white **Fruits:** capsules in clusters **Foliage:** glossy green; leathery, elliptical, 2 to 5" long, 2" wide **Soil & pH:** well-drained, humusy, fertile; pH 4.5 to 6.5. **Light & Moisture:** dappled or high shade; maintain moisture **Pruning Seasons:** after flowering

A mountain laurel (*Kalmia latifolia*)

Japanese Kerria

Kerria japonica

Kerria is a deciduous shrub that covers itself with sunny yellow flowers, like forsythia, for two or three weeks in April or May. The only species in cultivation is Japanese kerria (*Kerria japonica*), which actually comes from China. Grown in Zones 4–9, this 3- to 6-foot shrub is popular in the Northeast. It bears masses of small, flat-faced, five-petaled flowers and often reblooms in summer. 'Pleniflora', a larger showier cultivar, is a vigorous upright bushy plant 6 to 8 feet or taller, with profuse golden yellow double flowers. They last well as cut flowers. This plant is hardy from Zones 4 or 5–9. 'Picta', a smaller cultivar with gray-green leaves thinly edged with white, looks pretty and soft even from a distance. It's been cultivated in Japan since the 1700s, and some North American growers offer it.

Though the leaves drop when cold comes, kerria stems remain green throughout the winter, adding a welcome bit of color to the

Japanese kerria
(*Kerria japonica* 'Pleniflora')

garden. Both the species and the cultivar bloom well in partial shade, even in dry urban gardens. Kerria is a traditional wall plant in cottage gardens and is attractive massed in naturalistic plantings and on slopes. Use it to screen leggy lilacs.

Japanese kerria (*Kerria japonica*)

Culture: a balled-and-burlapped or container-grown kerria transplants easily in early spring to almost any well-drained, moderately moist fertile soil. Kerria isn't particular about pH, and it tolerates summer heat and drought. It prefers light shade, especially in hot regions. To keep 'Pleniflora' shapely, trim old flowering stems back to strong young shoots or to ground level as flowers fade. Remove the suckers that rise around the variegated cultivar 'Picta'; their foliage tends to revert to plain green.

FEATURED PROFILE

Kerria

Botanical Name: *Kerria japonica* 'Pleniflora' **Family:** Rosaceae
Type of Plant: spreading deciduous flowering shrub **Uses:** naturalizing, slopes, front of border **Genus Range:** central and western China
Hardiness: USDA Zones 4 or 5–9 **Height:** 6 to 8' **Growth Rate:** medium **Form & Habit:** upright and arching **Bloom Period:** April–May **Flowers:** fully double, 1 to 2" across, golden yellow **Foliage:** 1½ to 4" long, lance-shaped **Soil & pH:** well-drained loamy soil, only moderately fertile; pH adaptable **Light & Moisture:** bright shade but tolerates full sun; sustained moisture, but handles summer heat and drought **Pruning Seasons:** after flowering

Japanese kerria (*Kerria japonica* 'Pleniflora')

Beauty Bush

Kolkwitzia amabilis

Beauty bush (*Kolkwitzia amabilis*)

When in bloom, beauty bush (*Kolkwitzia amabilis*), a vase-shaped deciduous shrub with long slim branches, resembles a giant bridal bouquet. In May and early June, the shrub is smothered with irregular clusters of small but showy pale pink bell-shaped flowers with yellow throats. It grows to 10 feet tall. The brown hairy seeds that develop are interesting and last into winter. The species was introduced from China in the early 1900s and has become a garden staple in Zones 4–8. But smaller cultivars with better color have since been introduced and are becoming more popular than the species. An example is 'Pink Cloud', which has a flower of a richer, clearer pink.

Beauty bush makes a handsome specimen plant when covered with flowers, but it is not particularly ornamental out of bloom. Place it where it doesn't dominate the garden. A long row of beauty bush makes a good tall informal hedge or windbreak in a large landscape.

Culture: beauty bush transplants easily in early spring or fall to almost any well-drained soil and does best in pH 5.0 to 7.0. It requires full sun to bloom well and looks best when allowed to develop its arching branches freely. Remove old weak wood right after the flowers fade.

Beauty bush (*Kolkwitzia amabilis*)

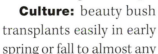

FEATURED PROFILE
Beauty Bush

Botanical Name: *Kolkwitzia amabilis* **Family:** Caprifoliaceae **Type of Plant:** deciduous flowering shrub **Uses:** tall screening, tall hedge, windbreak **Native Range:** central China **Hardiness:** USDA Zones 4 or 5–8 **Height:** 10' **Growth Rate:** fast **Form & Habit:** vase-shaped with arching branches **Bloom Period:** May to early June **Flowers:** irregular clusters of small, bell-shaped flowers; rich pink buds open to a paler pink with yellow anthers **Fruits:** light brown or pink hairy seeds **Foliage:** 1 to 3" long, almost as broad, with pointed tips and a rather dull green color **Soil & pH:** well-drained; pH 5.0 to 7.0, but tolerant **Light & Moisture:** full sun; tolerates drought **Pruning Seasons:** after flowering

Beauty bush (*Kolkwitzia amabilis* 'Pink Cloud')

The Leucothoes

Leucothoe

Keisk's leucothoe
(*Leucothoe keiskei*) fall foliage

These native woodland shrubs have ornamental foliage and beautiful spring flowers. They are broad-leaved evergreens or semievergreens 2 to 5 feet tall that thrive in shaded sites and acid soils.

The decorative drooping leucothoe (*Leucothoe fontanesiana*) has long slim arching branches covered with lustrous 2- to 5-inch leaves that turn from dark green to bronze-plum in the fall. In early summer, leucothoe shows off pendent 2- to 3-inch clusters of small, waxy, white bell- or urn-shaped flowers that are faintly fragrant. It is hardy in Zones 4 or 5–8; in Zones 4 and 5 the foliage persists but may drop in winter. 'Scarletta' is a 2-foot dwarf with foliage that starts out scarlet, turns lustrous green, and then turns wine red. 'Rainbow', a showy 3- to 5-foot cultivar introduced in 1949, has young shoots of bright red and mottled creamy yellow leaves tipped with rose-pink. Both cultivars are hardy in Zones 5 or 6–8.

The 2- to 4-foot coast leucothoe (*L. axillaris*), a similar species, has better summer heat tolerance, thriving in Zones 5 or 6–9. It is native to the Southeast from Virginia southward and combines well with native azaleas and rhododendrons. The even more tropical Florida leucothoe (*L. populifolia*) grows wild from South Carolina to Florida. It is often planted along shady streams and to control erosion on slopes in Zones 8 and 9.

Keisk's leucothoe (*L. keiskei*) is a Japanese plant with pure white, nodding, ½-inch flowers that bloom from June to July. It has brilliant wine red foliage in the fall. It is suited to Zones 6–9.

Culture: a container-grown leucothoe transplants easily in early spring to well-drained, loose, moist acid soil, pH 4.5 to 6.0. It requires a shaded location and watering during droughts. Little pruning is needed. To keep leucothoe well-shaped, cut any weak ungainly stems to ground level after the plant flowers.

Drooping leucothoe (*Leucothoe fontanesiana*)

FEATURED PROFILE
Drooping Leucothoe

Botanical Name: *Leucothoe fontanesiana* **Family:** Ericaceae **Type of Plant:** broad-leaved flowering evergreen **Uses:** evergreen for shade and moist acid soils **Native Range:** southeastern U.S. **Hardiness:** USDA Zones 4 or 5–8 **Height:** 3 to 5' **Growth Rate:** slow to medium **Form & Habit:** spreading arching branches **Bloom Period:** late May to June **Flowers:** white, ¼" in pendent 2 to 3" clusters, slightly fragrant **Fruits:** inconspicuous capsules **Foliage:** 2 to 5" long, slim, lance-shaped, glossy leathery green or bronze-green when emerging, turning bronze plum in fall **Soil & pH:** well-drained, loose, acid soil; pH 4.5 to 6.0 **Light & Moisture:** shade; keep the roots moist **Pruning Seasons:** after flowering

Drooping leucothoe (*Leucothoe fontanesiana* 'Rainbow')

The Mahonias

Mahonia

Chinese mahonia (*Mahonia fortunei*)

The mahonias, handsome shade-loving evergreen shrubs of the barberry family, add texture and fall color to the garden. They have spiny hollylike leaves and bear small golden yellow flowers that have a sweet, rather pervasive, scent. The two most popular species are often used with hollies. They're good for screening and attractive in shrub borders. Popular in the Southeast in Zones 6–8, leatherleaf mahonia (*Mahonia bealei*) is a 6- to 8-foot shrub with large, handsome compound blue-green leaves up to 18 inches long that are composed of 4-inch toothed leaflets. The leaves sit almost horizontally; they retain their color in winter. In late February and early March, leatherleaf mahonia bears drooping clusters of perfumed yellow flowers followed by blue-black grapelike fruits that birds love. Its legginess can be disguised easily by under planting using hellebore and *Sarcoccoca ruscifolia*. Chinese mahonia (*M. fortunei*) is similar but has softer foliage and is hardy only in Zones 7–9. On the West Coast it blooms in the fall.

Oregon grape holly
(*Mahonia aquifolium*)

Oregon grape holly
(*Mahonia aquifolium*)

Oregon grape holly (*M. aquifolium*) is a 3- to 6-foot plant with shiny refined leaves that turn bronze-plum in winter. Hardier than leatherleaf mahonia, it thrives in Zones 4 or 5–8. Clusters of small fragrant yellow flowers appear in late winter or early spring; blue-black fruits follow. 'Apollo' is an outstanding cultivar with yellow-orange flowers. 'Compacta', a dwarf 2 to 3 feet tall, is hardy in Zones 6–8.

Culture: a young container-grown or balled-and-burlapped mahonia transplants easily in early spring to well-drained, humusy, moist, slightly acid soil, pH 6.0 to 7.0. The mahonias prefer light shade, but Oregon grape holly can stand some direct sun. If the shrub becomes too leggy, cut gangling older canes back to ground level when blooming is over. Remove suckers as they arise to keep Oregon grape holly from spreading.

FEATURED PROFILE
Leatherleaf Mahonia

Botanical Name: *Mahonia bealei* **Family:** Berberidaceae **Type of Plant:** evergreen flowering shrub **Uses:** foundation plant, shrub border, screening **Native Range:** China **Hardiness:** USDA Zones 6–8 **Height:** 6 to 8' **Growth Rate:** slow **Form & Habit:** upright **Bloom Period:** early spring **Flowers:** fragrant yellow flowers clustered on erect spikes 4 to 8" long **Fruits:** grapelike clusters of blue-black oval berries **Foliage:** compound leaf to 18" long with 9 to 15 spiny leaflets **Soil & pH:** well-drained; humusy; pH 6.0 to 7.0 **Light & Moisture:** partial shade; even moisture **Pruning Seasons:** after flowering

Leatherleaf mahonia (*Mahonia bealei*)

Heavenly Bamboo

Nandina domestica

Heavenly bamboo
(*Nandina domestica*)

Heavenly bamboo
(*Nandina domestica*) flower

Delicate-looking but tough, heavenly bamboo (*Nandina domestica*) is a leafy, 5- to 7-foot unbranched multistemmed shrub that is evergreen in warm parts of its hardiness range. The dainty green leaves are tipped bright red in winter. In spring and early summer, the stems bear loose upright clusters of small whitish florets. In fall, beautiful drooping bunches of bright red berries appear. They may persist until blooming begins the following spring.

A native of China and Japan and hardy in Zones 6 or 7–9, the species is popular in the South, where the berries color well and last a long time. However, more compact and disease-resistant cultivars with even better winter color are replacing the species. The foliage of 'Harbor Dwarf', a graceful 2-footer, is touched with pink or bronze in spring and turns orange-bronze in fall. 'Nana Purpurea' is similar, but its foliage is reddish purple in winter. 'Alba', a white-fruited variety, makes a handsome companion for a red-berried form.

Nandinas are excellent in a shrub border, as a hedge, and in containers. They succeed in bright shade and compete well with tree roots. Cut stems of nandina provide attractive long-lasting greenery for bouquets.

Culture: a young container-grown nandina transplants easily in early spring or fall. Nandina thrives in well-drained, moist fertile soil but tolerates other situations. It fruits best in full sun but will still produce berries in 4 to 6 hours of sun, or all-day filtered light. To keep the plant compact, cut crowded or gangly canes back to the ground in early spring.

Heavenly bamboo (*Nandina domestica*) in fall

Heavenly bamboo (*Nandina domestica*)

FEATURED PROFILE
Heavenly Bamboo

Botanical Name: *Nandina domestica* **Family:** Berberidaceae **Type of Plant:** red-berried leafy semievergreen shrub; evergreen in warm regions **Uses:** shrub border, hedge, specimen **Native Range:** China **Hardiness:** USDA Zones 6 or 7–9 **Height:** 5 to 7' **Growth Rate:** medium to fast **Form & Habit:** erect, flat-topped **Bloom Period:** May–June **Flowers:** star-shaped, white, ¼ to ½" across, dense terminal panicles **Fruits:** clusters of round bright red berries **Foliage:** dainty, pointed compound 5-leaflet 1½ to 4" long **Soil & pH:** well-drained, fertile; pH adaptable **Light & Moisture:** full sun for best fruiting; maintain moisture **Pruning Seasons:** before growth begins in early spring

The Mock Oranges

Philadelphus

Mock orange is a large old-fashioned deciduous shrub with crisp white sweetly fragrant flowers that recall orange blossoms. Dozens of species and hundreds of hybrids have been introduced. Most are carefree vigorous growers 10 to 12 feet tall and twice as wide. In spring, a mock orange is a mass of dull, dark green leaves. Then, in May and early June, its clusters of 1- to 2-inch pure white flowers open to reveal showy golden anthers, and the perfume permeates the garden.

Of the modern cultivars, the closest to an old-fashioned fragrant mock orange is *Philadelphus* x *virginalis* 'Natchez'. Hardy in Zones 4 or 5–8, this 8- to 12-foot shrub needs a large garden to show off its beauty. The flowers of *P.* x *virginalis* cultivars are semidouble to double and repeat bloom modestly. Other modern hybrids are fragrant but smaller. The leaves of 'Variegata' have a creamy white margin. 'Minnesota Snowflake' reaches 6 feet and has arching branches and exquisite double flowers; it is hardy to Zone 4. Among the most fragrant are *P. 3 lemoinei* 'Innocence', which stays less than 8 feet tall, and 4-foot 'Avalanche'; both are hardy in Zones 5–8. The flowers of *P.* x *virginalis* cultivars are semidouble to double and repeat bloom modestly; plants are hardy in Zones 5–9.

Mock orange
(*Philadelphus* x *lemoinei*)

Mock orange (*Philadelphus* 'Buckley's Quill')

Culture: to be sure of having a strongly scented mock orange, buy a container-grown plant in bloom. Mock orange succeeds in almost any soil, but it grows best in a moist but well-drained site, pH 6.0 to 7.0. It flowers best in full sun and tolerates some drought. Mock orange blooms on the previous year's growth. A light annual pruning of older branches right after flowering keeps mock orange shapely and productive. Branches more than five years old should be removed in winter or early spring.

FEATURED PROFILE
Mock Orange

Botanical Name: *Philadelphus* x *virginalis* 'Natchez' **Family:** Saxifragaceae **Type of Plant:** tall deciduous flowering shrub **Uses:** specimen; shrub border; screening **Genus Range:** S.E. Europe and Asia Minor **Hardiness:** USDA Zones 4–8 **Height:** 8 to 10' **Growth Rate:** fast **Form & Habit:** upright and rounded with fountaining branches **Bloom Period:** May to early June **Flowers:** masses of showy fragrant white flowers **Fruits:** 4-sided capsule **Foliage:** dense, fresh green **Soil & pH:** well-drained; pH 6.0 to 7.0 **Light & Moisture:** full sun; best with sustained moisture but handles some drought **Pruning Seasons:** after flowering remove old wood

Mock orange (*Philadelphus* x *virginalis* 'Natchez')

Eastern Nineback

Physocarpus opulifolius

Eastern ninebark (*Physocarpus opulifolius*)

Eastern ninebark
(*Physocarpus opulifolius* 'Dart's Gold')

Eastern ninebark (*Physocarpus opulifolius*) belongs to an attractive group of deciduous tough durable shrubs and small trees with interesting shedding bark that peels off in papery strips. This shrub grows wild from Quebec to Virginia, Michigan to Tennessee, and has been cultivated since the 1600s. The most ornamental eastern ninebark is the upright 4- to 9-foot cultivar 'Dart's Gold'. Masses of small pink-to-white flowers are produced in May or early June to give the plant the appearance of a large spirea. The flowers are followed by reddish fruits that change to cinnamon brown and remain on the plant in winter. 'Dart's Gold' is more refined and compact than the species, with bright yellow leaves early in the season that look like a mass of yellow flowers. As the season advances, the foliage turns lime green, and then green. Eastern ninebark makes a colorful filler in a green grove and is decorative naturalized in an open woodland. Hardy in Zones 2–7, it is useful in harsh climates. Once established, it withstands adverse conditions.

Culture: eastern ninebark transplants easily in early spring or fall. It succeeds in dry soils, whether acid or alkaline. Full sun or partial shade suits it equally well. To keep it vigorous, cut back a proportion of older wood to the ground or back to an outward facing bud, right after flowering. Thin out young shoots if they become crowded.

Eastern ninebark (*Physocarpus opulifolius* 'Luteus')

FEATURED PROFILE
Eastern Ninebark

Botanical Name: *Physocarpus opulifolius* 'Dart's Gold' **Family:** Rosaceae **Type of Plant:** deciduous shrub with yellow foliage in spring **Uses:** shrub border, naturalized in open woodlands **Genus Range:** Quebec to VA, MI to TN **Hardiness:** USDA Zones 2–7 **Height:** 4 to 9' **Growth Rate:** fast **Form & Habit:** upright to spreading **Bloom Period:** May–June **Flowers:** pink-white, ⅓" across in upright clusters **Fruits:** small inflated pods **Foliage:** 3-lobed, 1½ to 3" long, to 1½" wide, emerging yellow, fading to lime and green **Soil & pH:** tolerant **Light & Moisture:** full sun to partial shade; tolerates dry conditions **Pruning Seasons:** cut old wood to the ground in late winter

Pieris
also called "Andromeda"
Pieris

The pieris (sometimes called "andromedas") are beautiful broad-leaved evergreen shrubs that in late winter are covered with large clusters of waxy cream-white buds that open into small urn-shaped flowers. The leaves are shiny green year-round; new foliage is a gleaming rose bronze. Widely used in formal landscaping and as foundation plants, pieris prefer the partial shade and acid soil conditions that suit azaleas and rhododendrons.

The most beautiful species is Japanese pieris, or lily-of-the-valley bush (*Pieris japonica*), a majestic plant 6 to 8 feet tall that thrives in Zones 5–8. The branches cascade almost to the ground, their tips laden with dense tassels of somewhat fragrant ivory flowers in strands 3 to 6 inches long. They open in March or April and last two to three weeks. The new foliage is bronze to wine red and is especially showy in cultivars such as 'Mountain Fire', hardy in Zones 5 or 6–8. Cultivars with colorful flowers include pink 'Valley Rose' and maroon-red 'Valley Valentine'.

A cultivar of mountain pieris, also called "fetterbush" (*P. floribunda* 'Millstream'), does better than Japanese pieris in the cooler regions of Zones 4 or 5–7. This vigorous, mounded, 2- to 6-foot shrub is also smaller and less showy but more tolerant of alkaline soils. Its white or pink flowers are fragrant; its leaves, dark green. For small gardens, the charming dwarf pieris (*P. taiwanensis* 'Prelude') is just 2½ feet tall. Hardy in Zones 6–8, it is a late bloomer with pure white flowers.

Culture: a young container-grown or balled-and-burlapped pieris transplants easily in early spring to moist but well-drained humusy acid soil, pH 4.0 to 5.0. It does best with two to six hours of sun a day, and needs shelter from the wind. Allow mountain pieris to develop naturally; prune back damaged wood in spring as new growth begins.

Japanese pieris
(*Pieris japonica* 'Forest Flame')

Japanese pieris (*Pieris japonica*)

Japanese pieris
(*Pieris japonica* 'Dorothy Wycoff')

Japanese pieris (*Pieris japonica* 'Valley Valentine')

FEATURED PROFILE
Japanese Pieris, or Lily-of-the-Valley Bush

Botanical Name: *Pieris japonica* **Family:** Ericaceae **Type of Plant:** formal flowering broad-leaved evergreen **Uses:** formal landscaping, foundation planting **Native Range:** Japan **Hardiness:** USDA Zones 5–8 **Height:** 6 to 8' **Growth Rate:** slow **Form & Habit:** upright, cascading **Bloom Period:** March or April **Flowers:** white, urn-shaped, fragrant, to ¼" long, held in drooping 3 to 6" long panicles **Fruits:** capsules **Foliage:** evergreen, lance-shaped, 1¼ to 3½" long, lustrous green in summer; new growth is bronze to wine-red **Soil & pH:** well-drained, humusy soil; pH 4.0 to 5.0 **Light & Moisture:** partial shade; maintain moisture **Pruning Seasons:** after flowering

The Cinquefoils

Potenilla

Rugged relatives of the rose, potentillas are low deciduous shrubs and perennials valued for their colorful five-petaled flowers that appear nonstop from June until frost. The blooms resemble wide-open wild roses and are usually yellow, but there are white and reddish cultivars.

Potentillas are attractive planted with evergreens in a low informal flowering hedge, in shrub borders, with perennials, and among foundation plant-ings. They also make handsome ground covers that need little care or watering once established.

Of the many species of potentilla, shrubby cinquefoil (*Potentilla fruticosa*) and its cultivars are the most popular in gardens. Hardy in Zones 2 or 3–7 and usually less than 2 or 3 feet, it bears bright yellow, red-orange, or white flowers and thrives in urban situations. While the species isn't exceptionally showy, many of the cultivars are. 'Goldfinger' has dark green foliage and bright yellow blooms. 'Katherine Dykes' has yellow flowers and branches that arch. Golden yellow 'Coronation Triumph' and 'Knaphill' all thrive in the Midwest. The double-flowered 'Yellowbird'

Shrubby cinquefoil
(*Potentilla fruticosa* 'Gold Star')

Shrubby cinquefoil
(*Potentilla fruticosa* 'Red Ace')

from Canada, vermilion 'Abbottswood', and white 'Mount Everest' all succeed in Zones 3–7.

Culture: a container-grown potentilla transplants easily in early spring or fall. Potentilla does best in well-drained fertile humusy soil, but it also succeeds in clay soils and in infertile, compacted, dry situations. It is not particular about pH. It flowers well in full sun but blooms in partial shade, too. To keep the plant vigorous, every other spring prune played-out wood back to stronger wood or right to the base, and shorten young shoots by one-half to two-thirds of their length. The lateral shoots that develop from these cuts will flower best.

FEATURED PROFILE
Shrubby Cinquefoil

Botanical Name: *Potentilla fruticosa* **Family:** Rosaceae **Type of Plant:** deciduous flowering shrub **Uses:** informal flowering hedge, shrub border, with perennials, among foundation plantings, flowering ground cover **Native Range:** Northern Hemisphere **Hardiness:** USDA Zones 2 or 3–7 **Height:** 2 to 3' **Growth Rate:** slow **Form & Habit:** low, upright, open-branched, rounded **Bloom Period:** June until frosts **Flowers:** 5-petaled, 1¼" across, flattish **Fruits:** small, dry, single-seeded, persistent **Foliage:** compound, composed of 3 to 7 leaflets, to 1" long, grayish to dark green **Soil & pH:** well-drained, fertile, humusy; pH adaptable **Light & Moisture:** full sun for best color; succeeds in partial shade; prefers moisture, but tolerates some drought **Pruning Seasons:** late winter

Shrubby cinquefoil (*Potentilla fruticosa*)

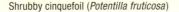

The Azaleas

Rhododendron

A Kurume azalea
(*Rhododendron*)

Flame azalea
(*Rhododendron calendulaceum*)

An azalea (*Rhododendron*)

Azaleas are evergreen and deciduous flowering shrubs with an unrivaled spring flower display. They belong to the genus *Rhododendron* (facing page) but have characteristics that distinguish them from the plants we commonly call "rhododendrons."

For example, azalea leaves are hairy, while rhododendron leaves have scales on the undersides. Azalea flowers are funnel-shaped, while rhododendron flowers are usually bell-shaped. Azaleas tend to bloom before rhododendrons, but some azaleas hold their blooms until late spring, and a few, such as Kaempferi azaleas 'Armstrong's Fall' and 'Indian Summer', rebloom in the fall. Azalea blooms may be single, semidouble, or double, and the colors range from sparkling white through yellow, pink, orange, purple, and red. Some are bicolored, and some are fragrant. Azaleas, especially the evergreen forms, have neat refined leaves, and some turn glowing yellow or maroon in fall and winter. The leaves of the white-flowered azaleas tend to yellow in the fall, while those of red, purple and pink azaleas redden or turn bronze.

Evergreen strains are grown in milder regions. These include Belgian Indian, Southern Indian, Belgian-Glenn Dale, Pennington, Kehr, Glenn Dale, Kurume, Back Acre, and North Tisbury, which grow as far north as Zone 7. The Kaempferis (which tend to rebloom), Robin Hill, Linwood, Girard, Gable, Shammarello, Schroeder, and Greenwood azaleas, are planted in Zones 5–6.

In Zones 4–5, where summers and winters are cool, the deciduous azaleas, such as the Ghent, Mollis, Knap Hill, and Exbury strains, do best. In the Northwest, the Occidentale group originally developed from the native Western azalea (*R. occidentale*), is outstanding. In any region, an azalea native to the area will always be the hardiest plant, if not the showiest.

Culture: a balled-and-burlapped or container-grown azalea transplants easily in early spring or fall to well-drained humusy soil, pH 4.5 to 6.0. It requires watering during summer droughts. An azalea does best in bright dappled light but tolerates full sun if the soil is moist. A summer mulch is necessary in hot regions. Shearing to remove flowering tips when the blooms fade improves the next season's flowering.

FEATURED PROFILE
Exbury Azalea

Botanical Name: *Rhododendron* 'Scarlett O'Hara' **Family:** Ericaceae **Type of Plant:** deciduous flowering shrub **Uses:** specimen, foundation plant, background for a flowering border **Genus Range:** Asia, North America, Europe **Hardiness:** USDA Zones 5 or 6–7 **Height:** 4 to 6' **Growth Rate:** medium **Form & Habit:** rounded habit, layered branches **Bloom Period:** midspring **Flowers:** scarlet **Foliage:** oval green leaves **Soil & pH:** well-drained; humusy; pH 4.5 to 6.0 **Light & Moisture:** partial shade; maintain moisture **Pruning Seasons:** pinch back branch tips after flowering

Exbury Azalea (*Rhododendron* 'Scarlett O'Hara')

The Rhododendrons

Rhododendron

Rhododendron (*Rhododendron* 'Cynthia')

Rhododendron
(*Rhododendron* 'Grace Seabrook')

Rhododendron
(*Rhododendron* 'Crest')

In most regions of North America, the most outstanding blooms of the early growing season occur on rhododendrons. These shrubs have broad leaves, may be evergreen or deciduous, and produce large clusters of bell-shaped pink, rose, purple, lavender, white, or yellow blossoms. The flower colors may be solid, flushed, splotched, or spotted with a contrasting shade or color.

Rhododendrons thrive in light shade. The hardiest ornamentals come from China, Japan, and the United States. Some can exceed 20 feet in the wild, but 6 to 8 feet is the more common height in cultivation. There are thousands of species, varieties, and hybrids. A local nursery can recommend varieties and hybrids for your area. Here are some regional suggestions, hardy in Zones 4 or 5–8 or 9.

In New England, try pink *Rhododendron fortunei*; white, rosy red, or lavender-pink *R. smirnowii*; spotted rose leatherleaf rhododendron (*R. metternichii*); and white, large-leaved Fujiyama rhododendron (*R. brachycarpum*).

In the mid-Atlantic region, you could try Dahurian rhododendron (*R. dauricum*), with purple, pink, or white flowers and its variety *sempervirens*; pink or lilac-pink *R. fortunei*; soft pink *R. makinow*; dark pink and white Korean rhododendron (*R. mucronulatum*), with yellow-bronze fall foliage; and bright rose *R. yakushimanum* and its hybrid 'Yaku Princess', which also succeeds in the South.

In the Great Lakes region, try pink to purplish Wilson's rhododendron (*R.* x *laetevirens*) and dark pink and white *R. mucronulatum*.

A great many cultivars thrive in the Pacific Northwest, including *R. yakushimanum* and *R. augustinii*, with bluish or lavender-rose flowers.

Culture: plant only winter-hardy rhododendrons in your area. A rhododendron may survive but fail to bloom when growing at its northern limit. A young rhododendron transplants easily in early spring or midfall to well-drained humusy acid soil, pH 4.5 to 6.0. Find a site protected from north winds with a full morning sun and afternoon shade. With moisture, small-leaved deciduous plants tolerate full sun. Deadhead to promote growth, but avoid damaging tiny buds behind the blooms. Prune after flowering. Rejuvenate a rhododendron by hard pruning over two or three years.

FEATURED PROFILE
Yakushima Rhododendron

Botanical Name: *Rhododendron yakushimanum (R. degroniamum* subsp. *yakushimanum)* **Family:** Ericceae **Type of Plant:** evergreen flowering shrub **Uses:** specimen, foundation plant, background for a flowering border **Native Range:** Japan **Hardiness:** USDA Zones 5 or 6–7 **Height:** 3' **Growth Rate:** slow **Form & Habit:** mounded, as wide as it is tall **Bloom Period:** spring **Flowers:** buds are bright rose to red, opening to white **Foliage:** dark green leaves, downy undersides **Soil & pH:** well-drained; humusy; pH 4.5 to 6.0 **Light & Moisture:** partial shade; maintain moisture **Pruning Seasons:** after flowering

Yakushima rhododendron (*Rhododendron yakushimanum*)

The Roses

Rosa

A polyantha rose (*Rosa* 'The Fairy')

A landscape rose (*Rosa* 'Bonica')

A hybrid tea rose (*Rosa* 'Peace')

The rose is so beloved in America that it is the national flower. Roses comprise a vast and varied group of species and cultivars that have been subdivided into classes according to form and culture. These groupings reconcile old and new rose classifications. Rugosa and other hedge roses appear on page 229.

Climbing Roses. These plants bear clusters of small flowers on long pliant canes; or large flowers singly or in clusters on stiff canes. Bright scarlet 'Blaze', coral-pink 'America', and clear yellow 'Golden Showers' are all excellent climbers. Climbing roses must be led and tied to training wires or to a trellis. For the first two years, prune in fall to remove unproductive canes and again in spring to remove damaged or dead wood. Beginning the third year, prune in fall after flowering to shorten the side shoots by about two-thirds and to maintain five or six healthy canes. Climbers tend to flower more abundantly when canes are trained horizontally. Climbing roses (as well as floribunda types) are used to create tree forms, called standards.

Hybrid Tea Roses and Large-Flowered (Grandiflora) Bush Roses. The hybrid teas produce exquisite, high-centered, double or semidouble blooms on long stiff stems that are perfect for cutting. The form of the classic 'Chicago Peace' is typical. Modern hybrid tea shrubs grow upright and are usually 3 to 6 feet tall. All-season bloomers flower generously in midspring, sporadically in the summer, and then bloom well

A landscape rose (*Rosa* 'Flower Carpet')

from September until severe cold. They are formal shrubs suitable for a collection in a bed. Plant lavender or blue salvia around them to mask their legginess—and to disguise the tendency of even disease-resistant plants to lose foliage to black spot in summer. To encourage blooming, remove spent flowers, cutting back to the first five-leaflet stem. In late fall, prune four to five strong canes to about 30 inches.

Miniature Roses. The buds and flowers of the "minis" have the form of either a hybrid tea or a many-petaled cabbage rose. Upright minis are used as edging or in front of a rose garden. Minis with trailing branches are used as basket and container plants. Easy-to-grow miniature roses flower from June to frost and are hardy with some winter protection. A typical shrub is 12 inches high and 6 to 18 inches across. The large miniatures, known as "macrominis," reach 2 feet; a few micro-minis, such as 'Elfin Gold' and 'Tiny Flame', are just 6 inches tall with dime-sized flowers. Orange 'Starina' is one of the most popular miniature roses. 'Rise 'n' Shine', which holds the American Rose Society Award of Excellence, is quite fragrant.

Prune miniatures in fall to remove all but the four or five best canes, and cut those back by one-third.

Ground-Cover Roses and Landscape Roses. There are two main groups of these tough and beautiful shrubs: Meidiland and Flower Carpet. Use the ground-cover types to spread over slopes or walls and the hedge types to add color to mixed beds or as specimen plants. Ground-cover roses grow 2 to 3 feet high and spread 5 to 6 feet. Hedge types grow 3 to 4 feet tall and spread 2 to 3 feet. Meidilands, such as 'Bonica', bloom from early summer until fall. Flower colors include white, cherry pink, scarlet, and shell pink.

Flower Carpet roses grow to 2½ feet with a 5-foot spread. 'Flower Carpet' has lavender-pink flowers that are lightly scented. 'Flower Carpet Appleblossom' is white with a pink center. The roses bloom all season if they are fed in early spring and again in midsummer. Remove spent flowers to encourage another flush of bloom, and cut out dead wood as needed. Prune back plants in spring after several years of growth.

Garden Roses, also Known as English, Polyantha, and Floribunda Roses. These shrubby plants produce clusters of blooms throughout the season. Many are fragrant and disease resistant. For example, the many-petaled David Austin English roses have the full look and perfume of old-fashioned roses. Hybrids, such as the rich pink 'Cottage Rose' and the pristine white 'Fair Bianca', are compact shrubs that are easily managed.

The polyanthas grow 2 to 3 feet tall and produce clusters of charming 2-inch blooms. 'The Fairy', with lovely seashell pink, slightly fragrant flowers, is best known. It is often used as a hedge rose.

The floribundas reach 2 to 3 feet tall and bear clusters of 2- to 3-inch flowers, some shaped like hybrid teas. A favorite for hedges is 'Betty Prior', a vivid pink with emerald foliage.

In fall or early spring, prune to remove unproductive canes; cut side canes back by about three-fifths, and trim the main canes by about one-third.

Culture: mail-order nurseries ship roses bare root at planting time for each region and include planting in-

A landscape rose
(*Rosa* 'Alba Meidiland')

A David Austin English rose

structions. Nurseries and garden centers sell container-grown roses throughout the growing season, but planting by midspring is best. Roses require well-drained, humusy soil, pH 6.0 to 7.0. If possible, enrich the soil several weeks in advance of planting by working in fishmeal and a slow-release 5-10-5 fertilizer or a rose formula such as 8-12-4. To bloom well, roses require at least six hours of direct sun daily, monthly fertilization from early spring until mid-July, and some watering during droughts. To encourage flowering throughout the growing season, cut the stems of faded roses back to an outward five-part leaf. Ask a local nursery for suggestions on avoiding problems.

FEATURED PROFILE
Climbing Rose

Botanical Name: *Rosa* 'Blaze' **Family:** Rosaceae **Type of Plant:** large-flowered climbing rose **Uses:** beautifying fences, corners of buildings, pergolas and posts **Genus Range:** Asia, Europe, North America, North Africa **Hardiness:** USDA Zones 4–9 **Height:** 12 to 15' canes **Growth Rate:** fast **Form & Habit:** climber **Bloom Period:** heavily in spring with some recurrent bloom **Flowers:** large clusters of 2–3' semidouble, cupped, slightly fragrant, bright scarlet blooms **Fruits:** orange hips **Foliage:** dark green, leathery **Soil & pH:** fertile, well-drained humusy soil, pH 6.0 to 7.0 **Light & Moisture:** full sun; maintain moderate moisture during droughts **Pruning Seasons:** remove spent blooms; see detailed instructions for pruning climbing roses on the opposite page.

A climbing rose (*Rosa* 'Blaze')

The Sweet Boxes

Sarcococca

Himalayan sweet box
(*Sarcococca hookeriana*
variety *humilis*)

The sarcococcas are Asian evergreens related to box-wood, with long, similarly lustrous green leaves. The flowers are small and unimportant, but the fleshy fruit is quite decorative. Sweet box are useful ground covers and edgers in shady, moist situations, bordering mahonias and rhododendrons, for example. Best known is the Himalayan, or dwarf, sweet box (*Sarcococca hookeriana* variety *humilis*), a cultivar of the handsome 6-foot multistemmed species, hardy from Zones 5 or 6–8. Dwarf sarcococca forms a dense 2-foot carpet of shiny green leaves. In March and April, small fragrant ivory flowers appear, followed by a few fleshy berrylike black fruits.

Fragrant sarcococca (*S. ruscifolia*), a beautiful Chinese species, reaches 4 to 6 feet and tolerates winters only in Zones 7 and 8. In early spring it bears small, sweetly fragrant white flowers; red fruits follow. The plants can be hard to find, but they are lovely growing as understory plants in groves of needled evergreens.

Fragrant sarcococca (*Sarcococca ruscifolia*)

Culture: a container-grown or balled-and-burlapped sarcococca transplants easily in early spring to well-drained loam with a pH of 5.5 to 6.0. Sarcococca does best in a shady site, with two hours of full sun or dappled light all day, and in soil that stays moist during droughts. Little pruning is necessary except to cut back ungainly stems to the ground in spring.

FEATURED PROFILE
Himalayan Sweet Box

Botanical Name: *Sarcococca hookeriana* variety *humilis* **Family:** Buxaceae **Type of Plant:** low-growing evergreen foliage plant **Uses:** underplanting leggy specimens and shrub borders **Native Range:** western Asia **Hardiness:** USDA Zones 5 or 6–8 **Height:** 2' **Growth Rate:** slow **Form & Habit:** multistemmed, spreading **Bloom Period:** March to April **Flowers:** off-white, ½" across, hidden in axils of terminal leaves **Fruits:** shiny and black, rounded, ⅓" across **Foliage:** long lance-shaped leaves, lustrous dark green, 2 to 3½" long **Soil & pH:** well-drained loam; pH 5.5 to 6.0 **Light & Moisture:** partial shade; maintain moisture **Pruning Seasons:** after flowering

Himalayan sweet box (*Sarcococca hookeriana* variety *humilis*)

The Skimmias

Skimmia

Japanese skimmia (*Skimmia japonica*) female flowers

Shade-loving skimmias are low, broad-leaved evergreen shrubs from Asia with handsome, dark green leaves that are aromatic when crushed. In early spring in cool regions of Zones 6 and 7 skimmias produce upright clusters of small, fuzzy, fragrant flowers. In warm regions in Zone 8, the flowers appear in fall and winter and are followed by ornamental berrylike fruits. Often flowers and fruit appear on the shrub at the same time. Skimmias tolerate urban conditions well and make good container plants. They are excellent in borders with rhododendrons and mixed evergreens, and as understory plants in woodland gardens. They do not do well in the Midwest or in the Northeast, where summer droughts are prolonged.

The most attractive species is dainty Japanese skimmia (*Skimmia japonica*), a slow-growing, densely branched shrub 3 to 5 feet high. The female plant bears yellowish white flowers; the male, larger, fragrant flowers. The fruits are borne by female plants when a male plant is growing nearby. Where there is inadequate room for both male and female shrubs, gardeners plant Reeves skimmia (*S. reevesiana*). A less-hardy

species for Zones 7–8, it grows 2 to 3 feet high and bears white flowers that are bisexual. One plant alone will fruit.

Culture: a container-grown skimmia transplants easily in early spring to soil that is well drained, sandy, moist, peaty, and acid, pH 5.0 to 5.7. It doesn't tolerate wet conditions or drought and will be most beautiful growing in partial to dense shade. A skimmia looks best if allowed to develop naturally. Ungainly branches should be removed in spring before growth begins.

Japanese skimmia (*Skimmia japonica*)

FEATURED PROFILE
Japanese Skimmia

Botanical Name: *Skimmia japonica* **Family:** Rutaceae **Type of Plant:** low, flowering broad-leaved evergreen **Uses:** mixed evergreen border, woodlands **Native Range:** Japan, Himalayas **Hardiness:** USDA Zones 6 or 7–8 **Height:** 3 to 5' **Growth Rate:** slow **Form & Habit:** low-growing, rounded **Bloom Period:** March to April **Flowers:** glossy red-maroon buds open to yellow-white; female flowers are small, somewhat fragrant, ⅓" across, borne on 2 to 3" long upright panicles; male flowers are larger, more fragrant **Fruits:** female bears bright red rounded drupes ⅓" wide and conspicuous in fall and winter; male and female plants required for fruit set **Foliage:** evergreen, elliptical-oblong, 2½" to 5" long; bright green on top, yellowing underneath **Soil & pH:** well-drained, sandy, moist; pH 5.0 to 5.7 **Light & Moisture:** light to deep shade; maintain moisture **Pruning Seasons:** after flowering

Japanese skimmia (*Skimmia japonica*)

Japanese skimmia (*Skimmia japonica*) female fruit

The Lilacs

Syringa

Japanese tree lilac (*Syringa reticulata*)

A tall multistemmed shrub or small tree, the lilac bears panicles of single or double florets in shades of lilac, rose, or white. Lilacs may be planted as featured specimens in a lawn, by an entrance where their scent would greet a visitor, in tall hedges, or to create "lilac walks," also called "allées." Mildew and other problems are prevalent, so buy resistant cultivars and site them in a dry, airy cool place.

The lilac of memory lane is the sweetly scented 20-foot common lilac (*Syringa vulgaris*), which blooms in May and grows best in Zones 3–7 or 8. It requires a winter chilling period to bloom well.

The Chinese, or Rouen, lilac (*S. × chinensis*) blooms in the Midwest and the East in Zones 2 or 3–7 in midspring. This graceful 10- to 12-foot shrub with broadly spreading

Lilac
(*Syringa vulgaris* 'Primrose')

Lilac
(*Syringa vulgaris*)

branches has the color and scent of *S. vulgaris* but with more flowers. Mildew-resistant *S. meyeri*, a rounded shrub 4 to 8 feet tall with a 6- to 12-foot spread, blooms in May before the leaves fully develop. The violet-purple flowers appear when plants are just a foot high. 'Palibin', a compact form, bears reddish purple buds that open to pale pink.

Of the late bloomers, the 5- to 9-foot Korean cultivar *S. patula* 'Miss Kim' is outstanding. Mildew-resistant and hardy in Zones 3 or 4–8, it bears fragrant purple-in-the-bud flowers that fade to pale pink or blue. The fall foliage often develops a good reddish color. Hardy in Zones 3–7, *S. × henryi* 'Lutece,' with violet flowers, is another lovely late bloomer. The last of the lilacs to flower—and the only one that truly qualifies as a tree—is the 20- to 30-foot Japanese tree lilac (*S. reticulata* or *S. amurensis* variety *japonica*), hardy in Zones 3–7. Its 6-inch plumes of creamy white florets have scent similar to a privet's. 'Ivory Silk' is a compact, heavily flowering 25-foot cultivar that blooms at an early age.

Culture: a lilac transplants easily in spring to well-drained but moist humusy soil with a pH near 8.0. Plant in full sun or light shade; once established it tolerates some drought. Fertilize annually. After flowering, remove unproductive trunks; allow two or three strong suckers to grow up as replacements. Eliminate all others.

FEATURED PROFILE

Lilac

Botanical Name: *Syringa patula* 'Miss Kim' **Family:** Oleaceae
Type of Plant: fragrant deciduous flowering shrub **Uses:** specimen; hedge; screen; shrub border; topiary **Genus Range:** China
Hardiness: USDA Zones 3 or 4–8 **Height:** 5 to 9' **Growth Rate:** slow **Form & Habit:** rounded, multistemmed **Bloom Period:** spring **Flowers:** deep purple in the bud, opening to pale pink or blue **Foliage:** dark green with burgundy tints in fall **Soil & pH:** well-drained humusy soil; pH 6.0 to 7.5 or 8.0 **Light & Moisture:** full sun; tolerates some drought **Pruning Seasons:** after flowering

Dwarf lilac (*Syringa patula* 'Miss Kim')

The Viburnums

Viburnum

The viburnums are enormously popular deciduous and semievergreen flowering shrubs of the honeysuckle family. The flowers of some species are extraordinarily fragrant, and many have colorful foliage and fruits in fall. Most bloom in spring, some as early as the flowering cherries, some as late as the end of June.

The shrubs produce three types of flowerheads: flat clusters of hundreds of white florets, rounded snowball types, and flat clusters ringed with large flowers. The double-file viburnums have the latter blooms, sitting horzontally on the tops of their branches. The United States National Arboretum introduced some of the most disease-resistant cultivars. *Viburnum x burkwoodii* 'Mohawk' is an 8- to 10-foot shrub hardy in Zones 4–8 with snowball-shaped flowerheads in early to mid-April. The dark red buds open to white flowers with a strong sweet clove scent. The foliage turns brilliant orange-red in fall.

Virburnum (*Virburnum* x *carlcephalum* 'Cayuga')

Viburnum (*Virburnum* x *burkwoodii*)

Double-file viburnum (*Viburnum plicatum* variety *tomentosa* 'Shasta')

The pink buds of the compact *V.* x *carlcephalum* 'Cayuga', another snowball type, open to white, and the flowers are slightly fragrant. 'Cayuga' is hardy just to Zones 5 or 6; its foliage turns a brilliant red in winter and the fruits are black. A superb 6-foot cultivar of the double-file *V. plicatum* is 'Shasta', hardy in Zones 5–8. In late May its horizontal branches are covered with clusters of pure white flowers, suggesting a dogwood in bloom. The flowers are followed in midsummer by bright red fruits.

Culture: the virburnums can be difficult to transplant, so set out a young container-grown plant in early spring in well-drained loam that is slightly acid, pH 6.0 to 6.5, and maintain moisture the first season. Full sun is best, but viburnums tolerate some shade. A viburnum growing taller than desired can be kept compact for many years by shortening the branches right after they flower.

FEATURED PROFILE
Viburnum

Botanical Name: *Viburnum* x *burkwoodii* **Family:** Caprifoliaceae **Type of Plant:** fragrant evergreen to semievergreen flowering shrub **Uses:** specimen; foundation plant; hedge; screen; background to flowering border **Native Range:** temperate Northern Hemisphere **Hardiness:** USDA Zones 5–8 **Height:** 6 to 12' **Growth Rate:** medium **Form & Habit:** upright, multistemmed **Bloom Period:** early to mid-April **Flowers:** snowball-shaped clusters of fragrant pinkish white flowers **Foliage:** brilliant orange-red in fall **Soil & pH:** well-drained loam; pH 6.0 to 6.5 **Light & Moisture:** full sun for best color; tolerates some drought **Pruning Seasons:** after flowering

Viburnum (*Virburnum* x *burkwoodii*)

The Chaste Trees

Vitex

The chaste trees belong to a group of deciduous and evergreen shrubs that are widely distributed in temperate zones of the world. Their chief asset is a profusion of lilaclike flower spikes that appear in summer or late summer. *Vitex agnus-castus*, a fast-growing multitrunked species, is grown as a winter die-back perennial in Zone 6. In Zone 7, it grows into an 8- to 10-foot shrub; farther south in Zone 9, it reaches 20 feet. Aromatic gray-green leaves open in spring. From midsummer through September, the branches are tipped with long-lasting, fragrant, violet or lilac-blue flower spikes 6 to 12 inches long. There are cultivars in other colors: 'Alba' bears white flowers; 'Rosea' blooms in pink.

Chaste tree does well in a container and makes an attractive patio shrub. In Zone 6, it should winter in a spot protected from the north wind. The flowers bloom on new wood, so even if the plant dies back in winter, it develops a full complement of flowers the following summer.

Chaste tree
(*Vitex agnus-castus* 'Silver Spire')

Chaste tree
(*Vitex agnus-castus* 'Shoal Creek')

The cutleaf chaste tree, *V. incisa*, a hardier species suited to Zones 5–8, has beautiful, finely divided gray-green leaves and an airy graceful texture. It bears 8-inch panicles of fragrant lavender flowers in late summer.

Culture: a container-grown chaste tree transplants easily in early spring to moist but well-drained soil in the neutral range, pH 6.0 to 7.0. It requires full sun. Removing spent blooms encourages repeat blooming. The chaste tree blooms in late summer on wood grown during the current season. It benefits from annual pruning in spring, before the buds open. Cut back to a main branch the side branches that bloomed the previous season. A shrub that appears killed by winter cold will likely regenerate after it has been pruned back to within a foot of the ground.

FEATURED PROFILE
Chaste Tree

Botanical Name: *Vitex agnus-castus* **Family:** Verbenaceae **Type of Plant:** tall flowering deciduous shrub or small tree **Uses:** specimen, massed, espaliered **Native Range:** southern Europe, western Asia **Hardiness:** USDA Zones 6 or 7–8 or 9 **Height:** 6 to 12' in warm climates **Growth Rate:** fast **Form & Habit:** airy open silhouette **Bloom Period:** midsummer into September; earlier in warm climates **Flowers:** lilac-like, fragrant, in racemes 3 to 6" long, borne on 6 to 12" terminal panicles **Fruits:** inconspicuous gray-bronze drupes **Foliage:** dark gray-green; composed of 5 to 7 leaflets 2 to 6" long **Soil & pH:** well-drained; humusy; in the neutral range, pH 6.0 to 7.0 **Light & Moisture:** full sun; prefers consistent moisture but tolerates some drought **Pruning Seasons:** prune winter-damaged plants back to live wood; prune winter die-back plants back to within 6 to 12" of the soil

Chaste tree (*Vitex agnus-castus*)

The Weigelas

Weigela florida

The weigelas are dense, rounded, deciduous shrubs with spreading branches that in mid-May and June are covered with clusters of small rosy pink to ruby red tubular blooms. A few flowers appear in summer. Weigelas belong to the honeysuckle family, and some species have slightly fragrant flowers. The rugged old-fashioned species (*Weigela florida*) is used in evergreen borders where its late spring flowers are a real asset or where the soil is poor and the plant is likely to receive little extra watering.

An exceptionally ornamental form is the cultivar 'Variegata', a pink-flowered plant with leaves edged in creamy white and suited to Zones 5–8. It grows 4 to 6 feet tall and 6 to 10 feet wide. There's a 3-foot dwarf, 'Nana Variegata'

Weigela (*Weigela florida* 'Nana Variegata')

that is hardy to Zone 4. The red-flowered form, 'Vanicek', also hardy to Zone 4—it is one of the most cold tolerant— blooms abundantly in May. 'Minuet', a hardy compact dwarf just 2 to 3 feet tall, has dark ruby red flowers and purple-tinged foliage. 'Candida' has white flowers.

Culture: a container-grown weigela transplants easily in early spring to well-drained but moist clay or loamy soil, pH 6.0 to 7.5. It does best in full sun. A weigela flowers mostly on old wood. Wait until the branches leaf out to cut back the tips that died during the winter. A winter mulch may keep die-back to a minimum. 'Variegata' is somewhat compact and should be allowed to develop freely. Branches that fail to show the variegation should be cut back to old wood.

Weigela (*Weigela florida* 'Variegata')

Weigela (*Weigela florida*)

FEATURED PROFILE
Weigela

Botanical Name: *Weigela florida* 'Variegata' **Family:** Caprifoliaceae **Type of Plant:** flowering deciduous shrub **Uses:** featured specimen, large shrub border **Genus Range:** northern China, Korea, Japan **Hardiness:** USDA Zones 4 or 5–8 **Height:** 4 to 6' **Growth Rate:** medium **Form & Habit:** dense, rounded shrub with spreading branches **Bloom Period:** mid-May and June **Flowers:** rosy pink, bell-shaped, 1" long, held in upright clusters **Fruits:** inconspicuous capsules **Foliage:** elliptical, 3 to 4" long, edged in creamy white **Soil & pH:** well-drained clay or loamy soil; pH 6.0 and 7.5 **Light & Moisture:** full sun; maintain moisture, but withstands drought **Pruning Seasons:** after flowering

PART 4

All about Hedges

If you live in North America, you can choose shrubs for your landscape from hundreds of tree species and cultivars. These shrubs belong to 15 major groups called "genera" (plural for "genus"). Hedge genera are listed in this section alphabetically by scientific name. But if you don't know the genus name of the plant you are researching, no problem: just look for the common name. For example, if you don't know the scientific name for honeysuckle, which is *Lonicera*, simply go to the Table of Contents or the Index. You'll find honeysuckle listed in both places. In addition, many common names are listed on page 211, where you'll also find the names of trees and shrubs that you can train as hedges.

Hedge Basics and Fine Points

Hedges are living walls that add structure and organization to the garden. You can use them to enclose a garden room, as the backdrop for a flower border, to edge and outline a path, and to lead the eye to or from important features in the landscape. A low prickly hedge can discourage four-footed visitors. A dense mid-height hedge can disguise an ugly wire fence and block wind, noise, blown leaves, and debris. A tall hedge composed of trees or large shrubs can create a privacy screen and mark distant property boundaries. A hedge is also better than a solid wall as a windbreak because it filters the stream of air rather than blocking it completely, thus avoiding a turbulent wash of air over the top.

Designing Ideas

Whether high or low, a hedge can link the various parts of your property to one another and to your house. In designing a hedge, consider whether the architecture of the house and yard calls for a trim, formal look or something loose and less formal. A formal garden around a stone house in the Federal style, for example, is likely to be symmetrical with repeated planting patterns. The formal hedge would either run in straight lines with squared corners or be created symmetrically around a circle, an oval, or another geometric form. To maintain the clean edges and regular shape, you must trim a formal hedge at least twice a year. Good plants for a formal hedge include fine-textured evergreens, such as boxwood, yew, arborvitae, and privet.

As evidenced in this knot garden, design and pruning schemes for hedges can be quite elaborate. Such a hedge needs shearing at least twice a year by someone skilled at navigating mazes.

Some roses create informal barriers that need old canes removed in early spring and only periodic light pruning as noted on page 229.

The informal architecture of a modern house, on the other hand, would call for a more naturalistic line moving in sinuous curves and at irregular angles. Plants suited to informal hedges have a loose shape, rich texture, and often colorful flowers. Pyracantha and some roses make attractive unclipped hedges and require little pruning.

Besides linking to the property's architectural style, a new hedge can tie into its surroundings if it is composed of a shearable or a slow-growing variety of an existing tree or shrub. For example, if the property includes tall Irish yews, a yew hedge would fit in nicely. Or you could place a close relative of your hedge plants nearby.

Although cheaper and easier to install than a masonry wall or a wooden fence, a hedge started from container-grown or balled-and-burlapped plants won't be cheap and will take a few years to develop. But a good hedge should also be with you for a long time. If you choose your plants carefully and take good care of them, your hedge will grow more beautiful each year.

Hedge Plants

To be useful as a hedge, a tree or shrub should respond well either to shearing or—for informal hedges—to light pruning. Deciduous barberry and evergreen boxwood are familiar hedge shrubs, but other less-common plants also make beautiful hedges. For colors other than green, you might choose variegated holly and privet. Or select plants for their flowers and fruits. In general, you can use any plant with a natural habit that suits the eventual hedge shape and size you want to achieve or one with a shape and size that can be controlled by pruning. The hedge plants listed on page 211 are some of the best from which to choose.

By pruning or shearing, you can turn some large shrubs and even trees into hedges of a manageable size. But hedge plants will mature no matter how often they are clipped, and you should be mindful that some will outgrow their desired size within 10 years or so. A shearable large conifer, such as a hemlock or Leyland cypress, must retain some new growth every year to look good. Even if you keep cutting it back, the plant will eventually develop thick visible trunks and coarse branches at the bottom. At that stage, hedge plants can be renewed if cut back to within a foot of the ground and then allowed to regrow.

You may be tempted to choose fast-growing species, such as Leyland cypress, for quick results. But remember that hedges from slow-growing species, such as boxwood, will be denser and more attractive, and they will last longer and require less frequent and less aggressive clipping. If you need a screen or windbreak in a hurry, consider planting a row of fast-growing plants alongside your slow-growing hedge. They'll quickly provide shelter and screening, and you can remove them when the hedge of choice becomes tall.

For hedges, foliage texture is as important as plant size. Choose fine-textured plants, such as yew, arborvitae, and boxwood, for a hedge that will be viewed close up. For a hedge that will be seen mainly from a distance, choose plants with bold structure and coarse leaves, such as Meserve hollies, fiery photinias, elegant cherry laurel, or European beech. Branch and foliage texture and density are especially important for barriers; dense, prickly plants, such as barberry, flowering quince, holly, spruce, and the thorny rugosa roses, discourage two-footed and even four-footed visitors.

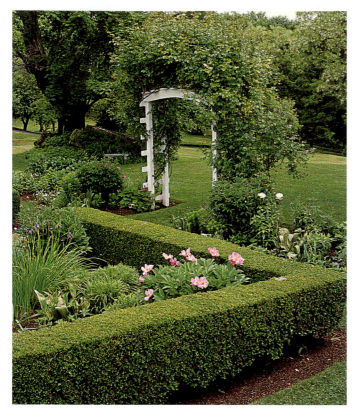

This tidy boxwood hedge and overgrown arbor create an arresting blend of formal and informal elements.

EVERGREENS

When you want the hedge to have a consistent year-round presence, evergreens are the best choice. Dwarf boxwoods, evergreen euonymus, and yew make compact 1- to 2-foot hedges. Midsize arborvitae, cotoneaster, camellia, and pyracantha are among many that grow 4 to 10 feet tall. Tall hedges of evergreen trees, such as false cypress, Leyland cypress, and hemlocks, can reach 20 feet or more and can serve as windbreaks for exposed sites. Many of the most useful evergreens—among them boxwoods, yews, and junipers—are available in a variety of heights and shapes.

Shearable upright broad-leaved evergreens, such as the boxwoods and small-leaved hollies, and tall trim fine-leaved conifers, such as arborvitae and incense cedar, create hedges with a formal look. A softer and less formal look can be had with lightly pruned open-textured evergreens, such as the feathery Pfitzer junipers, graceful eastern white pine, and fast-growing Canadian hemlock. (Note: hemlocks have been dying in the Northeast from the woolly adelgid; painstaking spraying of individual trees has met with some success.) Yew and Leyland cypress work well in both formal and informal hedges. Try combining cultivars with subtly or strikingly different hues.

DECIDUOUS PLANTS

Though prized for their foliage and flowers, many deciduous hedge plants are attractive even after the leaves have fallen; in winter the dense twiggy branches and colorful fruits of roses and barberries look exquisite traced in snow and ice. And many deciduous hedge plants make lovely, loosely shaped midsize informal hedges without pruning; the graceful foliage of burning bush (*Euonymus alatus* 'Compactus') holds its shape all season long and turns brilliant red in the fall.

FLOWERING AND MORE

Both evergreen and deciduous flowering plants make beautiful informal hedges. Although prized for the constancy of their green foliage, many broad-leaved evergreens also have attractive flowers. Cherry laurel's fragrant green-white flower clusters shine against the dark green leaves. The list of plants on the opposite page offers more suggestions for hedges.

You can also combine species that have compatible cultural requirements. To create a graceful natural hedge that's colorful all season long, try plants that flower at different times. Or mix flowering shrubs with evergreens: mugo pines interplanted with deciduous yellow-flowered potentillas and 'Crimson Pygmy' barberry are beautiful together, and all three do well in full sun, tolerate salt and drought, and require only light pruning.

Tall, manicured hedges on both sides of a walkway act as a soft privacy wall that guards the home's entry from the street.

HEDGES FOR EVERY SEASON AND REASON

Consider these hedges, which have exceptional qualities and seasonal interest. Also consider plants normally thought of as trees and shrubs that can be trained as hedges. **Note:** the plants are alphabetized by scientific name.

FOR FLOWERING HEDGES
Glossy Abelia
    (*Abelia* x *grandiflora*), 160
Camellia (*Camellia*), 167
Ceanothus (*Ceanothus*), 168
Flowering Quince (*Chaenomeles*), 169
Hawthorn (*Crataegus*), 104
Deutzia (*Deutzia*), 175
Forsythia (*Forsythia*), 177
Gardenia (*Gardenia*), 179
Rose-of-Sharon, Shrub Althea
    (*Hibiscus syriacus*), 183
Hydrangea (*Hydrangea*), 184
Beauty Bush (*Kolkwitzia amabilis*), 188
Crape Myrtle
    (*Lagerstroemia indica*), 118
Honeysuckle (*Lonicera*), 222
Oleander (*Nerium oleander*), 223
Osmanthus (*Osmanthus*), 224
Cinquefoil (*Potentilla*), 195
Cherry Laurel
    (*Prunus laurocerasus*), 227
Rose (*Rosa*), 229
Spirea (*Spiraea*), 230
Lilac (*Syringa*), 202

FOR EVERGREEN HEDGES
Boxwood (*Buxus*), 218
Incense Cedar
    (*Calocedrus decurrens*), 92
Camellia (*Camellia*), 167
Cedar (*Cedrus*), 95
White Cedar, aka False Cypress
    (*Chamaecyparis*), 97
Cotoneaster (*Cotoneaster*), 172
Leyland Cypress
    (x *Cupressocyparis leylandii*), 219
Blue Gum Eucalyptus
    (*Eucalyptus globulus*
    'Compacta'), 106
Euonymus (*Euonymus fortunei*
    cultivars), 220
Holly (*Ilex*), 113
Juniper (*Juniperus*), 114
Privet (*Ligustrum*), 221
Oleander (*Nerium oleander*), 223
Osmanthus (*Osmanthus*), 224
Christmas Berry (*Photinia*), 225
Pine (*Pinus*), 130
Podocarpus (*Podocarpus*), 226
Cherry Laurel
    (*Prunus laurocerasus*), 227

Firethorn (*Pyracantha*), 228
Yew (*Taxus*), 231
Arborvitae (*Thuja*), 143
Canadian Hemlock
    (*Tsuga canadensis*), 145

TREES USED AS HEDGES
Incense Cedar
    (*Calocedrus decurrens*), 92
Hornbeam (*Carpinus*), 93
Cedar (*Cedrus*), 95
White Cedar, aka False Cypress
    (*Chamaecyparis*), 97
European Smoke Tree
    (*Cotinus coggygria*), 103
Hawthorn (*Crataegus*), 104
Leyland cypress
    (x *Cupressocyparis leylandii*), 219
Blue Gum Eucalyptus
    (*Eucalyptus globulus*
    'Compacta'), 106
Holly (*Ilex*), 113
Juniper (*Juniperus*), 114
Crape Myrtle
    (*Lagerstroemia indica*), 118
Pine (*Pinus*), 130
Arborvitae (*Thuja*), 143
Hemlock (*Tsuga*), 145

SHRUBS USED AS HEDGES
Glossy Abelia
    (*Abelia* x *grandiflora*), 160
Gold-Dust Tree
    (*Aucuba japonica* 'Variegata'), 164
Ceanothus (*Ceanothus*), 168
Flowering Quince (*Chaenomeles*), 169
Cotoneaster (*Cotoneaster*), 172
Dwarf Japanese Cedar
    (*Cryptomeria japonica*), 173
Deutzia (*Deutzia*), 175
Forsythia (*Forsythia*), 177
Gardenia (*Gardenia*), 179
Witch Hazel (*Hamamelis*), 182
Rose-of-Sharon, Shrub Althea
    (*Hibiscus syriacus*), 183
Hydrangea (*Hydrangea*), 184
Beauty Bush (*Kolkwitzia amabilis*), 188
Heavenly Bamboo
    (*Nandina domestica*), 191
Cinquefoil (*Potentilla*), 195
Lilac (*Syringa*), 202

INFORMAL HEDGES
Glossy Abelia
    (*Abelia* x *grandiflora*), 160
Gold-Dust Tree
    (*Aucuba japonica* 'Variegata'), 164
Barberry (*Berberis*), 216
Camellia (*Camellia* species), 167
Flowering Quince
    (*Chaenomeles* species), 169
Leyland Cypress
    (x *Cupressocyparis leylandii*), 219
Slender Deutzia (*Deutzia gracilis*), 175
Burning Bush
    (*Euonymus alatus* 'Compactus'), 220
Showy Border Forsythia
    (*Forsythia* x *intermedia*), 177
Rose-of-Sharon
    (*Hibiscus syriacus*), 183
Pfitzer Junipers (*Juniperus*), 114
Honeysuckle (*Lonicera*), 222
Heavenly Bamboo
    (*Nandina domestica*), 191
Oleander (*Nerium oleander*), 223
Eastern White Pine (*Pinus strobus*), 131
Cinquefoil (*Potentilla*), 195
Firethorn (*Pyracantha*), 228
Rose (*Rosa*), 229
Spirea (*Spiraea*), 230
Yew (*Taxus*), 231
Canadian Hemlock
    (*Tsuga canadensis*), 145

FORMAL HEDGES
Barberry (*Berberis*), 216
Boxwood (*Buxus*), 218
Incense Cedar
    (*Calocedrus decurrens*), 92
Leyland Cypress
    (x *Cupressocyparis leylandii*), 219
Small-Leaved Hollies (*Ilex*), 113
Privet (*Ligustrum*), 221
Osmanthus (*Osmanthus*), 224
Christmas Berry (*Photinia*), 225
Southern Yew
    (*Podocarpus macrophylla*), 226
Cherry Laurel
    (*Prunus laurocerasus*), 227
Yew (*Taxus*), 231
Arborvitae (*Thuja*), 143

Placing a Hedge

When selecting a hedge plant, you should match its growth requirements to the site conditions—again, choosing the right plant for the place. Luckily, many hardy and adaptable hedge plants are available for almost any site. Adaptability is important because conditions may vary along the length of the hedge. While soil conditions—drainage, pH, humus content—can be changed to make the site more amenable to a particular species or more uniform over the length of the planting area, light conditions often can't be modified. Roses, oleander, and pyracantha are some of the hedge plants that do best in full sun. For a site in light to full shade, choose shade-tolerant, adaptable plants that can grow in a range of shady conditions, such as compact cultivars of cherry laurel. Many of the commonly used hedge plants thrive in light ranging from full sun to partial or light shade and, in the case of versatile boxwood and yew, full shade. Where light varies over the length of a hedge, set the plants in the shadier areas closer together because they'll grow thinner than the plants receiving more sun. An informal hedge combining several species can be a creative and attractive solution to the problem of a highly variable site.

To determine how much space your hedge will occupy, you'll need to know the width at maturity, or spread, of the plants you've chosen. An unclipped hedge occupies more space than a clipped one of the same species. If the site for your hedge is narrow, consider compact columnar forms, rather than spreading forms that require endless pruning to keep them within bounds. If you are planting a boundary hedge, allow for spread, and then plant well within the property line, because your neighbors can cut off everything that grows on their side. And whether you plant in individual holes or in a planting bed, dig broad enough holes to encourage the spread of roots.

If you space the plants a little closer to each other than their estimated spread, the gaps between them will close

Trenching for a Hedge

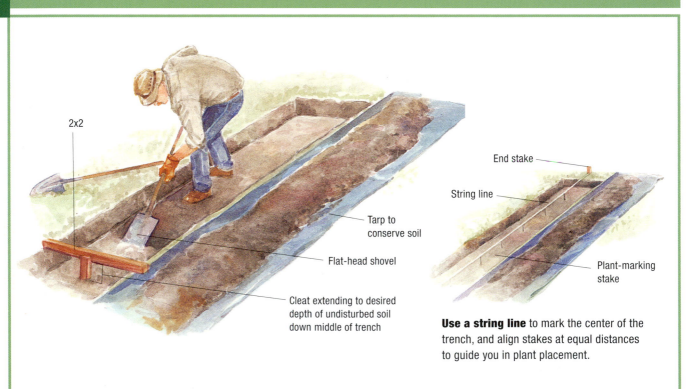

2x2

Tarp to conserve soil

Flat-head shovel

Cleat extending to desired depth of undisturbed soil down middle of trench

End stake

String line

Plant-marking stake

Use a string line to mark the center of the trench, and align stakes at equal distances to guide you in plant placement.

To place hedge plants equal distances apart, it's easier to keep them evenly spaced and in a straight line if you dig a trench rather than individual holes. Be sure to provide a solid, undisturbed base of soil for each plant so that it won't later settle below ground level. To do this, dig a shallow trench to the firm depth at which your plants will rest, as illustrated.

DIGGING TRENCHES OR HOLES

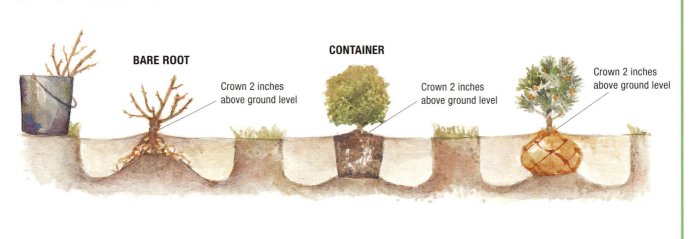

BARE ROOT

CONTAINER

Crown 2 inches above ground level

Crown 2 inches above ground level

Crown 2 inches above ground level

Bare Root. Dig to the level at which the plant will rest and then dig deeper at the sides, creating an undisturbed cone of soil.

Container. Dig to less than container depth. Place containers in the row at desired distances, and then scoop deeper around each container.

Balled and Burlapped. Dig to less than ball depth. Place plants in the row, and then scoop deeper around each ball.

as they grow, and the plants won't be crowded at maturity. For a thicker, denser, and wider hedge, stagger the plants in a double row; the hedge will be more expensive and take more work to install, but the gaps between the plants will be less noticeable.

Planting a Hedge

A new hedge is best established using young plants because they're less costly than older specimens, and they adapt more quickly. Follow the instructions regarding soil amendment, planting, and watering beginning on page 24. In moderate climates, a fall planting gives a new hedge time to establish itself before winter, and that helps get it off to a quick start in the spring. In cool regions, an early spring planting is best.

Depending on the size of your hedge, the number and size of your plants, and their distance apart, you may choose to dig a separate hole for each plant, a trench, or a planting bed. Large shrubs and trees for screening and windbreaks are best planted in separate holes. But a trench is more convenient for smaller, more closely spaced plants. In either case, prepare the planting bed or holes, as shown in the illustrations above.

A planting bed is practical for wide hedges with two rows of plants and for plants with particular soil requirements. If you amend the soil with organic matter, such as compost or peat moss, remember to make the bed wide enough to accommodate the spread of the mature root system.

If you can afford it, you'll get quicker results using container-grown shrubs or balled-and-burlapped specimens. But for extensive plantings, bare-root plants are substantially cheaper and just as likely to succeed, if you begin with moist roots in good condition.

Whether in single or double rows, set plants a little closer to each other than their estimated width at maturity. Most plants in formal hedges are spaced 1 to 1½ feet apart. Plants in an informal hedge may be 2 or even 3 feet apart, depending on their eventual spread. To plant a hedge in a double row, stagger the plants so that plants in one row are opposite the spaces in the other. This arrangement gives some insurance of screening in case one plant fails—another will fill in the space. A length of chicken wire between the plants in a double hedge can make an unobtrusive barrier to small animals. Position the wire's lower edge at least 4 inches below ground level.

Mulch, water, and fertilize the new hedge and maintain it according to the guidelines beginning on page 44. If you get less than an inch of rain in a week during the first growing season, it's especially important to water the newly planted hedge every 7 to 10 days. Water as necessary during periods of drought; soaker hoses work especially well with hedges. (See page 36.) Apply a balanced fertilizer and renew the mulch every spring.

Pruning a Hedge

Once established, most trees and shrubs need little or no pruning. But a hedge is a different story. Formal hedges need regular pruning to maintain their consistent shape and dimensions, and even informal hedges need some pruning now and then to keep them in bounds and to stimulate flowering and dense foliage. The most important rule for pruning a hedge—especially a formal one—is that the top of the hedge must be narrower than the bottom, as illustrated below left. Stop pruning at least six weeks before you expect the first fall frost, giving tender new shoots time to harden before the onset of cold weather.

NEW HEDGES

For a full, bushy hedge, it is important that plants produce branches that are close to the ground as well as some that are higher up. That means you may need to do some judi-cious pruning shortly after planting. Yet as stated often throughout this book, new plants establish healthy root systems quicker if a full head of leaves can create photosynthesis that feeds roots and if end buds are allowed to create hormones that also stimulate root growth. With new plants, bear this in mind.

If you need to prune deciduous plants during their first year, head back the main stems, as shown below right. (Do not head back conifers, however.)

To guide the shape of a formal hedge as it grows, prune just to promote balanced growth. Prune deciduous plants moderately, and just trim the sides of conifers and broad-leaved evergreens. To even out the sizes of plants in a hedge, the rule is to prune strong growth lightly and weak growth hard. That's because harder pruning stimulates more vigorous growth; cut back strong growth by no more than one-third of its length and weaker growth by up to two-thirds as the hedge grows.

Hedge Shapes

AVOID THIS.

Wedge and square shapes result in bare, leggy bottoms.

Hedge cross-sectional shapes greatly affect where the lush, green growth occurs. Avoid wide or square tops that shield lower branches from needed sunlight. Make the base broader than the top by at least a few inches. In snow country, consider shapes that help deflect snow.

CONSIDER THESE OPTIONS.

Inverted wedge and obelisk shapes result in lush growth, top to bottom.

Rounded and pointed tops help deflect heavy snow loads.

Informally pruned, this hedge lets snow through.

SHAPING

PRUNED TO SHAPE　　　**EVENTUAL APPEARANCE**

ANNUAL GROWTH

It's important to establish the desired shape when a hedge plant is still small, shearing it to a miniature of its intended full-grown shape. For a formal look, a flat top can serve well in regions with light snowfall.

Experts sometimes disagree on when to begin shaping a hedge. Because end buds produce hormones that help stimulate root growth, bare-root plants may get off to a better start if given a year to become established before pruning. Container and balled-and-burlapped plants tend to have better root systems that may allow pruning upon planting.

Consider the time and possible expense of maintaining a formal hedge, which requires regular pruning.

MAINTENANCE PRUNING

The neat appearance of a clipped hedge can be maintained only by pruning twice a year with manual hedge shears or an electric or gas-powered trimmer. Follow guidance for specific plants given in the Plant Profile sections of this book.

Keep up with the maintenance of coniferous hedges. Because most conifers sprout new shoots solely from new wood, only regular pruning of fresh new growth produces and maintains the fine, dense surface. Shear the light green new growth in spring before it hardens, two or three times at weekly intervals, if necessary; shearing later in the season will leave unattractive wounds until the new season's growth begins.

RENEWING AN OLD HEDGE

Hedges that are regularly maintained can last for years. But if you've neglected your hedge or acquired a severely overgrown one, don't despair. Many deciduous hedges and those of yew and of broad-leaved evergreens, such as boxwood, can be saved. In general, the plants that respond well to hard pruning or renovation are likely to be the most successful candidates for hedge renewal.

One way to renew a hedge, especially an informal one, is to cut it down nearly to the ground and start over. A more complicated process, but one that retains some semblance of hedge throughout, is to cut back one side the first year and the other side the following year, as shown at right.

In either case, to promote strong growth, fertilize, mulch, and water the hedge well during the seasons before and after the renovation. Renovate deciduous hedges when they are dormant. But renovate evergreen hedges in midspring, as mentioned on page 52.

Maintenance Pruning

With practice, many gardeners feel comfortable shearing hedges by eye, with either hand shears or a power trimmer. Most deciduous and evergreen plants with small, closely spaced leaves can be sheared. To maintain a neat formal hedge, you may need to shear at least twice a year, when new shoots have emerged but before their wood has hardened. To help control the power cable of an electric trimmer, drape it over your lead shoulder. Caution: make sure that your power cable meets manufacturer specifications for the trimmer and that it is protected by an outdoor-rated ground-fault circuit interrupter (GFCI).

Renewing an Old Hedge

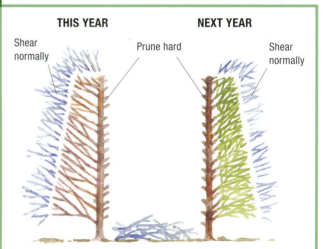

THIS YEAR   NEXT YEAR

Shear normally   Prune hard   Shear normally

To reduce the width of an overgrown hedge, prune back one side hard, as shown in the drawing above left; then shear the other side as you would normally. During the next year, prune the other side hard, as shown above right; then shear the newly regrown side normally.

The Barberries

Berberis

Barberry (*Berberis* x *mentorensis*)

The barberries, slow-growing rugged shrubs native to temperate regions of Asia, Europe, and North America, make colorful, striking hedges. Some have spiny leaves and thorns wicked enough to discourage pets and wildlife. In the spring, small flowers bloom; in fall, the leaves of deciduous barberries turn gold, orange, and crimson. Conspicuous showy berries enhance the color scheme. In winter, the twiggy structure and interesting branching of both evergreen and deciduous barberries, whether trimmed or untrimmed, add presence and texture to the scene.

The deciduous barberries have the brightest fall color and are the most cold tolerant. Cultivars of the lovely Japanese barberry (*Berberis thunbergii* variety *atropurpurea*) are especially popular, such as the thorny 2-foot dwarf 'Crimson Pygmy', with reddish purple leaves and bright red berries in the fall. White-flowered 'Rose Glow' and 'Pink Queen' are 5-foot forms with lovely rose-pink foliage when young, deepening in color and developing

Japanese barberry
(*Berberis thunbergii* variety *atropurpurea* 'Crimson Pygmy' and 'Aurea')

Barberry (*Berberis thunbergii* variety *atropurpurea* 'Aurea')

Dwarf Japanese barberry (*Berberis thunbergii* variety *atropurpurea* 'Crimson Pygmy')

flecks and streaks of gray, white, or reddish purple with age. The leaves of 'Aurea' are luminous yellow when new and turn pale green-yellow in late summer. These hardy shrubs thrive in Zones 4 or 5–8.

The evergreen barberries bear larger flowers. Wintergreen barberry (*B. julianae*), a favorite on the East Coast in Zones 6–8, is a 4- to 6-foot shrub with yellow flowers and spiny dark green leaves that make a forbidding hedge. The berries are bluish black. Warty barberry (*B. verruculosa*), a refined 3-foot plant with glossy green 1-inch leaves that turn bronze in the fall, is safely hardy to Zone 6. Its large golden yellow flowers are followed by blue-black berries with a dusky bloom. The dark green foliage of a Midwest favorite, 5- to 6-foot *B. mentorensis* (Zones 5–8), turns a flaming scarlet red in the fall.

Culture: the barberries transplant easily in early spring or fall, thrive in almost any soil, and tolerate shade, though they color best in sun. They bloom on old wood. Prune to control the height or shape of a hedge shortly after the shrubs bloom.

William Penn barberry (*Berberis julianae* 'William Penn')

Darwin barberry (*Berberis darwinii*)

Dwarf Japanese barberry
(*Berberis thunbergii* variety *atropurpurea* 'Crimson Pygmy')

FEATURED PROFILE
Dwarf Japanese

Botanical Name: *Berberis thunbergii* 'Crimson Pygmy' **Family:** Berberidaceae **Type of Plant:** spiny deciduous shrub with vivid color and red berries in autumn **Uses:** hedge, thorny barrier, specimen plant **Genus Range:** temperate Asia, Europe, North America **Hardiness:** USDA Zones 4–8 **Height:** 1½ to 2' **Growth Rate:** slow **Form & Habit:** wide-spreading, densely branched **Bloom Period:** April and May **Flowers:** yellow flowers in small clusters on stem undersides **Fruits:** bright red berries **Foliage:** reddish purple leaves **Soil & pH:** adaptable **Light & Moisture:** full sun for best color but succeeds in shade; tolerates drought **Pruning Seasons:** shortly after flowering

The Boxwoods

Buxus

Native to Europe and Asia, boxwood is a slow-growing evergreen shrub with a billowing, somewhat natural pyramidal shape. Fine neat foliage and a great tolerance for shearing and shaping make it a superb subject for hedging, edging, and topiary treatment. Clipped boxwood was used in ancient Rome to make topiaries, and later during the Renaissance to make the low-clipped hedges that outline gardens in Italy and the grand parterres at the Palace of Versailles.

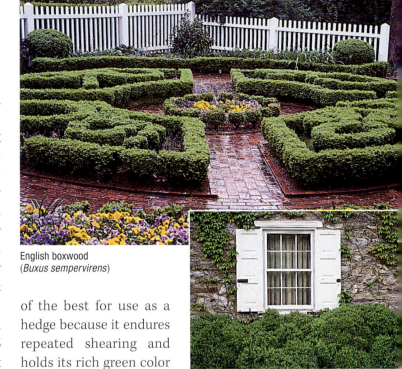

English boxwood
(*Buxus sempervirens*)

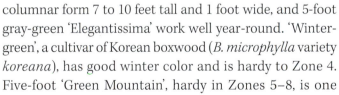

Littleleaf boxwood
(*Buxus microphylla* 'Winter Gem')
pyramidal trained

In the Mid-Atlantic and Northest regions, in Zones 5 or 6–8, long-lived English box (*Buxus sempervirens*) is a great favorite. Some boxwoods in Virginia date back to Colonial times. Unclipped, plants will eventually reach 15 to 20 feet. Lower-growing 6-foot 'Vardar Valley' tolerates cold and drought. As accent plants, 'Graham Blandy', a columnar form 7 to 10 feet tall and 1 foot wide, and 5-foot gray-green 'Elegantissima' work well year-round. 'Winter-green', a cultivar of Korean boxwood (*B. microphylla* variety *koreana*), has good winter color and is hardy to Zone 4. Five-foot 'Green Mountain', hardy in Zones 5–8, is one of the best for use as a hedge because it endures repeated shearing and holds its rich green color in winter. For warm dry climes in Zones 6–9, the 3- to 6-foot littleleaf boxwood cultivar *B. microphylla* variety *japonica* 'Morris Midget' is a good choice.

Culture: a container-grown boxwood transplants most easily in the fall. It requires well-drained, humusy, loose soil with a pH of 6.0 to 7.2 and doesn't tolerate salt or wet feet; once established, it can stand occasional droughts. It succeeds in sun or partial shade. Pruning elongated shoots in late spring after new growth is complete keeps boxwood bushy and beautiful. You can reshape overgrown shrubs by cutting back the plants, in May, to within a foot of the ground. Because this evergreen's leaves are toxic, deer seem to avoid boxwood.

English boxwood (*Buxus sempervirens*)

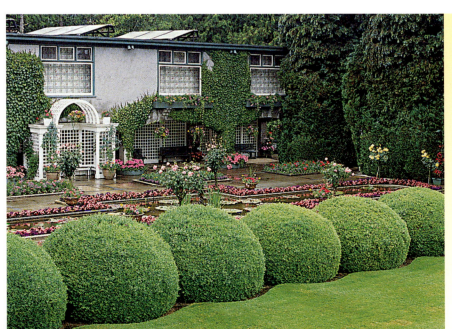

FEATURED PROFILE
English Boxwood

Botanical Name: *Buxus sempervirens* **Family:** Buxaceae **Type of Plant:** broad-leaved evergreen shrub **Uses:** hedges, edging, screening, topiary, specimen **Genus Range:** temperate Europe, Asia **Hardiness:** USDA Zones 5 or 6–8 **Height:** 15 to 20' **Growth Rate:** slow **Form & Habit:** pyramidal, billowing **Foliage:** $\frac{2}{5}$ to $1\frac{1}{8}$" long, lustrous dark green on top, lighter green underneath **Soil & pH:** well-drained; humusy; pH 6.05 to 7.2 **Light & Moisture:** sun; partial shade **Pruning Seasons:** late spring after new growth

English boxwood (*Buxus sempervirens*)

Leyland Cypress
x *Cupressocyparis leylandii*

Evergreen Leyland cypress, a favorite in the Southeast and hardy in Zones 6–10, is a hybrid of the cypress family of narrow columnar shrubs and trees that have flat scalelike leaves. The dense, feathery, gray-green bluish foliage almost conceals its reddish brown bark. The Leyland cypress grows rapidly, at a rate of 3 feet and more a year, reaching 60 or 70 feet. It makes a tough quick screen for urban properties and, because it withstands salt spray, for coastal homes. It tolerates heavy shearing and makes a fine tall hedge, or it can be planted as a companion to a slower-growing, more desirable tree or shrub and later removed to make room for the star.

Some lovely graceful cultivars have been introduced, such as 'Naylor's Blue', hardy in Zone 5, which grows to 30 or 40 feet high and can reach 15 feet wide. The summer foliage is a soft grayish blue that intensifies in winter. 'Castle-wellan' is an equally hardy Leyland cypress, about 20 feet tall at maturity and 5 feet wide. New growth has a golden cast that turns bronze in the winter.

Leyland cypress
(x *Cupressocyparis leylandii*)

Culture: a young container-grown Leyland cypress transplants easily in early spring to moist fertile soil, acid or alkaline. Allow plenty of space for the root ball; if you are planting a hedge, make the bed at least 5 feet wide. In full sun, the foliage grows dense and close to the trunk; in shade, the branching is more open and informal. Maintain soil moisture during droughts. Prune or shear a Leyland cypress in July, but do not prune into wood devoid of foliage. For a formal hedge, allow the tops to grow 6 to 12 inches beyond the intended height; then cut off the leaders to just above a lateral branch 6 inches below the intended height.

Leyland cypress (x *Cupressocyparis leylandii*)

FEATURED PROFILE
Leyland Cypress

Botanical Name: x *Cupressocyparis leylandii* **Family:** Cupressaceae **Type of Plant:** evergreen conifer **Uses:** tall evergreen hedge and screen **Hardiness:** USDA Zones 5–9 **Height:** 60 to 70' in cultivation, to 100' in the wild **Growth Rate:** fast, 3 feet or more per year **Form & Habit:** columnar or pyramidal **Fruits:** cones ⅖ to ⅛" diameter with 8 scales **Foliage:** scalelike, dark green, pressed close against the flattened branchlets; bluish gray-green **Soil & pH:** fertile, moist; tolerates acid or alkaline soil **Light & Moisture:** full sun for best color; maintain moisture **Pruning Seasons:** summer, after the main spurt of growth

Leyland cypress (x *Cupressocyparis leylandii*)

Euonymus

Euonymus

Euonymus is a member of the bittersweet family, a large group of deciduous and evergreen shrubs, small trees, and vines valued for their handsome foliage and colorful fall fruit. In autumn, every leaf of the deciduous

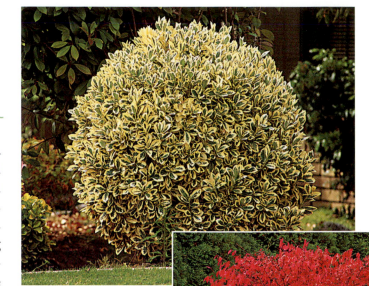

Evergreen euonymus
(*Euonymus japonicus* 'Albo-marginatus')

12- to 20-foot winged euonymus (*Euonymus alatus*) turns a glowing rosy crimson; even its small clusters of fruit turn red. The rest of the year the plant is a mound of green foliage on slender stems lined with curious corky flanges—hence the common name. For medium-tall hedges, the 6- to 10-foot dwarf cultivar 'Compactus' is a good choice. For low hedges, 3- to 5-foot 'Rudy Haag' withstands heavy pruning.

Caution: winged euonymus has escaped cultivation in parts of the East and Midwest and is crowding out native shrubs in some places. Confine plantings to suburban and urban locations, where birds are less likely to deposit seeds in wild areas. Versatile, trainable, shrubby evergreen euonymus forms make attractive informal hedges, edgings, topiaries, and espaliers. You can also use them as screens for unattractive fences. Wintercreeper (*E.*

Wintercreeper
(*Euonymous fortunei* variety *radicans* 'Gracilis')

Dwarf winged euonymus
(*Euonymus alatus* 'Compactus')

fortunei), a popular species, is the source of many handsome cultivars that develop clusters of brilliant tiny berries that split open to reveal colored seeds. Some variegated forms appear a soft gray-green from a distance. They are susceptible to scale, so check with a knowledgeable local nursery before buying them.

Culture: a container-grown euonymus transplants easily in early fall or spring and is tolerant of any soil that isn't swampy. It does as well in shade as in sun. *E. alatus* is most attractive when allowed to develop naturally. To keep a hedge of evergreen euonymus no taller than 4 to 6 feet, selectively cut back older wood in late winter.

FEATURED PROFILE
Winged Euonymus

Botanical Name: *Euonymus alatus* **Family:** Celastraceae **Type of Plant:** large deciduous shrub with brilliant fall color **Uses:** informal hedges, specimen **Native Range:** NE Asia to central China **Hardiness:** USDA Zones 3 or 4–8 **Height:** 12 to 15 or 20' **Growth Rate:** slow **Form & Habit:** flat-topped, wide, mounded to horizontal **Bloom Period:** midspring **Flowers:** insignificant **Fruits:** red capsules in fall, partly hidden by foliage **Foliage:** lustrous, dark green, slim oval leaves, 4 to 7" long; fall color brilliant scarlet to deep purplish red **Soil & pH:** well-drained; humusy; pH 5.5 to 6.5 **Light & Moisture:** full sun for best color; maintain moisture, but handles some drought. **Pruning Seasons:** prune old wood in late winter

Winged euonymus (*Euonymus alatus*) winged twigs in winter

The Privets

Ligustrum

The privets used for tall hedges and screening are highly shearable members of a group of evergreen and deciduous shrubs native to Asia, Europe, and North Africa. Generally fast-growing, they succeed almost anywhere, including the seashore. Dense multistemmed plants with dark green oval leaves 1 to 2 inches long, the privets bear clusters of small white flowers that sometimes have an unpleasant scent, followed by blue or black berrylike fruits. Of the several species introduced to North America, two have naturalized: the Japanese, or waxleaf, privet (*Ligustrum japonicum*) and the California privet (*L. ovalifolium*).

A vigorous large shrub originally from Japan, the 10- to 15-foot California privet works well for hedges. Its glossy green leaves last almost year-round in Zone 6; in Zones 7 and 8 it is an evergreen. During the summer, the plant bears clusters of creamy white flowers followed by black fruits. The similar ibolium privet (*L.* × *ibolium*) is hardy in Zones 4–8. *L.* × *vicaryi*, a fast-growing, showy golden hybrid, is hardy in Zones 5–8.

In cooler regions, Zones 3–7 or 8, the deciduous 10- to 12-foot Amur privet (*L. amurense*) is popular; it can take heavy pruning. The equally hardy Regel's privet (*L. obtusifolium* variety *regelianum*), a wide-spreading 5- to 6-foot plant, makes a beautiful untrimmed hedge. In warm regions, Zones 7–9, the Japanese privet (*L. japonicum*) is a favorite.

Culture: a container-grown privet transplants easily, tolerates any soil that isn't wet, and grows well in sun or shade. It thrives where the pH range is 6.0 to 7.5. A privet planted for a hedge should be cut back to within 12 inches of the ground after planting and cut again in April, for two or three years, to fill out the base. After that, shear the plants lightly as needed during the growing season, beginning after flowering.

A privet (*Ligustrum*)

Japanese privet (*Ligustrum japonicum*)

California privet (*Ligustrum ovalifolium* 'Aureum')

FEATURED PROFILE
Amur Privet

Botanical Name: *Ligustrum amurense* **Family:** Oleaceae **Type of Plant:** tall multistemmed broad-leaved evergreen shrub **Uses:** tall hedge; screening **Native Range:** Asia, Europe, North Africa **Hardiness:** USDA Zones 3–7 **Height:** 10 to 12' **Growth Rate:** fast **Form & Habit:** dense, upright, somewhat pyramidal **Bloom Period:** May–June **Flowers:** 1 to 2 panicles of creamy white flowers with an unpleasant odor **Fruits:** persistent berrylike fruits in early fall **Foliage:** oval-rounded, medium to dark green **Soil & pH:** tolerates most soils; pH 6.0 to 7.5 **Light & Moisture:** sun or shade; tolerates drought but not wet feet **Pruning Seasons:** prune after flowering

Amur privet (*Ligustrum amurense*)

The Honeysuckles

Lonicera

Tatarian honeysuckle
(*Lonicera tatarica* 'Arnold Red')

Goldflame honeysuckle (*Lonicera heckrottii*)

The honeysuckles, rugged shrubs and twining vines, are suited to a variety of landscape situations. You can train shrubby forms into attractive low or tall informal hedges, or use them for screening. Their small fleshy berries attract birds; their often intensely fragrant flowers come in white, pink, red, or yellow. Most fragrant is winter honeysuckle (*Lonicera fragrantissima*). Its pungent lemon-scented white blooms appear in late winter and early spring and last for several weeks. The upright wide-spreading shrub reaches 10 feet tall; its tangled mass of wiry, somewhat pendulous, stems looks charming in an informal hedge or screen and is attractive naturalized at the edge of an open woodland. It is hardy in Zones 4–8 or 9.

Tatarian honeysuckle (*L. tatarica*), hardy in Zones 3–8 and dependable, succeeds even by the seashore. An evergreen in the South, its fragrant pink-to-white flowers bloom later than those of winter honeysuckle and are followed by red or yellow fruits. Pests like the species, but some beautiful resistant cultivars, notably 'Arnold Red', have been developed.

Popular in the Midwest (Zones 4–6), *L. xylosteum*

Tatarian honeysuckle
(*Lonicera tatarica*)

'Claveyi' and 'Emerald Mound' grow to 3 or 4 feet tall and almost twice as wide. They have blue-green foliage and white flowers followed by deep red berries.

Culture: a honeysuckle transplants easily, in spring or fall, to moist but well-drained clay or loam soils. A pH range of 6.0 to 8.0 is best but not essential. Honeysuckle thrives in full sun but will succeed in light shade, especially in warmer regions. The only pruning required is to remove weak wood. After flowering, cut back to a suitable point just above promising new growth. An overgrown plant can be cut back to the ground in spring before growth begins; it will regenerate.

FEATURED PROFILE
Winter Honeysuckle

Botanical Name: *Lonicera fragrantissima* **Family:** Caprifoliaceae **Type of Plant:** deciduous fragrant flowering shrub **Uses:** low or tall informal hedge **Native Range:** eastern China **Hardiness:** USDA Zones 4–8 or 9 **Height:** 6 to 10' **Growth Rate:** medium **Form & Habit:** erect, widespreading, fountain-shaped branches **Bloom Period:** March or early April **Flowers:** small, cream-white, fragrant but not showy **Fruits:** ¼" shiny red berries **Foliage:** elliptical; 1½ to 3" long; blue-green to dark green **Soil & pH:** well-drained clay or loam; pH 6.0 to 8.0 **Light & Moisture:** full sun but tolerates light shade; maintain moisture **Pruning Seasons:** after flowering

Winter honeysuckle (*Lonicera fragrantissima*)

The Oleanders
also called "Rose Bay"

Nerium oleander

Rose bay (*Nerium oleander*)
trained as a small tree

Rose bay (Nerium oleander)

Rose bay
(*Nerium oleander* 'Petite Salmon')

Oleander is a flowering evergreen shrub 8 to 15 feet tall for hot areas, Zones 8–10. It belongs to the dogbane family, a group of plants native to regions from the Mediterranean to Japan that includes periwinkle (*Vinca minor*). All summer long, oleanders produce clusters of attractive flowers about 2 inches across in white, yellow, red, pink, or lilac. Some cultivars are very sweetly scented. The flowers, the leathery evergreen leaves and handsome branching, and the low-maintenance needs make oleanders ideal for informal hedges, screening, shrub borders, and container gardens. Oleanders tolerate the repeated clipping required by a more formal hedge. And they are so tolerant of intense heat, drought, salt, and wind that they are used in the Southwest and southern Florida as street plants and in highway dividers. Gardeners in cooler regions can grow oleanders in planters that summer outdoors and winter indoors in a bright window. Dozens of varieties are offered by southern nurseries; many vibrantly colored North African cultivars have appeared in recent years. Cultivars of the Petites series, developed in California, are valued for their smaller size (4 to 6 feet high and wide).

Culture: the milky sap in the leaves and branchlets is poisonous; avoid planting the shrub where small children play. Oleander transplants easily to any ordinary well-drained fertile soil. It thrives in full sun but does well in light shade and grows most rapidly in soil that is evenly moist. Oleander blooms on new growth, so prune back individual branches, as needed, in late winter or in the early spring.

FEATURED PROFILE
Oleander, or Rose Bay

Botanical Name: *Nerium oleander* **Family:** Apocynaceae **Type of Plant:** flowering evergreen shrub **Uses:** medium to tall informal hedge, screening from wind and salt **Native Range:** Mediterranean, southern Asia **Hardiness:** USDA Zones 8–10 **Height:** 6 to 12' **Growth Rate:** slow **Form & Habit:** upright, bushy, rounded top **Bloom Period:** all summer to midfall **Flowers:** fragrant; about 1" across; single or double; white, pink, red; held in full clusters at tips of the stems **Fruits:** slender pods 5 to 7" long **Foliage:** whorls of 3 to 4 leaves 3 to 5" long and ½ to ¾" wide; dark gray-green **Soil & pH:** well-drained, moist, fertile; withstands some drought; tolerant of salt conditions **Light & Moisture:** full sun or partial shade; maintain moisture but handles some drought **Pruning Seasons:** late winter, early spring

Rose bay (*Nerium oleander*)

Osmanthus
Osmanthus

Osmanthus are large, handsome evergreen shrubs with small, dark green hollylike leaves. In midfall or early spring, plants bear tiny fragrant flowers. These graceful shrubs accept shearing and can be used as hedges. The 10- to 20-foot sweet, tea, or fragrant, olive (*Osmanthus fragrans*) is the most strongly scented and the most tender; it is hardy only in Zones 8–9 or 10. Its white flowers bloom in spring and summer in gardens in the Southeast and in California. The tiny orange flower spikes of the 10-foot form aurantiacus are so fragrant that they are used in China to scent teas. A similar, more cold-tolerant hybrid, *O. × fortunei*, is a fragrant fall bloomer. In April, tall, twiggy, gracefully arching *O. delavayi*, a wide 6- to 20-foot shrub, is covered with masses of scented white flowers. Farther north in Zones 6 or 7–9, 10-foot holly, or Chinese, olive (*O. hetero-phyllus*) blooms from September to November. The new growth of its white-variegated cultivar 'Goshiki', a 3½-foot plant, is tinged with pink-orange. The native osmanthus (*O. american-us*), called "devilwood," makes a rugged hedge up to 25 feet tall in moist shady places, at the shore, and in

Chinese olive
(*Osmanthus heterophyllus*)

acid soils—pH 4.0 to 6.0. An open shrub that is good looking all year-round, it bears fragrant flowers in late March or April. Devilwood is hardy in Zones 6 or 7–9; it grows wild on the coastal plain from south-eastern Virginia all the way down to Louisiana. It is sold by nurseries specializing in native plants.

Culture: a container-grown osmanthus specimen transplants easily in early spring to well-drained, fertile, acid soil—pH 4.0 to 6.0—and it tolerates alkalinity and urban conditions. It does best in bright shade. Osmanthus regenerates freely on old wood and withstands severe pruning. Keep it within bounds by trimming radically in April or by cutting back extra long growth in May. Light trimming to tidy an osmanthus hedge should be completed before the end of July.

Sweet olive (*Osmanthus fragrans*)

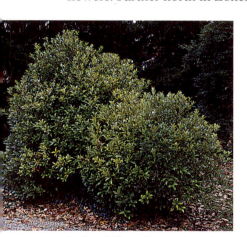

Devilwood (*Osmanthus americanus*)

FEATURED PROFILE
Fragrant, Sweet, or Tea, Olive

Botanical Name: *Osmanthus fragrans* **Family:** Oleaceae **Type of Plant:** fragrant, flowering broad-leaved evergreen shrub **Uses:** hedge; specimen for fall and early spring flowering **Native Range:** Asia, Pacific Islands, and southern U.S. **Hardiness:** USDA Zones 8–9 **Height:** 10 to 20' **Growth Rate:** slow-medium **Form & Habit:** densely branched broad upright form **Bloom Period:** spring or summer **Flowers:** small, white **Fruits:** blue-black capsules **Foliage:** finely toothed, dark green **Soil & pH:** well-drained, fertile, acid soil, pH 4.0 to 6.0, but is adaptable **Light & Moisture:** partial shade; maintain moisture **Pruning Seasons:** spring, to keep within bounds

Sweet olive (*Osmanthus fragrans*)

The Photinias
also called "Christmas Berry"
Photinia

Japanese photinia (*Photinia glabra*)

Photinias are tall, lustrous evergreen or deciduous shrubs or small trees that bear white flowers in early summer. These are followed by red berrylike fruit, which inspired the common name. Photinias belong to the rose family and are susceptible to a few of the rose's problems, including fireblight and mildew. Where those problems are prevalent, plant only resistant cultivars.

Fraser's photinia (*Photinia x fraseri*) is a popular ornamental shrub in Zones 6 or 7–10. The upright 15- to 20-foot broad-leaved evergreen makes a handsome formal clipped hedge, a solid windbreak, or a dense screen. But photinia's major assets are dense glossy foliage and new growth that emerges a glistening coppery red. Hedges using Fraser's photinia are usually clipped in early spring and again in summer in order to encourage new growth. A trim photinia hedge with new foliage is lovely in a garden.

A smaller plant, the 10- or 12-foot Japanese photinia (*P. glabra*), with showier flowers, is widely used in the Southeast in Zones 7–9. The species seen in northern gardens, in Zones 4–7, is Oriental photinia (*P. villosa*), a 10-to-15-foot shrub or small

Oriental photinia (*Photinia villosa*)

tree (deciduous) with multiple stems that is planted for its flowers and fall color—the shiny green leaves turn to lovely shades of bronze and red before falling. Bright red berries hang in clusters into winter.

Culture: a container-grown photinia transplants easily in fall or early spring to well-drained fertile soil. It is pH adaptable. Photinias color best in full sun but tolerate light shade. Pruned in April and again in late summer, Fraser's photinia will produce two or three shiny, colorful new shoots from each cut. Make the cuts back into the bush at a point where they are hidden.

Fraser's photinia
(*Photinia x fraseri* 'Red Robin')

Fraser's photinia (*Photinia x fraseri*)

FEATURED PROFILE
Fraser's Photinia, or Red Tip

Botanical Name: *Photinia x fraseri* **Family:** Rosaceae **Type of Plant:** broad-leaved evergreen shrub **Uses:** tall hedge, screening, windbreak **Native Range:** Asia **Hardiness:** USDA Zones 6 or 7–9 **Height:** 15 to 25' **Growth Rate:** medium to fast **Form & Habit:** upright **Bloom Period:** June to mid-July **Flowers:** white, composed of 5 petals each ⅓" across, born in flat heads to 6" wide; considered malodorous **Fruits:** ¼" red globes **Foliage:** small-toothed, 4 to 8" long, elongated, pointed oval, emerging bronze red and turning glossy green in 2 to 4 weeks **Soil & pH:** well-drained, fertile; pH adaptable **Light & Moisture:** full sun for best color; not too much moisture in summer **Pruning Seasons:** early spring and late summer

Podocarpus

Podocarpus

These southern evergreens are related to yews and have somewhat similar fruit. Southern yew (*Podocarpus macrophyllus*), a rather rigid, upright evergreen 8 to 25 feet tall, has needlelike dark green leaves and scalelike flowers that are followed in fall by edible berrylike reddish purple fruits. Southern yew belongs to a group of coniferous shrubs and small trees native to the Southern Hemisphere and to tropical mountains and highlands. Male and female flowers appear on separate plants in early summer; the male flowers grow in catkinlike clusters and female flowers are solitary. The species tolerates salt spray and is planted along the coast and inland for sheared hedges and screening in Zones 8–10 or 11, from North Carolina and southward, and in California. Chinese podocarpus (*P. m.* variety *maki*), a narrow shrubby form that grows slowly to 10 feet, makes a handsome, compact, dark green hedge; it also does well in containers. In the North, young potted plants are grown indoors and on patios.

Two larger species used as specimen trees are often planted in landscapes that include podocarpus as a hedge. African fern pine, *P. gracilior* (Zones 9–10), a graceful midsize conifer with fernlike foliage on pendent branches, creates a soft beautiful canopy. It can reach 50 feet. Smaller long-leaved yellowwood, *P. henkelii* (Zones 8–10), which reaches 20 to 25 feet tall, produces drooping tufts of long, narrow, glossy deep green leaves on erect branches.

Southern yew
(*Podocarpus macrophyllus*)

Southern yew
(*Podocarpus macrophyllus*)

Culture: a container-grown podocarpus transplants easily in fall or early spring to well-drained fertile humusy soil. It does best in full sun but tolerates light shade; it withstands mild droughts but not wet feet. To train podocarpus to an informal hedge, prune the plants hard before July to encourage low branching so that new growth has time to harden before winter. If it is necessary to clip twice during the growing season to keep the plants shapely, make the first cuts in May and the second in July.

FEATURED PROFILE
Southern Yew

Botanical Name: *Podocarpus macrophyllus* **Family:** Podocarpaceae **Type of Plant:** narrow-leaved evergreen conifer **Uses:** hedge, screening, specimen, seashore border **Native Range:** Southern Hemisphere **Hardiness:** USDA Zones 8 or 9–10 or 11 **Height:** 8 to 25' **Growth Rate:** slow **Form & Habit:** columnar or upright oval **Bloom Period:** midspring **Flowers:** catkinlike male; female is a short stalk bearing a few scales **Fruits:** to ½" long, egg-shaped, reddish purple; edible **Foliage:** needlelike, to ¾" wide, 2 to 4" or longer, lustrous dark green above with two whitish bands on the underside **Soil & pH:** humusy, well-drained, fertile, pH adaptable **Light & Moisture:** full sun or light shade; tolerates drought when established but not wet feet **Pruning Seasons:** after growth is complete in summer

Southern yew (*Podocarpus macrophyllus*)

Cherry Laurel
Prunus laurocerasus

Beach plum (*Prunus maritima*)

Prunus is a diverse group of fruit trees and shrubs that includes the beautiful flowering cherries and almonds. The most adaptable for hedges is the cherry laurel (*P. laurocerasus*), a tall European shrub species suited to Zones 5 or 6–8. The smaller evergreen 'Otto Luyken' is especially popular. It looks like a 3- to 4-foot shrubby mountain laurel, with lustrous leaves about 4 inches long. (For more on mountain laurels, see page 186.) In spring, fuzzy upright clusters of tiny fragrant white flowers cover 'Otto Luyken', even if it's growing in dense shade. An excellent edging shrub, it also makes a beautiful medium-low hedge. 'Schipkaensis', a somewhat larger cultivar, withstands winters in Zone 5 with some protection.

The cherry laurel tolerates salt spray, as does its relative the beach plum (*P. maritima*), a 6-foot shrub native to the Atlantic Coast from Maine to Virginia and hardy in Zones 3–7 or 8. Both are used as windbreaks at the seashore.

Culture: a container-grown cherry laurel transplants well in early spring to moist but well-drained humusy soil. It tolerates drought, adapts to pH, and succeeds in full sun, though it blooms well in dense shade. An 'Otto Luyken' laurel hedge tolerates shearing but looks better left unpruned. A tired-looking shrub can be regenerated by hard pruning in spring or early summer.

Beach plum (*Prunus maritima*)

Cherry laurel (*Prunus laurocerasus* 'Otto Luyken')

FEATURED PROFILE
Cherry Laurel

Botanical Name: *Prunus laurocerasus* 'Otto Luyken' **Family:** Rosaceae **Type of Plant:** broad-leaved evergreen shrub, dwarf English laurel **Uses:** medium-low broad hedge, edger **Genus Range:** S.E. Europe, Asia Minor **Hardiness:** USDA Zones 5 or 6–8 **Height:** 3 to 4' **Growth Rate:** slow **Form & Habit:** densely branched, 6 to 8' wide **Bloom Period:** spring **Flowers:** sprays of small white flowers **Fruits:** purple-black, hidden by foliage **Foliage:** lustrous dark green leaves 4" long, 1" wide **Soil & pH:** well-drained, humusy; pH adaptable **Light & Moisture:** best in full sun but will bloom in shade; maintain moisture **Pollinators:** unnecessary **Pruning Seasons:** after flowering in spring or early summer but looks better unpruned

The Firethorns

Pyracantha

These beautiful broad-leaved evergreen shrubs from Europe and Asia have fine foliage and businesslike thorns. They bear white flowers in May or June, followed by a flush of spectacular and long-lasting red, orange, or yellow berries. Firethorn can be pruned to make a dense hedge. Wide-branching forms are beautiful trained as an espalier, and upright species can stand alone in a row for screening. The most vividly colorful is the 12-foot species *Pyracantha coccinea*, hardy in Zones 6–9. Three evergreen selections hardy as far as Zone 5 have been popular for many years: 'Lalandei', an orange-berried plant with an upright habit good for screening; 'Kasan', a compact plant with bright orange-red berries; and low-growing 'Rutgers', a 2- to 3-foot hybrid that spreads widely and bears orange-colored fruit. A good upright variety is the semievergreen hybrid 'Mohave' (*P. coccinea* × *P. koidzumii*), hardy to Zones 6–9. It produces masses of orange-red berries in mid-August. 'Harlequin' has striking, brightly variegated leaves.

Formosa firethorn
(*Pyracantha koidzumii*)

The most cold-resistant firethorns, *P. angustifolia* and its cultivars, tolerate winters in Zone 4. 'Gnozam' and 'Monon' have orange berries. For hot, dry areas in Zones 7 and 8, try planting upright arching red-berried *P. koidzumii* 'Victory', which is resistant to scab. Pyracantha is subject to fireblight, but the hybrids 'Apache' and 'Mohave' are resistant. 'Apache' is compact as well and doesn't need pruning.

A firethorn (*Pyracantha*)

Firethorn (*Pyracantha coccinea*) in winter

Culture: a container-grown firethorn can be transplanted with care in early spring to well-drained fertile soil, pH 5.5 to 6.5. It fruits best in full sun but tolerates light shade. The layered way that pyracantha branches develop is one of the shrub's great assets, and it should be allowed to grow naturally. If branches get straggly, cut out year-old shoots selectively after flowering, leaving the best flower clusters to ripen fruit. Any cuts made should be taken back into the center of the shrub to hide the wounds.

FEATURED PROFILE

Pyracantha

Botanical Name: *Pyracantha coccinea* 'Mohave' **Family:** Rosaceae **Type of Plant:** flowering, fruiting broad-leaved semi-evergreen shrub **Uses:** hedge, espalier, screening, specimen planting **Genus Range:** southeastern Europe and Asia **Hardiness:** USDA Zones 6–9 **Height:** 8 to 10' **Growth Rate:** fast **Form & Habit:** stiff, thorny branches; open, spreading habit **Bloom Period:** spring **Flowers:** clusters of tiny whitish flowers **Fruits:** clusters of round orange-red berrylike fruits **Foliage:** lustrous dark green leaves 1 to 2½" long **Soil & pH:** well-drained; pH 5.5 to 7.5 **Light & Moisture:** full sun for best color; handles drought **Pruning Seasons:** to remove straggly branches, prune selectively after flowering, leaving best flowers to ripen fruit

Firethorn (*Pyracantha* 'Mohave')

Roses for Hedges

Rosa

Rose (*Rosa* 'Simplicity')

A row of hedge roses makes a beautiful informal boundary. Armed with thorns, a rose hedge becomes an effective barrier. The best forms bloom all season long or repeat bloom and are disease resistant.

Tall Hedges and Seashore Barriers. Beach rose (*Rosa rugosa*) from Asia, a tall stiff shrub that grows into dense hedges usually bristling with thorns, tolerates salt air and strong wind. It is often planted along the shore in the Northeast. In spring, modern cultivars bloom with clove-scented single or double flowers, which repeat through summer. In fall, large shiny coral-orange rose hips appear and the foliage is colorful. Beach rose is pest resistant and generally cold hardy to Zone 3 or 4.

Beach rose
(*Rosa rugosa*) hip

The 4-foot light pink cultivar 'Fru Dagmar Hastrup', also known as 'Frau Dagmar Hartopp', grows in Zones 3–8 and is so dense that repeated pruning will not much diminish its flower production.

Medium Hedges. The floribundas are vigorous bushy growers that make fine hedges 4 to 5 feet tall. The blossoms of popular varieties have the tidy form of a hybrid tea rose and produce several flushes of bloom. The all-time favorite for hedges is 'Betty Prior', a prolific bloomer 4 to 5 feet tall that produces five-petaled vivid pink flowers and maintains its emerald foliage until frost. 'Simplicity', another floribunda, was introduced in 1979 and grows densely upright, making a fine "living fence."

English shrub roses also make good hedges. These fragrant repeat bloomers are disease resistant, vigorous, and bushy but hardy to Zone 4 only. 'Bredon' grows to about 5 feet and produces large sprays of small buff yellow rosettes. (See pages 198–199.)

For a naturalized hedge or edging or a tall ground cover barrier, the sprawling Meidiland shrub roses are excellent. Disease resistant, they bloom all season with little care. (See pages 198–199.)

Low Hedges. The bushy polyantha roses—low-growing, vigorous plants—grow into dense impenetrable hedges. All season long, they produce masses of charming flowers under 2 inches. A popular choice, 'The Fairy' bears abundant clusters of small, double, slightly fragrant seashell pink blooms that last long in a vase. It is hardy to Zone 3.

Culture: before planting, work in fish meal, a slow-release 5-10-5 fertilizer, or a rose formula. Plant roses in early spring or fall in well-drained humusy soil, pH 6.0 to 7.0. Roses require six to eight hours of direct sun daily. Fertilize monthly from early spring until mid-July, and water during droughts.

FEATURED PROFILE
Beach, or Rugosa, Rose

Botanical Name: *Rosa rugosa* 'Fru Dagmar Hastrup' **Family:** Rosaceae **Type of Plant:** spiny deciduous flowering shrub **Uses:** coastal sand binder; hedge, tall edger, boundary marker **Genus Range:** northern China, Korea, Japan **Hardiness:** USDA Zones 3–8 **Height:** 4 to 6' Growth Rate: fast **Form & Habit:** stiff, upright spiny multistemmed shrub **Bloom Period:** June with repeat bloom through late summer **Flowers:** masses of fragrant silvery pink flowers **Fruits:** large round orange-red hips **Foliage:** thick dark green serrated leaves turn orange-red in fall **Soil & pH:** well-drained; humusy; pH 6.0 to 7.0 **Light & Moisture:** full sun; maintain moisture in droughts **Pruning Seasons:** in early spring, cut older canes to the ground; remove faded flowers to encourage repeat bloom

Beach rose (*Rosa rugosa* 'Fru Dagmar Hastrup')

The Spireas
also called "Bridal-Wreath"
Spirea

The spireas are old-fashioned deciduous shrubs with arching branches and dainty leaves. They are covered with tiny white or pink flowers in early May, June, or July, depending on the species. Spireas make beautiful informal flowering hedges and are also used as flowering fillers and for massing. There are dozens of species and hundreds of cultivated varieties. Six-foot *Spiraea* x *vanhouttei*, hardy in Zones 3–8 or 9, is an old-fashioned bridal-wreath type with branches that arch to the ground and, in late May, are covered with small white flowers. Another bridal-wreath form, the 3- to 5-foot Japanese cultivar 'Snowmound' (*S. nipponica*), is a midwestern favorite suited to Zones 4–8 that flowers in June. The strikingly beautiful 3- to 4-foot 'Grefsheim' (*S.* x *cinerea*) blooms earlier.

The other types of spirea bear flowers in rounded clusters and later in the season. The hardy Japanese spirea (*S. japonica*), which grows in Zones 3–8, has white, pink, and rose-colored flowerheads on the same plant, with lustrous green foliage. The 3- to 4-foot cultivar 'Anthony Waterer' (formerly known as a cultivar of *Spiraea* x *bumalda*), hardy in Zones 4–8, is an old favorite

Bridal-wreath (*Spiraea prunifolia*)

Japanese spirea
(*Spiraea japonica* 'Anthony Waterer')

Japanese spirea
(*Spiraea japonica* 'Goldflame')

with 4- to 6-inch wide dark pink flowerheads that open in July. Several pink-flowered varieties with colorful new foliage have been introduced. The young leaves of 2- to 3-foot 'Goldflame' are red, copper, and orange; the leaves of 'Golden Princess' are bronze yellow; 'Limemound' foliage is lemon yellow with a russet tinge that tends toward lime green in summer; in fall the foliage turns orange-red.

Culture: a container-grown or balled-and-burlapped spirea transplants easily in early spring or fall. It tolerates any soil that isn't wet and prefers pH in the 6.0 to 7.0 range and a sunny open airy site. To maintain their form and to increase flowering, prune *S. japonica* and its cultivars in early spring before growth begins. Don't prune the arching branches of bridal-wreath types; after they have flowered, remove dead branches from the interior of the shrub.

FEATURED PROFILE
Spiraea, or Bridal-wreath

Botanical Name: *Spiraea japonica* 'Anthony Waterer' **Family:** Rosaceae **Type of Plant:** deciduous flowering shrub **Uses:** low flowering hedge, specimen **Genus Range:** Japan, China, Korea **Hardiness:** USDA Zones 4–8 **Height:** 3 to 4' **Growth Rate:** fast **Form & Habit:** low, wide shrub with erect, gracefully arching branches **Bloom Period:** June into August **Flowers:** flat heads of dark pink flowers **Fruits:** small dry brown fruits **Foliage:** reddish purple new growth changes to bright green **Soil & pH:** airy, well-drained site; pH 6.0 to 7.0 **Light & Moisture:** full sun; tolerates some drought **Pruning Seasons:** before growth begins in early spring

Japanese spirea (*Spiraea japonica* 'Anthony Waterer')

The Yews

Taxus

Intermediate yew (*Taxus x media*)

English yew
(*Taxus baccata* 'Standishii')

The yews are the most adaptable and useful of all evergreens for hedging. Dark-needled shrubs and trees with reddish brown scaly bark and pea-size fleshy red berries, yews are native to the Northern Hemisphere and quite hardy. Slow growing, disease resistant, and tolerant of extensive pruning, yews make fine clipped hedges, green screens and walls, and topiary. The seeds and the foliage contain poisonous compounds, so be aware if you have children or pets.

Numerous cultivars of the English yew (*Taxus baccata* 'Adpressa') are used for foundation plantings throughout the East, where they grow in Zones 5 or 6–7 or 8. Most of the shrubby forms grow to be twice as wide as they are tall, but *T. baccata* 'Adpressa Fowle' is a good hedge plant with a mature size of 6 feet by 16 feet. Unique among evergreens in its tolerance for shade, it does best in a pH range of 7.0 to 7.5. 'Aurea' has golden needles. 'Stricta', a columnar form also known as the Irish yew, makes a handsome 15- to 30-foot screen. Where English yew isn't hardy, cultivars of Japanese yew (*T. cuspidata*) can be grown, in Zones 4–7. The dwarf 'Nana', 3 feet by 6 feet, is one of the most popular.

In the Midwest and West, in Zones 4 or 5–8, favorites are cultivars of the intermediate yew (*T. x media*), a cross between the English and Japanese yews. There's a size for every purpose, from compact, 3-foot 'Flemer', to 4- or 5-foot 'Densiformis', to 6-foot 'Brownii', and the longtime columnar 12-foot favorites, 'Hicksii' and *T. x media* 'Hatfieldii'.

Culture: transplant a container-grown or balled-and-burlapped yew with care in early spring or fall to fertile humusy soil with excellent drainage. Most yews prefer a neutral pH and thrive in sun or shade. You can shear the branch ends throughout the growing season. To keep a yew hedge compact, follow an early spring pruning with the removal of the soft new summer growth.

Intermediate yew
(*Taxus x media* 'Hicksii')

FEATURED PROFILE
Intermediate Yew

Botanical Name: *Taxus media* 'Hicksii' **Family:** Taxaceae **Type of Plant:** tall needled evergreen shrub **Uses:** tall hedges, screening **Genus Range:** north temperate region to Mexico **Hardiness:** USDA Zones 4 or 5–8 **Height:** 10 to 12' **Growth Rate:** slow to medium **Form & Habit:** long upright branches form a columnar habit **Flowers:** inconspicuous **Fruits:** fleshy red seedlike fruits **Foliage:** glossy dark green needlelike foliage **Soil & pH:** well-drained, humusy, fertile; 6.0 to 7.0 **Light & Moisture:** full sun or partial shade **Pruning Seasons:** early spring

Intermediate yew
(*Taxus x media* 'Hicksii')

Glossary

Acid soil. Soil with a pH lower than 7.0 (neutral).

Alkaline soil. Soil with a pH higher than 7.0 (neutral).

Alternate. Alternate leaf placement, rather than opposite or in a whirl, on a stem.

Amendments. Organic or mineral materials, such as peat moss, vermiculite, or compost, used to improve the soil.

Annual. A plant that germinates, grows, flowers, produces seeds, and dies in the course of a single growing season.

Anther. The endmost part of a flower stamen where pollen is produced.

Antitranspirant. A substance sprayed on the stems and leaves to slow transpiration (water loss) resulting from drying winter winds.

Axil. The angle where a leaf joins a stem.

Balled-and-burlapped (B&B). A tree or shrub dug from the ground with its roots still enclosed in a ball of original soil that is wrapped in burlap and tied.

Bare-root. A plant that is dug out of the ground and then shaken or washed at its roots to remove the soil.

Bract. A modified leaf or leaflike structure that embraces a flower bud and opens with the flower. Bracts occur at the base of the flower and may be part of the flower head.

Catkin. A drooping spike of many small flowers, common on wind-pollinated trees.

Compound leaf. A leaf with two or more leaflets branching off a single stalk.

Conifer. A usually evergreen woody plant bearing conelike fruit and needlelike leaves.

Container-grown. A plant that is raised in a container and removed before planting.

Crown. Where roots and stem meet, usually at soil level. It is also the term for the canopy, or "upper story," of a tree.

Cultivar. Short for cultivated variety. A plant variety developed in cultivation, rather than occurring naturally in the wild.

Cutting. A part of a plant (often a stem section) removed and planted in order to grow a new plant.

Deadheading. Removing spent flowers during the growing season to prevent seed formation and to encourage new flowers.

Deciduous. A tree, shrub, or vine that drops *all* of its leaves in fall or winter.

Dioecious. Plants that bear male and female flowers on separate plants. See *Monoecious*.

Division. Propagation of a plant by separating it into two or more pieces, each of which has at least one bud and some roots.

Double flower. A flower with more than the standard number of rows of petals.

Drip line. An imaginary circular line on the soil around a tree that mirrors the circumference of the tree's canopy.

Evergreen. Either a broad-leaved plant or a conifer that retains foliage for at least a year.

Exposure. The intensity, duration, and variation in sun, wind, and temperature that characterize any site.

Feeder roots. Slender branching roots that spread close to the soil surface and absorb most of the nutrients for a tree or shrub.

Floret. A small flower in a multiflowered flower head.

Foundation plantings. Woody plants that form the main features, or the "structure," in a landscape; also a narrow border of evergreen shrubs along the foundation of a house.

Full shade. A site that receives no direct sun during the growing season.

Full sun. A site that receives at least six hours (in the South) or at least eight hours (in the North) of direct sun each day during the growing season.

Genus (plural: *genera*). A closely related group of species sharing similar characteristics and probably evolved from the same ancestors. In scientific, or botanical, language the genus name begins with a capital letter and is followed by the species name, which begins with a lowercase letter. Both words are italicized, as in *Acer palmatum*.

Ground cover. A plant, such as ivy, liriope, or juniper, used to cover the soil and form a continuous low mass of foliage. Often used as a durable substitute for turf grass.

Habit. The characteristic shape or form a plant assumes as it grows.

Hardiness. A plant's ability to survive winter cold or summer heat without protection.

Hardiness zone. A geographic region where the coldest temperature in an average winter falls within a certain range, such as between 0° and −10°F.

Hard pruning. Cutting away most of a shrub's top growth, leaving just stubs.

Herbicide. A chemical used to kill plants.

Humus. Fibrous residues of decomposing organic materials in soil. Humus absorbs moisture and is an essential element of good garden soil.

Hybrid. A plant resulting from cross breeding plants that belong to different varieties, species, or genera. Hybrids are indicated in scientific names by a times sign (×) between the genus and species name, as in red horse chestnut (*Aesculus × carnea* 'Briotii').

Invasive plant. A plant that spreads quickly, usually by runners, and mixes with or dominates adjacent plantings.

Landscape fabric. Synthetic fabric, usually water-permeable, that is spread under paths or mulch to serve as a weed barrier.

Leaflet. One segment of a compound leaf.

Lime, limestone. White mineral compounds used to combat soil acidity and to supply calcium for plant growth.

Loam. Natural or amended soil that is well-structured, fertile, moisture retentive, and free draining. Loam contains a balanced mix of sand, silt, and clay particles, as well as organic matter.

Monoecious. A plant that bears both male and female flowers. See *Dioecious*.

Mulch. A layer of bark, compost, shredded leaves, straw, gravel, paper, plastic, or other material spread around the base of plants.

Native. A plant that occurs naturally in a given region and therefore is well suited to the local climate and growing conditions.

Naturalized. A plant introduced to an area that has escaped cultivation and reproduces on its own.

New wood. Stems and branches that have grown during the current season.

Nutrients. Nitrogen, phosphorus, potassium, calcium, magnesium, sulfur, iron, and other elements needed by growing plants.

Old wood. Stems and branches that developed during a previous growing season.

Panicle. A loose, branched flower cluster on which the flowers bloom gradually from bottom to top or from the center outward.

Peat moss. Partially decomposed mosses and sedges mined from boggy areas and used to improve garden soil.

Perennial. A plant that lives for a number of years, generally flowering each year.

Pistil. The female, central, part of a flower onto which pollen is deposited by a pollinator. See *Anther*.

Pod. A dry fruit that contains seeds.

Pome. A fleshy fruit that contains seeds, such as a crabapple.

Raceme. A spikelike stalk with numerous flowers on individual stems.

Root ball. The mass of soil and roots dug up with a plant when it is removed from the ground or from a container.

Samara. A dry, winged fruit, usually with a single seed, such as the fruit of maples.

Single flower. A flower with a single concentric row of petals.

Species. Among plants, a group that shares many characteristics, including essential flower characteristics, and can interbreed freely. In scientific, or botanical, language the species name always follows the genus name and begins with a lowercase letter, and both words are italicized, as in *Abies concolor*.

Specimen plant. A plant that is featured in a prominent position.

Spike. An elongated flower cluster, with individual flowers borne on short stalks or attached directly to the main stem.

Stamen. One of the male reproductive organs of a flower, consisting of an anther, which produces pollen, supported by a stalklike filament. See *Anther*.

Standard. A plant that is trained to grow a round bushy head of branches atop a single upright trunk.

Tender. A plant that is susceptible to damage by excessive cold.

Watersprout. A shoot that grows almost vertically from a relatively horizontal branch.

Index

Note: **_Bold italics_** = subjects illustrated.

Credits

Have a home gardening, decorating, or improvement project?
Look for these and other fine Creative Homeowner books
wherever books are sold

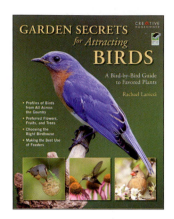

GARDEN SECRETS FOR ATTRACTING BIRDS
Provides information to turn your yard into a mecca for birds.

Over 250 photographs and illustrations.
160 pp.
8½" × 10⅝"
$14.95 (US)
$17.95 (CAN)
BOOK #: CH274561

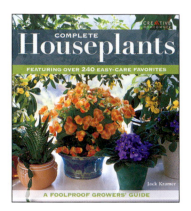

COMPLETE HOUSEPLANTS
Secrets to growing the most popular types of houseplants.

Over 480 photographs and illustrations.
224 pp.
9" × 10"
$19.95 (US)
$21.95 (CAN)
BOOK #: CH274820

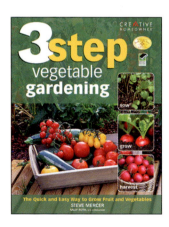

3 STEP VEGETABLE GARDENING
A quick and easy guide for growing your own fruit and vegetables.

Over 300 photographs.
224 pp.
8½" × 10⅞"
$19.95 (US)
$21.95 (CAN)
BOOK #: CH274557

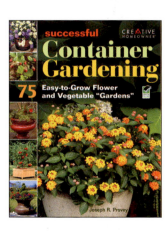

SUCCESSFUL CONTAINER GARDENING
Information to grow your own flower, fruit, and vegetable "gardens."

Over 240 photographs.
160 pp.
8½" × 10⅞"
$14.95 (US)
$17.95 (CAN)
BOOK #: CH274857

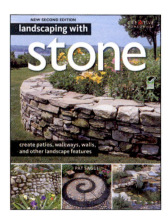

LANDSCAPING WITH STONE
Ideas for incorporating stone into the landscape.

Over 335 photographs.
224 pp.
8½" × 10⅞"
$19.95 (US)
$21.95 (CAN)
BOOK #: CH274179

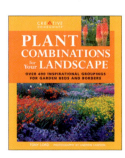

PLANT COMBINATIONS FOR YOUR LANDSCAPE
How to plan and grow the best plant combinations.

Over 400 photos and 2,000 alternative combinations.
368 pp.
5½" × 6½"
$14.95 (US)
$16.95 (CAN)
BOOK #: CH274100

For more information and to order direct, go to **www.creativehomeowner.com**